Fine Art and High Finance

Also available from

Bloomberg Press

Money Well Spent: A Strategic Plan for Smart Philanthropy
by Paul Brest and Hal Harvey

A complete list of our titles is available at
www/bloomberg.com/books

Fine Art and High Finance

Expert Advice on the Economics of Ownership

Edited by Clare McAndrew

BLOOMBERG PRESS
NEW YORK

First edition published 2010

13

Library of Congress Cataloging-in-Publication Data

Fine art and high finance : expert advice on the economics of ownership / edited by Clare McAndrew. – 1st ed.

    p. cm.

    Includes bibliographical references and index.

    Summary: "Art investors and collectors can't protect and profit from their collections without grappling with a range of complex financial issues like risk, insurance, restoration, and conservation. In Fine Art and High Finance, Clare McAndrew and a highly qualified team of contributors explain the most difficult financial matters facing art investors"–Provided by publisher.

    ISBN 978-1-57660-333-8 (alk. paper)

    1. Art as an investment. I. McAndrew, Clare.

N8600.F56 2010

332.63–dc22
                                                     2009047843

This book is dedicated to my son, Kane, whose wonderful
and timely arrival spurred on its completion.

Contents

About the Editor

Dr. Clare McAndrew is a cultural economist, investment analyst, and author. She founded Arts Economics in 2005. Arts Economics is a research and consulting firm focused exclusively on the art economy. The company carries out bespoke research and analysis on all aspects of the fine and decorative art market for private and institutional clients.

Dr. McAndrew completed her PhD in economics at Trinity College Dublin in 2001, where she also lectured and taught economics for four years. She then directed a number of research projects for the Arts Council of England on the effects of regulation, taxation, and other issues in the visual arts market.

In 2002, Dr. McAndrew joined the U.S. firm Kusin & Company, a boutique investment banking firm specializing in art investment, as chief economist. After three years in the United States, she returned to Europe in 2005, and continued her work in the art market in a private consulting capacity for a global client base. She set up Arts Economics to focus her efforts on art market research and analysis and works with a network of private consultants and academic scholars in providing research and consulting services to the global art trade and financial sector. Some of the main strands of research currently include macroeconomic art market and micro-level sector analysis, art banking, and investment-related services. The company also specializes in the analysis of arts-related policy and regulation for private- and public-sector bodies. Dr. McAndrew has published widely on the economics of the art market, including two recent books: *Globalisation and the Art Market*, commissioned by the European Fine Art Foundation, and *The Art Economy*, published by Liffey Press.

Dr. McAndrew is a guest lecturer in the masters program at Trinity College Dublin in the Trinity Irish Art Research Centre (TIARC) and is an associate lecturer at Sotheby's Institute of Art, Singapore. She also lectures Business Studies for Artists at the National College of Art and Design (NCAD) in Dublin. She lives in Dublin, with her husband and son.

Web: www.artseconomics.com
E-mail: clare@artseconomics.com

Acknowledgments

I would like to thank all of the contributors for their time, hard work, and expertise in putting the chapters of this book together. I would especially like to thank Andy Augenblick for his thoughts and advice at the start of the project. Thanks are also due to Veronica McDavid for work in the early stages of the book, and also to all of the editors at Bloomberg, particularly Evan Burton.

About the Contributors

Anthony Browne is chairman of the British Art Market Federation (BAMF). Founded in 1996, BAMF represents the interests of art dealing and auctioneering companies in the United Kingdom in their contact with government. He is a graduate (MA, Modern History) of Oxford University. He was a director of Christie's, London (1978–1996) and a member of the British Government's Cultural Industries Export Advisory Group (1998–2001); Ministerial Advisory Panel on Illicit Trade (1999–2003); Quinquennial Review Panel on the Reviewing Committee on the Export of Works of Art (2001–2003); and Advisory Group on Museum Acquisitions (Goodison Review) (2003). Mr. Browne is a board member of the European Fine Art Foundation (TEFAF) and consultant to Christie's International PLC. He has written numerous articles on political aspects of the art market.

Dr. Rachel Campbell completed her PhD in Risk Management in International Financial Markets at Erasmus University, Rotterdam, in 2001. She is currently an assistant professor of finance at both Tilburg University and the University of Maastricht. Her work has been published in a number of leading journals, including the *Journal of International Money and Finance, Journal of Banking and Finance, Financial Analysts Journal, Journal of Portfolio Management, Journal of Empirical Finance, Journal of Risk,* and *Derivatives Weekly.* Dr. Campbell teaches at Tias Business School and Euromoney Financial Training on art investment and works as an independent economic adviser for The Fine Art Fund in London, and for Fine Art Wealth Management, U.K. She is also a risk consultant for Emotional Assets Management & Research.

Charles T. Danziger and **Thomas C. Danziger** are brothers and partners in the New York City law firm of Danziger, Danziger & Muro, specializing in art law. They are the authors of the widely read "Brothers-in-Law" column, which appears regularly in *Art + Auction* magazine, and to date have published almost fifty articles dealing with legal issues in the art world.

Thomas Danziger graduated from Wesleyan University with honors in General Scholarship and from the New York University School of Law, where he was an editor of the *Journal of International Law and Politics.* Prior to founding Danziger, Danziger & Muro, he practiced law with Shearman & Sterling in New York. Mr. Danziger specializes in art-related transactions, and advises collectors, dealers, museums, and artists in this field. He is fluent in French, and lives in New York City with his wife, Laura, and young son, James. He may be reached via e-mail: thomas@ danziger.com.

Charles Danziger graduated from Yale University, magna cum laude, and the New York University School of Law, where he was also an editor of the *Journal of International Law and Politics*. Mr. Danziger was formerly associated with Milbank, Tweed, Hadley & McCloy; Nagashima, Ohno & Tsunematsu, in Tokyo; and the Museum of Modern Art in New York, where he served as assistant general counsel. He wrote and illustrated *Japan for Starters*, a book about Japanese modern life, business, and tradition; and *Harvey and Etsuko's Manga Guide to Japan*. He is a trustee of designer Issey Miyake's Miyake Design Foundation and violinist Midori's Partners in Performance. He has lectured on art law at the University of Chicago Law School and at Tokyo University and Keio University in Japan. Mr. Danziger is fluent in Japanese, German, and French. He may be reached via e-mail: charles@danziger.com.

Jeremy Eckstein studied third-level math, statistics, and economics and started his career training to be an actuary. He joined Sotheby's in 1979 to provide support to the Trustees of the British Rail Pension Fund following their decision to diversify part of their investment portfolio into art. During his tenure there as head of research, he developed Sotheby's Index of art prices, contributed regularly to *Barron's* and *Forbes* on the state of the market and created Sotheby's *Art Market Bulletin*. He left the company in 1990 to work as a self-employed consultant. In recent years Mr. Eckstein has worked closely with dealers and independent advisers, developing solutions for investment clients. He undertakes the regular members' surveys on behalf of the Society of London Art Dealers (SLAD) and has recently had published research on the economic impact of art fairs commissioned by TEFAF. He advises on asset allocation strategy involving art for high-net-worth individuals and also acted as adviser to a number of embryo art funds. In 2004, he was a member of the team of independent experts assembled by ABN Amro to evaluate a fund of funds based on art funds. He currently lectures on art and business for Sotheby's Institute in London as well as for the Institut d'Études Supérieures des Arts (IESA) in Paris.

Christiane Fischer was named chief executive officer of AXA Art Insurance Corporation in January 2004 and its president in June 2006. Prior to that, she served as chief operating officer and director of communications. Before joining AXA Art in January 2000, she served as general manager of corporate information and reporting at Daimler-Benz North America Corporation in New York. Ms. Fischer started her professional career in the Customer Service Department of Bank of America in Frankfurt, then she worked in the Finance Department of Daimler-Benz in Stuttgart before moving to America. Ms. Fischer was born and raised in Germany. After receiving her Abitur, she completed a program as Foreign Language Correspondent, with a focus on industry and commerce. In addition to her studies in Germany, she studied economics and marketing at New York University.

Ms. Fischer currently serves as president of the Art Resource Alliance (ARA), a not-for-profit organization whose mission is to foster the preservation of cultural heritage through education, with special focus on the fine and decorative arts. Fischer also serves as a member of the board of trustees of the Isamu Noguchi Museum and the International Foundation for Art Research (IFAR) and on the advisory boards of the Chicago Conservation Center and the Appraisers Association of America. In addition, she is a member of the International Council of the Miami Art Museum. Ms. Fischer lives in New York with her husband and their three daughters.

Jill Arnold joined AXA Art Insurance Corporation in October 2008 as director of business development. Before joining AXA Art, she was a client advocate at Willis of New York and a director at DeWitt Stern Group in New York City. She started her professional career at Chubb Group of Insurance. Ms. Arnold has written articles for Fine Art Connoisseur Magazine and has lectured at Art Chicago, the Sotheby's Institute, and Franklin & Marshall College. She was born in Lancaster, Pennsylvania, and is a graduate of Franklin & Marshall College where she studied Classics and Art History. She currently serves as president of the National Association of Insurance in New York City and is on the Advisory Council for the Appraisers Association of America.

Rachel Goodman holds a BA in Art History and Communications from the University of Pennsylvania, from which she graduated magna cum laude. She has also completed coursework at University College London. She currently works in the president's office at Gurr Johns, New York. Previously she worked at Andrea Meislin Gallery, New York and the Jewish Museum, New York. Her interests lie in the intersection between art and economics.

Suzanne Gyorgy is a senior vice president of the Citi Private Bank Art Advisory Service and the art finance director. She is also the business manager of the group, overseeing all aspects of its day-to-day operations. Before joining the Art Advisory Service, she was director of exhibitions and collections for the Morris Museum, director of the PaineWebber (UBS) Gallery in New York, and a registrar at the Museum of Modern Art. Ms. Gyorgy's experience includes organizing exhibitions, establishing public-relations campaigns, fundraising, developing educational programs, and managing numerous private and corporate art collections. She earned a degree in fine art from Pratt Institute.

Elizabeth von Habsburg is president of Gurr Johns, Inc., the largest independent international art consulting and appraisal firm in the United States and Europe. She is a board member of the Appraisers Association of America, New York; the Appraisal Foundation, Washington D.C.; and the Albert Kunstadter Family Foundation and is also a member of ArtTable, a fellow of the Pierpont Morgan Library, and on an advisory committee for the Museum of Art & Design, New York. Prior to joining Gurr Johns, Elizabeth worked at Christie's, New York. She has a BA from Stanford University and an MA from Columbia University. She has edited four antiques price guidebooks, lectured extensively throughout the United States, and acted as expert witness in the courts of New York, Florida, and Texas.

Rachel Goodman holds a BA in Art History and Communications from the University of Pennsylvania, from which she graduated magna cum laude. She has also completed coursework at University College London. She currently works in the president's office at Gurr Johns, New York. Previously she worked at Andrea Meislin Gallery, New York and the Jewish Museum, New York. Her interests lie in the intersection between art and economics.

John K. Jacobs is the founder and president of Artex Fine Art Services. Mr. Jacobs has been involved in the safe handling, transport, packing, crating and storage of museum artifacts for almost thirty years. After completing postgraduate degrees in sculpture, he began working in museums in 1980 as registrar of the New Museum of Contemporary Art in New York City. He was responsible for managing traveling exhibitions and site-specific installations and was integrally involved in the expansion of the museum in 1983 to its new headquarters in Soho.

In 1986 he left to head up the International Services and Crating and Packing Department at Crozier Fine Arts. During his tenure, the company grew to one of the largest fine art services company in New York. In 1989, he established Artex Fine Art Services in Washington, D.C., with his partner, Todd Herman. After building the business into the predominant fine art service company in Washington, D.C., Artex expanded in 1996 by acquiring Atlantic Van Lines, a local competitor. This led to the opening of offices in Baltimore, New York, Fort Lauderdale, and Boston. Under Mr. Jacobs's direction, Artex has been awarded the largest and most complex museum projects of the last decade. Artex now manages over 500,000 square feet of specialized warehousing, and its services have grown to include transportation, storage, crating and packing, installation, rigging, and conservation.

Barbara A. Ramsay earned a BSc from the University of Toronto and a master of art conservation degree from Queen's University, Kingston, Canada. She has practiced as a painting conservator and conservation manager for the past thirty-five years in Canada, the United States, and Europe. Ms. Ramsay is an accredited member of the Canadian Association of Professional Conservators (CAPC) and an elected fellow of the International Institute for Conservation of Historic and Artistic Works (IIC). She was a painting conservator at the National Gallery of Canada (NGC) in Ottawa for eighteen years, five of those as senior conservator of fine art. She has taught painting conservation as an associate professor in the Queen's Master of Art Conservation Program. Ms. Ramsay is past president of both the IIC–Canadian Group and CAPC. After several years of running her own private conservation practice in Ottawa, she worked with John Jacobs at Artex Fine Art Services, Washington, D.C. to establish the Artex Conservation Laboratory in 1999. As director of conservation services, she manages the laboratory and directs the work of three professional painting conservators on staff, plus a variety of subcontracted conservators in other specialties for specific projects. She serves as project manager for complex conservation projects for museums, private and corporate collections, government agencies, artist estate collections, and others. Ms. Ramsay lives in Bethesda, Md., and has two sons attending university in Canada.

Dr. Roman Kräussl is associate professor of finance at VU University Amsterdam. He studied economics at the University of Bielefeld and got his PhD in Financial Economics at the Center for Financial Studies (CFS) at Goethe-University Frankfurt am Main. Apart from his position at VU University, Dr. Kräussl currently also holds a position as research fellow at CFS and at the Emory Center for Alternative Investments within Goizueta Business School, Emory University. His current research interests include alternative investments, private equity and venture capital financing, and art and finance. He established the Web site www.art-finance.com, where he publishes some of his recent work on art as an alternative asset class, mostly on building liquid art investment indices in order to evaluate optimal portfolio allocation decisions into art.

Ralph E. Lerner is the preeminent attorney practicing full time in the field of art law. He is counsel at Withers Bergman LLP and the co-author of the award-winning treatise, *Art Law: The Guide for Collectors, Investors, Dealers and Artists*, acclaimed as the "industry bible" by Forbes Magazine. He has served as chairman of the Art Law Committee of the Association of the Bar of the City of New York, chairman of the Fine Arts Committee of the New York State Bar Association, and chairman of the Visual Arts Division of the American Bar Association Forum on Entertainment and Sports Law. He is currently on the board of the New York Volunteer Lawyers for the Arts and is a fellow of the American College of Trusts and Estates Counsel. Mr. Lerner is a nationally acclaimed speaker and writer on the topic of tax planning for collectors and artists. He has extensive experience in dealing with the Internal Revenue Service in the broadest possible manner and numbers among his clients many of the foremost artists, collectors, and art dealers in America.

Rena Neville began her career as a litigation associate in New York City with the law firm of Sullivan & Cromwell. She then joined Sotheby's where she was worked since 1989. During her first eleven years with the company, she acted in a variety of legal capacities between London and New York, including general counsel for Sotheby's Europe, deputy general counsel worldwide for Sotheby's Holdings, Inc. and worldwide director of compliance, business practices counsel and senior vice president, Sotheby's Holdings, Inc. In 2006, she returned to New York City and assumed a nonlegal role as head of client development for Sotheby's North and South America.

Ms. Neville has served on various committees relating to art or art law or lobbying, including the Executive Committee of the British Art Market Federation, the European Round Table, the New York City Bar Association's Committee on Art Law and the board of directors of the Art Loss Register. She graduated from Denison University with a BA in Philosophy and received her JD from the Washington College of Law, American University. Ms. Neville's notable publications in the area of art and law include "The International Movement of Cultural Property" (Chapter 6 of *Art Law Handbook*) in 2000 and "European Experiment in Enforcing the Export Control Laws of Fellow Member States" (International Bar Association Newsletter, IBA Committee 20 on Art and Cultural Property, May 2001).

Pierre Valentin specializes in art law. For the past fifteen years, he has advised art collectors, art market professionals, artists and their estates, and museums and galleries on all legal issues arising when buying and selling art and managing art collections. He heads Withers's Art and Cultural Assets Group, a team of specialist art lawyers in London and New York. The focus of his practice is the visual arts. He handles a mix of contentious and transactional work including fraud and dispute resolution, restitution and repatriation, private treaty sales, consignments to auction, tax solutions around art, import and export, raising capital against art, and art investment funds. His practice is multijurisdictional and covers the fine and decorative arts, from antiquities to contemporary art. Prior to joining Withers in 2003, Mr. Valentin was a senior director and associate general counsel at Sotheby's. He is a trustee of the World Monuments Fund in Britain and of the Artists' Collecting Society. He teaches art law at a postgraduate level at the Sotheby's Institute, the London School of Economics, and the University of Lyon. He is fluent in French, Italian, and Spanish. Mr. Valentin co-authored Chapter 10 with his colleagues **Philip Munro** and **Samantha Morgan**.

Philip Munro trained as a solicitor at Withers LLP in London and is now a member of the Funds, Investment and Trust team where, as well as estate planning, tax and trust issues for entrepreneurs and their families, he is interested in the use of funds vehicles for private clients and derivatives in tax planning.

Samantha Morgan works with a number of international family offices, advising on all aspects of UK tax and fiduciary issues and coordinating foreign tax and other advice for the family office and family members. She advises trust companies, banks and investment houses on fiduciary and tax issues, which has included such areas as the structure and tax treatment of investments and trust structures (including EBTs) and drafting standard trust and other related documentation. She also works with individuals advising them on their personal tax issues (dealing particularly with US/ UK tax issues).

Randall Willette is the founder and managing director at Fine Art Wealth Management (www.fineartwealthmgt.com), a London-based art investment consultancy that specializes in advising wealth managers and their private clients on art as an alternative asset class and the disciplines required to analyze this complex field of investment. Prior to establishing the company in 2003, he was executive director and head of art banking for UBS Wealth Management in London and was responsible for building its Art Banking franchise in Europe and America. While there, he developed and implemented a global marketing strategy for UBS Art Banking, integrating art assets into the firm's overall wealth-management strategy for private clients. Before joining UBS, Mr. Willette served as managing director in corporate finance and joint head of securitization with Citigroup in Europe. His credentials include over twenty years' combined experience in investment banking, structured finance, and private wealth management with broad international experience in the United States, Europe, and Japan. He has lectured and published extensively on various aspects of art and wealth management.

1

An Introduction to Art and Finance

Dr. Clare McAndrew

The international art market is estimated to have turned over more than $60 billion in total sales of fine and decorative art and antiques in 2008, one of its highest-ever recorded totals. By sheer size alone, therefore, it is easy to see why it has sparked the interest of the mainstream investment community: the art trade is big business. It is also a truly global business, with sales of art taking place literally all around the world. Although geographically concentrated to some degree in terms of value in the two main centers of London and New York, virtually every country has an art market of some form.

For the purposes of understanding how this unique global market functions, it is important at the outset to clarify the art that will be considered. The chapters that follow consider both fine and decorative art (and, in places, antiques). These artworks were generally made for creative, decorative purposes or what some might refer to as "art for art's sake"—the motivation for their creation and continued existence is essentially the artworks themselves (as opposed to more utilitarian "craft" works or more commercial and functional works of design). These works are collected, bought, and sold for a range of reasons, including aesthetic, historical, and financial.

Fine art includes the basic categories of paintings, sculpture, works on paper (including watercolors, drawings, and photographs), and tapestries. Decorative art covers furniture and decorations (in glass, wood, stone, metal, and ceramic), couture (costumes and jewelry),

1

ephemera, and textiles. Definitions of antiques vary widely, but in this context the term refers mainly to items that are at least fifty to one hundred years old and are collected or desirable due to their rarity, condition, historical significance, or some other unique feature. Some of the larger dealers and art auction houses sell a variety of other "collectibles," such as wine, coins, vintage cars, sports memorabilia, stamps, and toys. Although some of these items have many characteristics in common with works of art (and although art is itself a collectible), these goods often function on markets with different characteristics from the art market and are therefore best classified separately.

Despite its sizable turnover and international dimensions, the art market, up until fairly recently, has tended to be the focus of wealthy collectors and a relatively elitist group of art experts, with closely guarded knowledge and trading practices. Over the last decade, however, art has sparked the interest of the mainstream financial community as an investment asset class. Although some of the older art elites might claim to be somewhat uncomfortable with their blatant partnership, the worlds of art and finance have been closely linked for hundreds of years throughout the history of the art market. In recent years, as some of its opacity has begun to slowly lift, the modern art market has begun to evolve into an international financial trading platform in which specialized assets are exchanged by a widening group of investors, both individual and institutional, with many as interested in their financial benefits as in their aesthetic beauty or historical importance.

The Art Market: A Brief Modern History

A brief review of the modern history of the art market shows some of the factors that have shaped the art trade over time, largely (but not solely) due to the drift of economic power and wealth. Although the geographical epicenters of the international art trade have shifted through history, many of the old foundations are still apparent in the modern art market and contribute to its current flow and infrastructure.

Many historians mark the period following the Industrial Revolution, when art began to become more widely traded and the primary role of the patron was diminished, as the impetus of today's modern art market. The birth of a new middle class in this era brought a new breed of collector to the art market who, for the first time, had both the time and the money to collect art.

During the eighteenth century, Britain and France emerged as the major global art markets and the key centers for trade, while countries such as Italy acted as primary source markets for wealthy European buyers. The British art market expanded during the second half of the eighteenth century, and the first major auction houses also began to appear such as Christie's and Sotheby's that still dominate the market today. During the 1800s, a variety of factors caused a geographic shift in the art market from London to Paris, particularly for the avant-garde, and Paris enjoyed the position as cultural capital for a period. However, the French reign was relatively short-lived, as wider economic and political events, a Wall Street market crash, and a massive devaluation of the French franc caused many dealers to go out of business and shifted power toward the U.S. and U.K. markets, where economic and buyer strength rested.

American buyers began to dominate the global art trade during the recessionary bear markets of the 1920s and 1930s. As noted by one of the leading London art dealers of this period, Joseph Duveen, "Europe had plenty of art and America had plenty of money," and Duveen and his colleagues on both sides of the Atlantic capitalized on this circumstance, creating highly successful art dealerships particularly from the trade in Old Master paintings.

Paris had a temporary revival as a world art center during the 1950s and 1960s; however, over the 1960s, New York and London dominated, largely due to their established bases of wealth and economic power and to the introduction of a new system of taxes on art sales and other regulatory deterrents in France. During these years, the major auction houses of Christie's, Sotheby's, and Parke-Bernet in New York thrived and began to attract a wider interest from wealthy collectors and investors, particularly for Modern art sales. In previous decades, buyers at auctions tended to be a small number of highly informed dealers who understood the market, had expertise in particular specialties, and purchased at lower prices in order to resell to collectors. During the 1960s and particularly in the recessionary early 1970s, however, art began to be promoted as a hedge against rampant and escalating inflation, and auctions began to attract an increasing number of "retail" clients. To respond to this trend, some of the "supergalleries" emerged, with global outlets in various cities throughout the world to accommodate an expanding buyer base. Although sales in many sectors were eventually affected by wider economic events like the oil crisis in 1973, art was being increasingly bought by investors and speculators as well as by collectors.

Throughout the 1970s, the distinctions between the two international art capitals also became more defined: New York took premier position for the trade in sectors such as Contemporary art, Impressionists, Post-Impressionists and others, while London was the international center for Old Masters, English and French eighteen-century art, and Asian antiques.

During the global prosperity of the 1980s, all of the established art centers flourished, and it became hugely popular and often very profitable to buy art. The global art market entered a boom period from about 1987, marked by the emergence of record prices at auction for works of art, especially in the Modern and Contemporary sectors, and especially in New York. At the height of the boom in 1990, van Gogh's *Portrait of Dr. Gachet* was sold for a record $82.5 million at Christie's in New York by Japanese paper magnate Ryoei Saito, which is still one of the most expensive paintings ever sold in real terms.[1]

As art prices soared and returns and dividends on stock markets started to contract, speculators added fuel to an art market that was already becoming overheated. The art market bubble at the end of the 1980s was particularly exacerbated by strong Japanese buying, mainly in the Impressionist and Post-Impressionist sectors. This demand-induced bubble was largely fueled by tax avoidance and the inflation-backed buildup of wealth in property. Added to this, the yen had also appreciated significantly against the dollar without a concurrent drop in exports, leaving the Japanese awash with money. Surplus cash, combined with a lack of discrimination on the part of new purchasers, caused prices to rise sharply, often with huge sums paid for mediocre works. That art boom ended abruptly in 1990 as a sharp rise in interest rates by the Bank of Japan forced many speculative collectors to go under, often because of a collapse of liquidity caused by unrelated investments. Many collections still remain in bank vaults, previously secured as collateral against corporate loans that failed during the Japanese recession that followed.

From this international low in 1990 and 1991, the art market has steadily advanced in terms of volume and value. Over the last eighteen years, several sectors of the market have gained significant ground—such as Impressionist, Modern, and Contemporary—while others have been on slower trajectories. Although most international markets showed a slight dip in 2002–2003, from that point until the end of 2008 the market as a whole, and many of the categories within it, have been on rapidly advancing paths of growth in terms of both individual prices and overall aggregate value. A particularly noticeable trend in recent years has been that fine art has risen in value both in absolute terms and in relation to decorative art.

The Current Structure of the Art Market

The twenty-first century has witnessed astonishing growth in the international market for works of art. Values peaked in 2007 after several years of rapid growth, with the global art market estimated to have reached a high of over $65 billion, including both dealer and auction sales of fine and decorative art and antiques. This represented its highest ever total, and the amount had more than doubled in a period of just five years.

After a relatively poor year in 2003, the market had a steady path of growth over the following four years, with growth per annum in its value averaging 28 percent since 2003. The fine art market was a key driver of growth during this period, with prices and values rising steadily, as this sector gained significant ground over decorative art. Certain categories within the fine art sector experienced phenomenal growth in value, including Contemporary, Impressionist, and Modern art. Contemporary art in particular showed exceptional growth and became the largest category of art by value at the major auction houses in 2007.

After seven consecutive years of rapid price inflation, the art market experienced a change in its aggregate trend in late 2008, as the trickle-down effects of the global financial crisis and economic recession were felt in some sectors. Just as it had been the leader in its expansive phase, the fine art market was also the key driver of the contraction of the art market during 2008, with sales at auction in this sector dropping by over 10 percent from 2007 values. Total global sales of fine and decorative art and antiques were estimated to have dropped to about $60 billion[2] by the end of 2008, with the Contemporary sector in particular showing a marked decline in average prices and values at the end of that year.

Although the most notable decline in sales values occurred in the art sales in the fall of 2008, global prices for fine art at auction contracted as early as the first quarter of the year (with aggregate prices in first-quarter 2008 down 7.5 percent from fourth-quarter 2007). A notable feature of auction sales at the end of 2008 was a high rate of buy-ins or unsold works at auction, reflecting a degree of wariness on the part of buyers compared with previous years. The average buy-in rate at fine art auctions in October 2008 was approximately 44 percent, more than twice the rate of the same month in 2007.[3]

Although the contraction in prices during 2008 represented the sharpest fall in the market since its previous "bust" in 1991, it is important to remember that the decline in aggregates is due in part to the fact that 2007 was such a boom year, and the levels of sales in 2008 and 2009 are still markedly above any years preceding 2006. For example, the turnover of the global market in 2006 was estimated at $54 billion, still some $6 billion lower than 2008. Contractions in average prices also mask important information in the market, as they do not reveal which sectors of the market were doing well or poorly, or what quality of works were on the market in this year versus previous years. In early 2009, aggregate sale rates and prices improved in some sectors, including the main spring sales of Contemporary art at auction.[4] However, again, it is impossible to determine from this (without drilling down into these sales in more detail) if the market bounced back or if in fact simply better quality works were sold.

The art market remains dominated by the two major art markets of the United States and the United Kingdom, which together accounted for over two-thirds of the global trade by value. The United States remains the largest market by far, with a share of over 40 percent.[5]

Although the position of these two dominant markets has not changed significantly in the last decade, their combined share has slipped a few percentage points in recent years largely due to the rise of China. *Figure 1.1* shows that China is now the third largest global art market with a market share of 8 percent, and has substantially over-taken previously leading markets such as France and Germany. This trend has continued since 2006, when China made significant inroads in the global art landscape for the first time, pushing Germany from its fourth position. The rise of China as a global player in the art market highlights one of the biggest transformations in the market over the last five years, namely, the emergence of a number of new and thriving art markets and art centers around the world, such as China, India, Russia, and the Middle East.

The presence of buyers from these newer "emerging" economies in the international art market has substantially increased demand, particularly in the Contemporary sector, and has been driven primarily by economic factors, specifically by the increasing wealth of their populations. While economic growth in some of the older Western economies has slowed in recent years, many of the emerging markets have shown strong and steady growth. New wealthy buyers that have emerged over the last few years from those countries have shown distinct preferences for Contemporary art, often originating from their own countries, causing a boom in sectors such as Chinese Contemporary painting.

From 2003 until the end of 2007, the aggregate art auction market grew by 311 percent, and the Contemporary art market grew by 851 percent. Although this growth has been a global phenomenon, with Contemporary markets such as the United States advancing 543 percent over the period, the growth in the newer global players has been staggering,

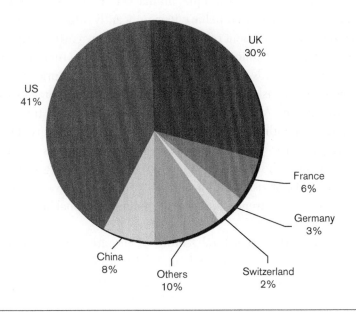

FIGURE 1.1   Global Art Market Share, 2007

Source: *Arts Economics* (2008)

with the Chinese Contemporary art market rising over 11,000 percent. These rapidly rising prices and expanding sales have been supported by an increase in the number of newly wealthy Chinese who for the first time have the purchasing power to participate actively in the market, alongside their Western counterparts.[6] Although, as noted above, the Contemporary sector was one of the worst hit within the art market in the fallout of the economic crisis of 2007 and 2008, this expanded base of global buyers undoubtedly saved the market to some degree from a 1991/1992-style meltdown.

It is important to note that due to the opacity of the market and the lack of data on private dealer sales, measuring the market is not easy. Auction data combined with dealer polling have formed the cornerstones of the quantification of the art trade and the basis of the numbers above. At the outset, however, it is important to remember that there is essentially no such thing as "the art market." The market is by no means a single homogenous entity, but rather a conglomeration of distinct markets, each developing at its own individual rate. The "art market" is in fact the name given to the aggregation of many independently moving and unique submarkets that are defined by artists and genres and often behave in significantly different ways.

Each underlying segment of the market has its own artists, experts, academics, dedicated collectors, specialist dealers, sometimes auction houses, and importantly their own independently moving price trajectories and inherent risks. This is fundamental to understanding investment in the market. Art can be a good investment because it trades on more than one hundred submarkets, many of which have very different returns and risks as well as their own definable patterns of trade. Any assessment of how the aggregated art market is faring in terms of prices, returns, or risk therefore can only be used as a very general guide to assess broad trends, and is often not useful in making specific investment decisions.

Another important structural feature of the art market is that it operates on a two-tier system made up of the primary and secondary markets, with the latter dominating the trade in terms of value and volume. The primary market is where artists first sell new work directly to collectors and dealers and on an agency basis, typically through dealers and brokers. Some living artists also make initial sales directly through auction houses, but this is generally limited to very well known artists.

Outlets for trade in the primary art market therefore tend to be artists' studios, art fairs or festivals, and galleries or art dealers, and the price points are often lower than in the secondary market. Sellers in the market are made up of new and unknown artists as well as more established Contemporary artists. Buyers in this tier of the market are faced with a lack of full and perfect information and often subject to high transaction costs in time, effort, and dealers' commissions. Some segments of this market are made up of artists that may not be very established, or the quality of their particular works is less easy to discern. Therefore purchasing in the primary market can entail a significant degree of risk.

The much larger secondary market is where dealers and auction houses offer works of art for subsequent resale. One of the distinctive features of the art market is the predominance of trade on this secondary tier, with by far the bulk of value in trading taking place here between former and future consumers. In the primary marketplace, prices tend to be lower than on the secondary market, as it can take considerable time before a work is recognized for its artistic value, rarity, historical importance, or notoriety. By the time a work is resold, these second sales tend to be higher priced by their very nature. Information costs are also lower in the secondary market, and participants are also likely to have more and better information concerning artists and their more established works, and therefore purchases tend to be less risky.

The fall in risk is connected to a distinct feature of works of art, that is, their value tends to appreciate rather than depreciate over time. This is quite different from other goods commonly traded on secondary markets, with a good example being the largest secondary market: the market for used cars. Buyers in the secondhand car market generally purchase cautiously and reluctantly for fear of being landed with a "lemon"; hence the price gap between the primary and secondary markets tends to significantly favor the former. Art collectors, on the other hand, will often be more wary and pay less for new and Contemporary artists' works, whose value may not be as well established as older, more renowned works sold on secondary markets.

Art Market Participants

The art market is made up of a number of different agents, all with varied and important functions, whose interaction shapes the global art trade.

Artists are central to the market as the basic source of its supply. In return for this supply, the market provides artists with a means to earn revenue, a channel to develop their artistic work and professional lives, and an avenue to promote themselves and their creations to the public.

Some artists, generally in the early stages of their career, will sell their work directly to interested collectors, investors, and the public. Some will also produce work on the basis of a commission from a collector or investor, although this tends to apply only to more successful and better-known artists. Most successful artists produce speculative work, which they hope to sell in the future through a gallery or broker. These dealers play a crucial role in many artists' careers and are involved not only in directly selling artists' work but also in promoting and developing their careers over time. Dealers will often work closely with artists and professionally manage their market presence. They will essentially be responsible for establishing the initial price levels for the works, and once a defined price base has been established for the artist, they will use increases in supply to help broaden the market and increase liquidity. Some artists also sell through auction venues, but again, this is not as common and is generally reserved for relatively prolific and well-established artists, or for smaller auction houses that act simultaneously as retailers and concentrate solely on art from a domestic base.

Art sales internationally are split between the two main types of traders in the market: *dealers* and *auction houses*. Although the relative market shares of these two sides of the trade varies over time, it has not shifted significantly from a fifty-fifty split (by value) in the last decade, although it does vary more dramatically in national art markets. In both sides of the market, value is concentrated in a small number of high-value transactions, and in recent years, the majority of these are in the fine art sector. There are a very large number of low-value transactions that take place in the market, and although individually less significant, these make up a substantial portion of the market's overall turnover.[7]

The highly fragmented dealers' market consists of a core of about four thousand art dealers worldwide who are responsible for about 75 percent of the turnover of this side of the market by value, and of those, possibly fewer than one thousand are responsible for about half of the market in terms of value. Beyond this core, however, there are over 100,000 listed dealers of fine and decorative art, including brokers (who sell on a commission basis), other smaller artists' agents, and a large number of small galleries and dealers of low-priced art and antiques.

Art dealers internationally are often single-owner shops or small partnerships, with many built around the names and reputation of individuals or a history of art dealing through family businesses. Dealers typically specialize in a few highly defined fields where they have a high level of expertise and develop a strong vertical presence within one specific designation, building personal and institutional knowledge in this area. Dealers tend also to develop strong bonds with the Contemporary artists that they work with and play a significant role in their career development, marketing, and promotion. Due to their specialized nature, the business model for individual dealerships is often highly dependent on the success of a small number of disciplines, and hence subject at times to considerable risks, in contrast to the more diversified sales of their auction house counterparts.

Dealers have a number of other distinct competitive advantages which have helped them to survive over time: their markups are significant and can range between 50 percent and 400 percent of the wholesale price (the price charged by the artist), and unlike auction houses, dealers do not charge any of the commission or premium to the buyer. Dealers also exert ultimate control over the price and other features surrounding a sale and can maintain confidentiality on all details of their transactions, which has made this side of the market one of the most difficult to measure and quantify. Apart from having direct control over prices they set, dealers can also control the supply of an artist's work on to the market to try to influence demand and establish base prices.

Although dealers remain geographically diverse, an important force changing their practices and bringing them together internationally has been the growth of art fairs over the last decade. Art fairs, including local and international events, have become a vital part of many dealers' livelihoods by giving them access to thousands of new and international clients as well as the stock of their competitive rivals. Art fairs have become important meeting places for dealers and their clients, frequently in locations that are foreign to both. Fairs have allowed dealers to gain access to global sales without the costs or restrictions of setting up premises overseas, although attendance at the increasing number of international fairs brings its own, often substantial expenses related to exhibiting, travel, and other ancillary costs.

Unlike the dealer market, the auction market is highly concentrated. Market leaders Christie's and Sotheby's have about one-third of the total auction market share by value (and about half of the fine art market). Their closest rivals in recent years are Bonham's and Phillips de Pury which account for somewhere in the region of 5 percent of the market each. There is an important second tier of auction houses in different national markets that, although inferior to Christie's and Sotheby's in terms of value of sales, have significant sales and a foothold in international trade, such as Kornfeld (Switzerland), Bonham's (United Kingdom), Villa Grisebach (Germany), or Artcurial (France). Then there is a third tier of small but significant auction houses in most major national art markets that tend to specialize in their own national art and domestic areas. In most countries there are also a number of auction houses that regularly sell art alongside other auctionable property such as real estate, cars, and collectible items.

Unlike dealers, auction houses will generally conduct auctions across a full spectrum of disciplines, although the larger houses have experts in different departments that are highly specialized and skilled in certain genres or sectors of the art market. Larger auction houses tend to locate in one or a group of permanent locations, from where they conduct auctions on a year-round basis. Apart from holding auctions, the houses have a crucial role in appraising, promoting, and preselling works of art. They also perform functions of a clearing and settlement center, which eliminates sellers' counterparty risk and, for buyers, eliminates much of the risk of the origin, provenance, and authenticity of the works of art.

An auction house's business model is based on revenues generated from both the buy and the sell side of the market. Auction houses generally charge commissions of about 10 percent to 20 percent to buyers. The charge for buyers is known as the "buyer's premium" and is added to the "hammer price," the highest winning bid "hammered down" by the auctioneer at a particular art auction. The total sales price for a work of art at auction is therefore the highest successful bid price plus a premium or percentage added on top of that price.

Auction houses also charge a seller's commission to vendors. Some auction houses such as Christie's vary this charge by way of a sliding scale of rates depending on the volume and value of the seller's transactions over a period. Others charge flat rates depending on value. Most art auctions are based on the English, or "ascending price," auction model (such as those in Sotheby's and Christie's), in which bidding starts low and rises as the auctioneer calls out higher and higher prices. When the bidding stops the item is either "hammered down" at the final hammer price or "bought in" by the auction house because the final bid price did not exceed the seller's reserve. Works bought in are either sold at a later date, put up for sale elsewhere, or taken off the market. Although the percentage of works bought in at auction varies widely between auctions, on average it would not be uncommon to see about one third of the works brought to auction fail to sell. As noted earlier, the rate of buy-ins can also act as a gauge of buyer confidence, with higher rates sometimes indicating caution in the market or even a decline in demand.

Unlike dealers, auction houses operate with an explicit set of rules, and sales transactions are open to the public and generally published directly by the auction venue or through art-price-data intermediaries. Before each auction, auction houses publish catalogues, which contain a number of important points of information concerning each artist, sale, and work of art. They include a presale lower and upper estimate for each work. Instead of offering a single estimate of the price that the auction house expects the work to sell for at auction, the convention used by art experts in different departments within the houses is to set a range in which they estimate it will fall (i.e., somewhere between the high and the low estimate). Auction houses do not publish or indicate the seller's reserve price, which is set at or below the presale low estimate. If the bidding at auction does not reach that level, the item will go unsold or be "bought in."

Postsale, auction houses also generally publish the prices achieved at auction, which are available directly from the auction house or through various online data intermediaries. Although art auction data are beset with their own set of problems, the fact that prices are publicly available means that this segment of the market is much less opaque than the dealers' segment. It has also allowed academics, investors, and collectors a chance to be able to study prices and trends objectively in various sectors of the art market. Some of the issues related to art price data are dealt with in Chapter 3.

Some of the larger auction houses such as Christie's and Sotheby's also have a private-sales department, in which the auction house acts in a similar capacity to that of a dealer. These two houses have also extended various financial services—such as guarantees, advances, sales-related loans, and term loans—to clients over time in order to secure consignments.

Collectors also play a central role in the art market, although as a group they are widely varied in terms of goals, backgrounds, and influence. Today's top private collectors are very similar to the patrons of the arts in the market's early history. Instead of titled noblemen and religious dignitaries, the current top art collectors tend to be global high-net-worth individuals, many of whom have made their fortunes in an entirely unrelated area.

It is possible to distinguish between collectors who tend to buy and hoard works of art from more speculative collectors or investors who also use their collections to achieve financial goals. Hoarders may or may not publicly display their collections, but are generally averse to selling works that have been purchased. Investors, on the other hand, purchase works of art with distinct collecting goals in mind; however, these include the possibility of divesting and repurchasing over time to help make their collection work for them financially. Financial returns may not be the primary motive for their collecting activities, but they lie somewhere along a spectrum of considerations included in making a decision on what items to collect. Many investors may also purchase across a wide range of artists within a genre, or even between genres, to hedge against the risks of market declines for a particular artist within their art portfolio.

Apart from individual collectors, there are also a number of institutional and corporate collectors including museums, libraries and other large-scale private and public institutions. Like individuals, these collectors will have varied motives, policies and methods for collecting art, and many public institutions may have certain political, social or cultural policy agendas that they are simultaneously pursuing via a collection or exhibition.

Some private institutional collectors, such as those operating through some of the art funds, buy opportunistically from the market with the hopes of making a capital gain in the medium or long term with pooled investor funds. Most of these funds have been set up by financiers and entrepreneurs hoping to profit from escalating prices and turning art into more of a mainstream asset class, similar to the way property did through real estate investment trusts (REITs) in the 1960s. The development of art funds in the market and their different motivations is discussed in Chapter 6.

Corporate collectors such as banks and other private institutions will often have a number of different motives for purchasing art. Companies may build a collection as a means to support the arts or to pursue some kind of philanthropic motive (along with any tax benefits that might bring). They may simultaneously see their collection as a tool for marketing and promotion, as a testament to the success of a company, or as a way to create a corporate image associated with culture, high quality, or other art- or wealth-related branding.

The *government* is another key player in the art market and has a multifaceted role. The state plays a critical role as a supporter, promoter, and funder of the market's supply, through the various ways in which it directly and indirectly helps to fund artists' careers. Most governments offer some form of direct financial aid to artists through grants or funds, either directly or through funding other semi-state bodies and arts councils, which then validate and distribute funds. Some governments also use different policies to help improve artists' income and benefits such as income tax exemptions, special unemployment benefits, and pensions schemes.

Another important function of government is that of an art market regulator. They can use this role to protect works of art and often reduce trade (e.g., preventing national artistic treasures from being exported), or to stimulate art investment through a variety of fiscal incentives, such as tax incentives to buy, hold, or exhibit works of art. Regulation can, of course, also have a negative impact on the market (either intended or unintended), adding layers of costs and red tape and causing disincentives to trade and investment.

Apart from influencing the market indirectly through funding, fiscal measures, and legislation, the government is also a direct consumer and investor in the market, with national galleries, museums, and libraries amassing substantial national, regional, and local art collections on behalf of the state. National governments also often play an important role as members of supranational bodies, such as UNESCO and Interpol, that attempt to enforce standards, regulations and other policies in the international art market.

The government's various roles in regulating and influencing the art market are dealt with in detail in Chapter 7, while tax issues in relation to the art market are discussed in Chapters 9 and 10.

Because of the lack of transparency in the art market, there are a number of agents that can collectively be referred to as gatekeepers, as they control the flow of some of the important information in the market. Because of its subjective nature and the fact that the quality of art is not directly quantifiable, art experts and critics play a significant role in spreading information in the market and making normative assessments of artists and the work that they produce.

Critics and others in the trade also rely on a relatively small number of outlets in the art and mainstream financial press to transmit this information. The art trade press consists of a number of periodicals and magazines of a widely varying quality. Some of the market stalwarts such as *The Art Newspaper, The Antiques Trade Gazette,* and *Art + Auction* contain regular and mostly accurate reporting on events in the global market, while others consist of a high percentage of advertising and advertorial combined with gossip, criticism, features, interviews, and calendars of up-and-coming events.

There are also a number of art data providers, who sell or give away art auction data and related information online. At present, there are about ten functioning online art databases that sell art auction data and several other sites that post artist and market information, again of widely variable quality. Besides price databases, other art information databases exist online for specific purposes or general information. A notable example is the Art Loss Register (ALR), which allows a work of art to be checked against an international online database of lost and stolen art.

Surrounding the key players in the art market are a number of ancillary businesses and associated support services. These businesses are important in ensuring the adequate functioning of the market and play supporting roles in the infrastructure of the art trade. Some of these are independent companies that have developed an art-related component such as financial institutions, insurance companies and banks offering art advisory services. Citi, Deutsche Bank, UBS, Credit Suisse, and some other major private banks, for example, all offer art advisory services, which range from advice on art collecting to financing and releasing liquidity using art as collateral, in a distinct department.

Chapter 5 discusses the current issues and practices in the area of art banking.

Others are stand-alone institutions that have developed specifically to serve the art market, such as specialist insurers (for example, AXA Art Insurance); independent appraisers and art advisers; specialist shipping, packaging, restoring, and security services; and others.

There are a number of businesses that also work around specific events in the art market such as art fairs or large exhibitions. These may work exclusively in the art market on a series of these events (e.g., specialist event organizers) or alternatively broker services to these events among a range of other clients. These associated and support businesses can be significant revenue and employment generators.

Art as a Financial Asset

One of the most interesting features of works of art is that they are dual in nature: on the one hand they are something to consume and enjoy (what economists call "consumer durables" that yield a nonmonetary viewing benefit); and on the other, they are capital assets that yield a return from their appreciation in value over time like other financial assets.

In common with other financial assets, the value of works of art tends to increase over time, as their use does not depend on any degenerative practical function, making them both a store of value and a potential source of capital gain. Their uniqueness and durability make them "collectibles," which are both sought after and scarce. As discussed, a large amount of trade in art takes place between art consumers in secondary markets rather than in primary sales, and this is connected to the feature that works of art appreciate in value over time, unlike many other consumer assets.

In economics, works of art are also termed "luxury goods," meaning that they have a "high income elasticity of demand": people demand proportionally more of them as their income rises. They have also been classified in economics as "positional goods"—goods that are inherently impossible to mass-produce as their value is mainly, if not exclusively, a function of their relative desirability. Positional goods are rare and unique enough to be socially distinguished, and an ability to purchase them generally depends on one's relative rather than absolute economic position. Works of art are positional goods in the sense that their supply cannot be augmented in the same manner as other goods. Increased demand in the art market cannot necessarily increase supply as in other markets, and instead elevates prices.

The competition for a particular work of art between collectors is what is known as a zero-sum game (as it is with all positional goods): because they are inherently scarce (there is limited supply for deceased artist and even for living artists' works in the short run), any attempts to acquire a particular work can only benefit one collector at the expense of another. This competition for art works leads to escalating prices, despite the fact that the goods themselves may have negligible intrinsic value.

All of these features make art a desirable asset for investment purposes, but it also has two very important characteristics distinct from financial assets. First, each work of art is unique and has no close substitutes, which will always bring a measure of subjectivity into valuations. Each original work of painting or sculpture, for example, is distinctive or a "one-off", even if it is copied or produced in the style of another artist. Second, because art trades very infrequently or trades on very "thin" markets (with a low number of buyers and sellers), it is a relatively illiquid asset, compared with stocks, bonds, and other financial instruments. This issue of liquidity has been a critical one in financial evaluations of art as an asset class.[8] An asset that is highly liquid is going to be more attractive than one that is less liquid as it is easier to "get your money out" whenever you want to. Works of art are obviously much less liquid than most money market assets, which makes speculative investing in art with a short-term horizon a high-risk and less-attractive strategy, especially for novices.[9]

These two features have thrown up a number of issues in trying to accurately quantitatively assess art as an investment. However, record prices, superior relative returns, attractive risk characteristics, and the interest of some major banks and institutional investors, have all sparked greater interest in the development of metrics and analysis to overcome the anomalies of this marketplace. Thanks to research in finance, economics and within the art trade itself, methods have been developed to measure and value art and to estimate its returns as an investment. The numbers are often more complex than some in mainstream finance, but they are doable, and art is now accepted as a valid investment asset class and generally one in which there is a positive return from capital appreciation over time that has often been better or as good as many alternatives. This evolving market still has unique features and many inefficiencies, mostly related to lack of transparency in the market, but investment in art is now within the radar of most of the mainstream financial community.

Art and Economics

Despite the special position that art occupies in the fabric and culture of societies, the reality is that art is produced, bought, and sold by individuals and institutions working within an economic framework inescapable from material and market constraints. The economic case is clear: the market for works of art functions at least as well as many others (albeit imperfectly and with certain special features), as it allows market transactions by voluntary consent, in which buyers and sellers mutually benefit.

Art prices, like prices in other markets, result from the interplay between the forces of supply and demand. These dynamics are also critical to understanding how returns on art investments are determined. However, the art market has a number of unique features not found in financial markets. Despite its size, it has relatively few of the formal coordination mechanisms or institutional structures that are found in other developed markets, and the base of buyers and sellers is a highly fragmented global mix that often relies on personal relationships and implicit trust to conduct business. The fragmented nature of the market, combined with its opacity and the often subjective elements in valuations, leads to information asymmetries which in turn lead to high transaction costs and the need for art experts, who act as both gatekeepers and market makers.

One of the most important economic features of the market is that it is essentially *supply driven*. Even if works of art are in high demand by collectors and investors, there always will be only a finite number of total works available (particularly in the case of deceased artists) and thus a more limited quantity on the market at any particular point in time. In other words, the fixed supply of most paintings can cause prices to catapult, as buyers attempt to grasp increasingly limited opportunities to buy high-quality works that often have a lengthy market cycle. Research on the art market shows that a typical cycle to market can take about thirty to forty years. In other words, from the time the work is first sold, it will take several decades (on average) for buyers to get the opportunity purchase that work again, which adds to the scarcity value of art.

Identical stocks in large corporations are sold literally every second on exchanges throughout the world, but in the secondary art market in particular, supply is often generated by "distress sales." A work of art often arrives on the market because of one of the famous "three Ds" (divorce, death, or debt). Because of the scarcity of high-quality works in circulation in the art market, increased supply can have a strong, positive effect on prices, unlike in other asset markets where excess supply drives prices downward.

Because the total quantity of art supply is essentially fixed in the short run for nearly all artists (and also in the long run for deceased artists), no matter what price someone may be willing to pay for more art, extra supply cannot be created simply to meet demand. This gives the market what economists call "zero elasticity": no matter how large the change in price, the quantity supplied cannot change.[10] It is because of these limits on supply that prices for art can shoot up to seemingly extraordinary levels when works appear on the market, with collectors trying to seize the often rare opportunity to own a particular unique asset.

The demand side of the art market is driven by the characteristics and preferences of a number of different market participants, including collectors, investors, museums, dealers, companies, and individuals with a desire to own works of art. The size and spending power of buyers, their awareness, taste, and a host of other characteristics will all affect demand for art in specific and different ways, and these will differ among transactions and over time.

Income is a critical driver of the demand for art, and the relationship is simple: income has a large, positive effect on demand. For nearly all goods that people consume, as income grows, demand increases[11]; for luxury goods such as art, this effect is magnified: demand increases more than proportionally as income rises, or they have a high income elasticity of demand. As people become richer, they spend more generally but can also afford to spend proportionally more on luxuries or "nonessential" items such as art. This also implies that if there is a drop in income, demand for luxury cars, expensive jewelry, art, and other luxuries should also decline.

The positive income effect on demand for art occurs at both the micro and macro level. As an individuals' wealth expands, they purchase more luxury goods and invest in more alternative assets such as art. At a more macro level, an increase in the wealth of a nation can also be linked to increased demand for art. The property bubble that escalated the wealth of many Japanese in the 1980s also buoyed their presence in the art market. More recently, the growing wealth of the emerging economies such as China, Russia, and India has also contributed to increased demand for their national works of art, both domestically as incomes increase and through their growing wealthy diasporas.

Taste is also central to understanding demand for art. Taste, preferences, fads, and fashion drive art consumption, although quantifying their effects is not straightforward. For goods that are purchased regularly and about which there is abundant and publicly available information, it is easy for consumers to recognize a product's quality and most will rely on their own taste to drive purchasing decisions. As art is a luxury good, however, many buyers do not even enter the market until they have reached a certain level of wealth, and even wealthy collectors buy art relatively infrequently, so they may have limited purchasing experience. While personal taste and preferences are central to purchasing a subjective and aesthetic asset such as art, many buyers are in fact very reluctant to rely on their own tastes to do that (particularly at the middle to high end of the market). Novice buyers have to either devote significant amounts of time and effort in researching the market or rely on art experts who become pivotal in forming and shaping the public taste and aggregate demand in many sectors.

Another method used by less-experienced buyers in the art market to reduce their search and information costs is to purchase only well-recognized works or those by famous artists. By doing so, they are essentially relying on preferences already established by previously successful buyers, hence reducing the risks of relying on their own taste in making the right choice. Collectively, these risk-reducing techniques tend to reinforce the "superstar phenomenon" in the art market, whereby the works of the most famous artists are demanded the most and achieve by far the highest prices in the market, while emerging artists face significant hurdles in gaining entry. Although many superstar artists have reached their positions by being more talented than their peers, the infrequent nature of sales and reliance on expertise does drive many art consumers to "consume as others are consuming" or to seek common and accepted tastes. These actions collectively reinforce the position of successful artists while sometimes letting others who are equally talented go unnoticed.

The price and availability of substitutes in a market usually has a significant impact on the demand for a product. As stated earlier however, works are unique and are characterized by a lack of close substitutes. If the prices of works by a particular Contemporary artist are prohibitively high, for example, a collector will not necessarily simply start buying Dutch Old Master paintings or antique furniture. Some collectors may, however, substitute between different works of a given artist, or even artists within a particular genre. If art is being purchased largely as a financial investment, buyers may be more driven to seek out substitutes for works that are perceived to be overpriced in the market, including other forms of alternative investments such as hedge funds, structured products, or commodities.

Finally, the higher the expected return on an investment in art, the greater the demand. Returns can be negative—some works may actually decline in value (sell at a lower price than their original purchase price) or even maintain their face value but incur a negative return given the costs to hold and maintain them over the period. Negative expected returns will dampen demand, as will risk and uncertainty surrounding that return. Those investors seeking highly liquid investments are also likely to find art less inviting than other asset classes.

The interaction of the forces of supply and demand in the art market has some complexities that cannot be explained by mainstream economic theory. Art has a subjective value but also a financial value, both measurable by prices achieved in the market. However, analyzing the various factors that make up the price of an artwork can be difficult. Objective and quantifiable factors such as the subject matter, size, medium, provenance, and condition of the work, as well as the artist's fame and popularity, will all contribute to its financial value. But there is also a large subjective and essentially irrational element that determines the price of a work of art according to a particular collector or investor's taste or aesthetic. It is possible, however, to construct a fair valuation range that one could expect art prices for particular works or artists to fall within. The excess paid over this range measures the extent of the irrational and subjective premium inherent in art prices.

Chapter 2 deals with these and some of the other complexities in the valuation and pricing of art in practice.

Art as an Investment

Internal evolution alongside external demands on the art market has meant that, for the first time, art is being properly examined for its value as a financial asset. As with any other investment, one of the starting points when analyzing an investment in art is assessing financial returns over time, measured by the change in its net monetary value. Many argue that there is an additional psychic return from art ownership that arises from the benefits from the consumption element of art. This psychic component is often measured indirectly through residual methods (e.g., through the difference between the returns on art versus returns on other alternative assets) but is mostly irrelevant when considering the financial implications of owning art in an investment context.

However, even assessing financial returns over a given period is problematic for this asset class. As previously discussed, works of art are unique products with extremely slow turnover. When considering investing in company stocks, it is simple to track returns by looking directly at what other identical shares in the market are trading at. If we want to see how the prices of a particular work or artist are performing, there is no comparable mechanism to check the daily or even monthly closing or opening prices. Economists have developed some methods to try to overcome these two major problems of heterogeneity and infrequency of trading (and some of these methods are discussed in Chapter 3).

In appraising the relative returns to art versus other assets, there are also a number of issues that must be addressed. Holding costs, for example, are the various costs incurred to maintain, store, restore, and insure a work of art. Holding costs occur for all physical, tangible assets, including real estate. Here, they arise from the need to use specialized art-related services that are unique to art investments and need to be deducted from returns in order to draw meaningful comparisons with other financial assets. (Issues directly related to the conservation and restoration of artworks are dealt with in Chapter 11, and art insurance is discussed in Chapter 8.) These costs vary depending on the artwork and the context of the investment and may run between 1 percent and 5 percent of the net asset value.

Relative transaction costs also warrant consideration. For example, auction fees and commissions imposed on buyers vary but often amount to as much as 25 percent for both parties (buyers and sellers) and may also include mandatory insurance and shipping charges. Some of these transactions costs are unique to art investments and can be materially higher than in other asset markets. The costs associated with buying and selling art at auction can, for example, be up to ten times more than those for commercial real estate sales.

On the positive side, there are also a number of tax advantages to investing in art (some of which are discussed in Chapter 9 and Chapter 10). In many countries, investment in art is used as a vehicle to escape or reduce the burden of tax, and hence the tax advantages of owning art can be an important part of an investor's final return.

Investors in the art market can be classified as functioning along a spectrum from pure collectors to pure speculators, and the relative importance of the different elements of the return to art investing will differ depending on their position. Those that exist toward the speculative end tend to be highly sensitive to price variations, their financial risk, and other risks such as uncertain provenance. Changes in the costs to buy, sell, store, or insure art, as well as changes in regulations affecting the art market (e.g., taxation or export restrictions), may also significantly shift their investment outlook and even drive speculators out of the market into alternative asset classes. Pure collectors, on the other hand, are (in theory) less concerned with changes in the value of art or risks related to its price and are less sensitive to selling costs and regulations, as their primary motivations are to buy and hold their collections regardless of the cost or value of doing so.

The marginal choice between buying art as an investment or as a collector's consumption good depends on an individual's preferences and financial means. However, neither extreme is an optimal position. Liquidity in the art market is too low to enable the necessary investment tactics to make pure speculation profitable, while even collectors with the purest of aesthetic motivations would be highly imprudent not to consider some of the financial implications of their investment in art, at least to the extent that they might affect the value or tax treatment of other assets in their portfolio of wealth, or even what can be bequeathed to or imposed on the next generation.

The flip side of investment returns is risk. While the returns to art can vary considerably between different genres and artists and across time, the potential to use art for risk diversification in an investment portfolio is undoubtedly its most tangible and attractive feature as an asset class.

There are a number of risks associated with an investment in art that do not exist for other financial asset classes. Because art is a material asset, there are risks related to its physicality, such as risk of damage or wear and tear over time. As with other material assets, an insurance market exists to help mitigate risks such as these in the art market and this is discussed in Chapter 8.

Other risks specific to this asset class are concerned with a work's authenticity: Is it a fake or a copy? How certain is its title and provenance? Are there any questions related to its rights of ownership? All of these risks are peculiar to this asset class and relate to the reliance on expert opinion for valuation and validation. The human-judgment element that is inevitable in the assessment of the value of art adds a layer of risk, as it comes with the ensuing possibility of human error and bias. These risks can, of course, be reduced by vetting the particular vendor used (and the experience, reputation, and qualifications of its experts) and ensuring adequate research in regard to provenance and authenticity; however, mistakes can still be made even by the most reputable auction houses and dealers.

The basic financial risk of any investment is the uncertainty concerning the rate of return and, as with any investment, the risk of an investment in art arises from fluctuations in the rate of price change. As with all assets, the objective of investing is to minimize the downside risk for a given level of return, or to maximize the returns for a given level of risk. The important area of risk analysis in the art market is the subject of Chapter 4. There are a number of statistical methods to measure risk both for individual art assets and relative to other investments. A problem with most measures is that they rely on historical data (which means they cannot predict future risks), and most are best used for short-term decision making, which is not often appropriate in the context of investment in the art market. What these measures are useful for is to help build a picture of how markets and assets have interacted in the past, which can suggest ways to combine art and other assets to reduce risk in a more long-term portfolio of wealth.

The main principle of portfolio management is efficient diversification: through finding and combining assets that have low correlation with each other, it is possible to obtain a portfolio risk that is less than that of the component assets considered in isolation. Art has been shown to have low and negative correlation with many other asset classes over different periods and the diversification benefits from investing in art are among its strongest selling points. These benefits are apparent not only in portfolios that mix various assets with art but also within an individual collection of art, through strategically combining different categories of art with each other to hedge against risk. Apart from standard financial risk analysis, the art auction process itself provides a unique and very useful method for measuring the downside risk in art investing via presale auction estimates. Risk can be measured through assessing the deviation of actual market prices from the presale valuation range or, in other words, how the price achieved at auction deviates from the price it was expected to achieve. If the work sells for a price above the estimated range, that is obviously an unexpected upside benefit, so in terms of assessing risk, the focus is on the downside—that is, if the price achieved at auction falls short of its expectation.

The mainstream application of risk analysis to the art market is still in its infancy, yet it shows great potential, with theory significantly outpacing practice. An industry that has emerged already in this area is art banking and specifically the use of art as collateral for lending, which is discussed in Chapter 5.

Looking Forward

The trade in art makes up a substantial and lucrative market, as well as one that has continued to develop despite various downturns in the global economy. Over the last decade, the art market has been on a phenomenal path of growth, with certain sectors advancing at a particularly rapid pace. It is likely that these first few years of the twenty-first century will stand out as significant in the art market's history as a period of remarkable growth, advancing prices, and growing participation from new global players.

Although the global financial crisis had been brewing for some time, it really started to show its full effects in the middle of 2008, and the long-term boom in the art market was tested for the first time. Around the world, stock markets fell, major financial institutions collapsed or were bought out, and governments in even the wealthiest nations have had to come up with rescue packages to bail out their financial systems.

The same day that Lehman Brothers collapsed in New York in September 2008, Sotheby's held a successful and landmark sale of primary works by Damien Hirst in London. This was immediately touted in the press as a sign of the art market's immunity to the prevailing financial crises. The very same media outlets were however running with a very different story within a matter of weeks. The major Contemporary art auctions at the end of 2008 were hailed to be the first tests of the market since the financial sector really bottomed out. These sales did appear to show some ripple effects from the economic downturn, with marked signs of buyer hesitation such as works selling below their estimates and a higher-than-usual proportion of buy-ins.

Views differ on how these results should be interpreted. One view holds that the apparent decline in some Contemporary prices marks the end of spending spree in this sector by global buyers and is a sign of possible further decline ahead. Most research studies have shown that the Contemporary sector has tended to have the most correlation with financial indices of all categories in the art market, albeit often with a significant lag, and is therefore the most susceptible to general economic fortunes. Another view contends that the poor results represent a correction occurring in the market, which was on an unstable growth path that could not be sustained. Some top international dealers have remarked that the market generally has in fact been on a bull run since as early as 1994, and that a correction has been delayed up to now because of the new buyers from emerging economies.

By early 2009, auction sales were already starting to show signs of improvement. Many of the spring auctions showed strong results as fresh works of high quality and reasonable estimates continued to sell for exceptional prices. Lesser-quality works, on the other hand, still had problems finding buyers. The full effects of the global financial crisis on the art market as a whole are as yet not fully clear. Predicting the effects of the economic recession on the art market is difficult, as two opposing economic forces are likely to influence the art market: a "wealth effect" on consumption and an investor "substitution effect."[12]

The wealth effect means that as an individual's or nation's income rises, demand and potential consumption of all goods is facilitated at a higher level, and for luxury goods such as art, demand increases more than proportionally with income. With some contraction in global wealth, therefore, it could be argued that lower incomes or less discretionary income (the income that remains after essentials are paid for) will lead to lower consumption of luxury goods.

On the other hand, in the current environment there is also an important "substitution effect" present for investors, which may enable the art market to resist some of the impact of the global financial downturn. Many sectors of the art market have shown consistently low or negative correlation with financial indices over time, suggesting that their price and return trajectories are often unrelated to other asset classes, and making art an attractive alternative investment in order to diversify risk. If sectors of the art market have low correlation with equity markets, for example, investors may either substitute art for poorly performing stocks in their portfolios or simply invest in art to maintain a more balanced portfolio of assets with lower risk in the turbulent economic environment.

Perhaps the only thing that can be said looking forward is that the future of the art market, like that of many sectors of the economy, is less certain and is likely to show some dampening of results from the bull run of the last decade within certain categories, while other sectors will continue to show strength. It seems likely that the era of the art market in which almost anything would sell at any price is coming to a close, and because of that, more prudent valuations may begin to emerge. It is exactly in a period of uncertainty in the market where experts' advice to buy the best-quality works and not to overpay particularly rings true. It is also a crucial time to be aware of the more fundamental tenets of investing in this asset class, with particular regard to its long-term and illiquid nature, as well as its attractive risk characteristics.

Chapter Notes

1. This figure includes the auctioneer's sales premiums and commissions. The hammer price for the work at auction was $75 million. Saito also bought *Au Moulin de la Galette* by Renoir for a world-record hammer price of $71 million. The purchase of *Dr. Gachet*, however, broke the previous records of a string of high-profile Japanese purchases, including $36.2 million for van Gogh's *Sunflowers*, purchased by Yasuda Fire and Marine Insurance in 1987, the $38.1 million (with premiums) paid by Mitsukoshi Department Store for Picasso's *Acrobat and Young Harlequin* in 1988, and

the hammer price of $51.7 million for Picasso's *Les Noces de Pierrette* by Nippon Autopolis in 1989.

2. Note that estimates of the size of the art market are based on figures from Arts Economics and Artprice and have been converted from euros to U.S. dollars for 2008 using interbank exchange rates in December 2008. There were significant fluctuations in the exchange rates between these currencies over 2007 and 2008, therefore the size of the market should be considered as an estimate based on the contemporaneous exchange rate only.

3. Calculations from Artprice (2009).

4. Christie's May Postwar and Contemporary sale, for example, showed buy-in rates of only 9 percent, with thirty lots selling for over $1 million. Sotheby's spring Contemporary sale recorded buy-in rates of 19 percent, with 14 works over $1 million.

5. This is the global market share for the fine *and* decorative art market in 2007. According to Artprice, the U.S. share of the fine art auction market contracted in 2008, leaving it neck and neck with the United Kingdom at 36 percent each. This could, in part, be contributed to by the contraction of the U.S. dollar vis a vis other major currencies including the Euro and Great British Pound over the period.

6. For a full discussion of the impact of these new economies on the global art market, see Clare McAndrew, *Globalisation and the Art Market: Emerging Economies and the Art Trade in 2008* (Helvoirt: TEFAF, 2009).

7. An interesting example given in McAndrew (2008) shows that in 2006 91 percent of the total global art auction turnover are in the price bracket below $25,000, and within those sales just over 76 percent are below $6,000. See Clare McAndrew, *The International Art Market: A Survey of Europe in a Global Context* (Helvoirt: TEFAF, 2008).

8. Liquidity refers to the ease at which an asset can be converted to cash or bought and sold on a secondary market without affecting the asset's value.

9. Developments within the art market such as art funds and other instruments have made it somewhat easier to buy and sell relatively quickly and easily, and even without the risks of full ownership.

10. Auction houses and dealers can often manipulate the timing, sequence, and appearance of the supply of art on to the market. However, as mentioned above, sellers often offer the works to them in the first place as the result of some form of ad hoc or exogenous event (such as the repayment of debt) that is beyond their control.

11. The positive relationship between income and demand holds for all "normal goods." There are certain goods that are classified in economics as "inferior goods," which have a negative relationship. Typical examples are intercity bus fares (which demand is thought to increase for if air and rail become too expensive), mass-market beer, and plain-label food products.

12. These terms are borrowed from basic economic consumer demand theory but applied in this case to investors. In traditional theory, the substitution effect would

refer to that portion of the effect of price on quantity demanded that reflects the changed trade-off between a good versus its alternatives. As prices rise, consumers will substitute away from higher-priced goods, choosing less costly alternatives. In addition, as the wealth of the individual rises, demand increases, shifting the demand curve higher at all rates of consumption. This is called the income or wealth effect. Investors, on the other hand, will always look for lower risk for a given return or higher returns for a given level of risk.

2

Art Appraisals, Prices, and Valuations

Elizabeth von Habsburg and Rachel Goodman, Gurr Johns
Dr. Clare McAndrew

EDITOR'S NOTE: Art prices, like prices in financial markets, are determined by the interaction of supply and demand. However, the process by which these forces are formed and interact in the art market has some unique features and complexities that go beyond the explanations of mainstream economic theory. Values in the art market are driven by a range of dichotomies: objective and subjective appraisals, rational and irrational forces, and quantitative and qualitative factors. Art has a subjective value to those who own and admire it but also has a financial value, and both these values are measurable by the prices it achieves in the market.

Past auction prices can help understand and forecast trends in the art market, but since individual art assets turn over relatively slowly and trade thinly, assessing the value of a work of art at a point in time always also requires a degree of human expertise and subjectivity. This expertise has developed into the industry of art appraisal, which is a crucial sector to understand and employ when making an investment in art.

The first section addresses appraisals and valuations in terms of such matters as taxes, insurance, estate planning, and sales, while the second section addresses the larger economic issues of valuations for art as an asset class.

Art Appraisals

Elizabeth von Habsburg and Rachel Goodman

Since the late 1990s, more and more individuals have begun purchasing works of art as a way of diversifying the assets in their portfolios. Art prices have skyrocketed, particularly in such sectors as Postwar and Contemporary Western art and Asian art, and the number of private art collectors around the world has increased exponentially. As a result of this growth, art has truly come to be considered, more than at any time in the past, its own distinct financial asset class.

There are many challenges unique to managing art assets: curatorial matters, insurance, risk management, taxation, transaction costs, and emotional considerations. The first step in tackling these challenges—whether buying, selling, moving, storing, restoring, or donating a work of art or a collection—is to establish value, and this is done through an appraisal. Establishing taxes that are due on art works in an estate situation (or, indeed, those that can be avoided) and accurately insuring your collection, for example, are both impossible tasks without establishing the collection's underlying value. When these measures are not undertaken in the most professional way, the legal, financial, and emotional consequences can be costly. Given its importance, the discussion to follow will clearly define the components, terminology, and methodology of a properly conducted art appraisal and touch on the particular difficulties of managing art as a financial asset. What is most important, however, is that it will clarify how and why an appraisal is a crucial step in effective financial management of your art collection.

An Overview of Art Market Prices

Until the latter half of 2008, when much of the world was reaching a point of financial crisis, certain areas of the art market were reaching extraordinary values. Works of Western Contemporary art, photography, Chinese and Indian Contemporary art, and Russian art, for example, were reaching unprecedented prices at auction. From 2002 to 2006, sales in the art market grew by 95 percent in terms of value, and 2006 represented a boom year in the market, with sales, number of transactions, and average prices all increasing. Much of the expansion in the global art market was driven by strong prices for fine art at auction, but certain sectors led the market in price increases. As a result of its unprecedented growth rates and the number of new global investors who were attracted to it, the Contemporary sector received much attention. In the boom year of 2006, among the ten art markets recognized for achieving the sharpest price inflation over the previous five years were Chinese Contemporary (with 336 percent growth), Indian Contemporary (684 percent), and Russian Contemporary (253 percent).[1] After 2006, the Contemporary market continued to advance, and by 2007, it had become the largest department in the major salesrooms of Sotheby's and Christie's.

In the introduction to his book *The $12 Million Stuffed Shark* (which refers to the staggering price that hedge fund executive Steven Cohen paid in 2005 for a two-ton shark preserved in formaldehyde by British artist Damien Hirst), Don Thompson marvels at how record prices were achieved at auction for 131 Contemporary artists in 2006.[2] In fact, many of the records for the most expensive paintings were set that year: Jackson Pollock's *No. 5, 1948*, reportedly sold for $140 million in a transaction negotiated by Tobias Meyer of Sotheby's;[3] Willem de Kooning's *Woman III* was said to have sold for $137.5 million in a private purchase;[4] and Pablo Picasso's *Dora Maar au Chat* sold at Sotheby's for $95.2 million. That these transactions all occurred in 2006 was a reflection of both the soaring economy and the soaring art market at that time.

Other types of art, however, also experienced dramatic increases in collector demand, and auction prices rose rapidly. The Russian art and photography markets became deeper and broader, with new and more aggressive collectors entering the market each year, and works by Chinese Contemporary artists began to command prices exceeding the million-dollar mark. One notable sale was in April 2008, when a painting titled *Bloodline: The Big Family No. 3*, by Zhang Xiaogang, one of China's most prominent artists, sold for just over $6 million at Sotheby's Chinese Contemporary art sale in Hong Kong, marking the highest price ever paid for a painting by a Chinese Contemporary artist. Such was the boom in Chinese Contemporary art that Pace Wildenstein, a powerful Manhattan gallery, was prompted to open a location in Beijing in August 2008, in an attempt to capitalize on the growing demand for art from newly wealthy Chinese collectors.

By the fall of 2008, after several years of growth, when it was beginning to look as if Contemporary prices would never hit a ceiling, the stock markets in the United States, Europe, and Asia experienced a significant downturn, and the Contemporary art sector finally began to show some signs of weakening. Many collectors who had suffered losses either on Wall Street or in the broader economic downturn needed to raise cash and put works up for sale. Many items simply did not attract buyers, and declining prices began to hinder sales further. To make matters worse, auction estimates, traditionally set between two and three months prior to each sale, reflected price levels from the spring of 2008 rather than the newer, more conservative reality. Many buyers sat on their hands, waiting to see what would sell. Tracking sales of prolific artist Andy Warhol's works in the fall 2008 auctions shows the trajectories of price levels in that period. Because his works had formerly made up an increasingly hot market each season, many Warhols for sale in the November 2008 auctions were listed with overly optimistic estimates. Sellers were hoping both to gain some liquidity and to cash in at the market high, but with so many works up for auction and with so many cautious or disinterested buyers, a number of the works went unsold. Warhol reflected the broader picture: With fewer people looking to buy because of the economic uncertainty, sales in general were far less successful. In October and November 2008, many sales at auction were down as much as 30 percent in terms of lots sold, and down 45–55 percent in terms of value, bringing prices in some sectors of the market back to the levels of 2006, the start of the boom.

Despite the gloomy outlook in 2009, many art buyers found themselves in a rather more favorable position than previously, in that those who were still in a position to make the investment might be able to obtain some high-quality works of art for reduced prices. There were also some still distinctly bright spots in the market, as certain sectors continued to attract interested buyers. In the autumn and winter of 2008, for example, Fabergé items were still achieving high auction prices, and photography, wristwatches, and twentieth-century furniture sales were generally steady if not strong. Overpriced items in all categories were not selling to prudent and price-conscious buyers, but high-quality works at reasonable prices in all collecting fields were still routinely realizing strong sales, and, in early 2009, the more realistic London auction sales estimates of Impressionist, Modern, and Contemporary art resulted in strong sales, with totals reverting to the more standard rates of 75–90 percent of the lots sold, by lot and by value.

Appraisals and Value

Some of the changes described above in certain sectors of the fall 2008 art market undoubtedly reflected the tumult of the world economy, but contractions in different areas of the market were an unfortunate, but highly relevant, example of the need for effective management of an art collection as a financial asset. A work of art can sell for different values at different times, because its value is related to timing and to such external factors as the economy and different trends and tastes in artistic genres. With this in mind, you will need to have a grasp of what you own and how much it is worth, and to update that knowledge on a regular basis.

In the art-appraisal practice, appraisers have seen many instances where collectors were unaware that certain items they owned were extraordinarily valuable, one example being an estate that contained a painting by Ludovico Carracci, an important early-Baroque painter. The work had been passed down through the generations within the family, and since it had never been properly identified by an expert, the owner had never realized that she owned such a valuable asset. Through enlisting the help of a professional appraiser, however, her estate was able to identify the painting and arrange for the sale of the work at auction for $1.6 million, all of which had been bequeathed to charity. Another previously unknowing collector discovered a table that was identified as a Chippendale mahogany tea table from 1760, worth $6.7 million. Aside from the excitement that comes along with a discovery like this, these examples highlight the responsibility inherent in owning fine or decorative art. Unlike other types of assets, such as real estate or stocks, the value of art is not readily apparent, and so appraisal by an independent and qualified appraiser can help collectors come to terms with the valuation problem and allow reasonable estate planning.

There is a range of issues involved in trying to aggregate and assess prices and values in the art market. (Chapter 3 discusses some of the complexities involved in developing aggregate price indices for art.) Although much progress has been made in developing quantitative assessment methods, a large part of valuing art for investment or any other purpose must always rely to some extent on qualitative measures. It is important to note that these qualitative inputs in the valuation process should not be simply the random, subjective feelings of a particular collector or investor but should rather be informed input from the research of well-qualified experts in the sector. It is also critical to remember that the art market cannot be viewed as a homogeneous entity when appraising (or when compiling indices) but is rather a compilation of over 300 separate markets, within each of which are different levels of value, all of which increase or decrease at different rates.

In an appraisal, there are a number of different definitions of value that can be assigned for different scenarios:

❑ *Retail replacement value* (RRV) is the amount of money it would cost to replace an item with a like item of similar quality, in a retail venue, and within a relatively short period of time. RRV is usually used for insurance purposes.

❑ *Fair market value* (FMV) is what a willing buyer would pay a willing seller in an open market (in this case, usually the auction market), with both parties having full knowledge of all the relevant facts. Fair market value is generally less than RRV, with the former reflecting how much it would cost to purchase the item in an auction scenario, while RRV reflects the cost of purchasing the item at a high-end gallery. FMV is typically used for estate and income tax appraisals.

❑ *Marketable cash value* (MCV) is determined by taking the FMV of the item and subtracting from it the cost of selling the item, such as commissions, insurance costs, and similar transactions costs. MCV is typically applied in situations such as divorces, when assets need to be divided.

INSURANCE APPRAISALS

Insurance appraisals are prepared as a risk-management measure, in order to protect assets in case the art collection falls victim to fire, flood, storm, theft, accidental damage, or any other unfortunate situation. As mentioned earlier, these appraisals will generally apply RRV to the works of art or collections. Many collectors unwisely avoid this type of appraisal, because they fear that the Internal Revenue Service might at some point use the insurance values for estate tax purposes, or that a listing of the contents of a confidential collection or estate might become public knowledge. With insufficient or no insurance coverage, however, the collector would sustain a 100 percent loss if a catastrophic event befalls a work of art instead of the much safer alternative that would provide a significant reduction in monetary losses—if the collector had insured the works properly. Also, the IRS recognizes the difference between insurance and fair market value when an appraisal is prepared for estate tax purposes, so it is a generally unfounded fear that the IRS would use the insurance values to penalize an estate.

TAX APPRAISALS

Appraisals are required for tax- or estate-planning purposes in order to determine the amount of money collectors or their heirs will pay in estate taxes, and appraisals are also necessary for philanthropic or

Why a Tax Appraisal Is Important: One Scenario

To highlight the importance of appropriate appraisals in a tax scenario, consider the following very simple scenario:

A client's relative dies, and the client removes a painting from the decedent's house, hanging it instead on her own wall. She does not claim the painting as an inherited item, nor does she have it appraised, nor does she pay taxes on it.

When she realizes that the painting is by a prominent nineteenth-century American artist, she decides to sell it to a local art dealer for $100,000.

The art dealer, having recognized the true value of the painting, subsequently resells it for $500,000.

The woman did two things wrong in this situation:

❏ By not paying any taxes on the item, she committed tax fraud. Hiding works of art from the IRS is a foolhardy proposition, leaving beneficiaries to suffer the consequences. There is no statute of limitations on tax fraud.

❏ She sold the painting to the dealer for much less than she should have.

When all was said and done, the woman has forfeited far more money than she would have had she simply obtained an appropriate appraisal for estate purposes, paid the tax, and sold the painting for its true worth.

charitable giving to a museum or other 501(c)(3) organization, for which the donated works must conform to the related-use parameters. Fair market value is generally assigned in tax appraisals.

In addition to their being legal documents for estate tax purposes, appraisals for tax and estate planning serve as an inventory list of items in an estate and are useful to the current owners and future heirs as a tool to assist in decisions concerning disposition of the tangibles. A good lawyer will always instruct clients to avoid using imprecise language when drafting their wills, because specific language helps to avoid confusion and subsequent arguments over who will inherit what. Language such as "household contents," "antiques," "fine art," and "furniture and furnishings" can mean different things to different people, leading to prolonged discussions, at best, and court cases at worst, among beneficiaries. A good way of being clear about the contents and intentions in a will is to reference the appraisal document in naming specific items. For example, using a will to bequeath "the diamond ring to my granddaughter" is not so precise as bequeathing "the diamond ring that is item number 27 on page 11 of the appended appraisal, to my granddaughter Anne." (This precision is also a reason why the appraisal document itself should include a photographic record of each item in question, and the photographs should be incorporated within the document.)

For these and other reasons, it is important to have an appraisal conducted on your art collection and on all the tangible personal property, including jewelry, that you have in your possession. Appraisals are a necessary venue through which value is assigned and can help you avoid a number of difficulties that may arise when value is not established.

CHOOSING AN APPRAISER

Given the importance of getting an accurate and up-to-date appraisal of works of art, it is critical to choose a professional appraiser who is trustworthy and objective. This can be a difficult and confusing process, but there are helpful tools to narrow down the best person or organization for the job.

No matter what type of object you need to have appraised, the appraiser should be an expert in his or her particular field. Appraisers should have either a number of years of experience working with the types of objects they appraise or advanced degrees focusing in their specialty area or both. A useful way to verify an appraiser's expertise is to find out if he or she is a member of a nationally recognized appraisal group such as the Appraisers Association of America (AAA), which is a not-for-profit association of personal-property appraisers. In addition to confirming the credentials of an appraiser, an appraiser's membership in the AAA also means that

❏ he or she will adhere to the AAA Code of Ethics,[5] which is a list of guidelines outlining the appraiser's relationship with his client and his approach to the appraisal, and

❏ he or she will prepare an appraisal in conformity with the Uniform Standards of Professional Appraisal Practice (USPAP).

The USPAP standards are developed by the Appraisals Standards Board (ASB) of the Appraisal Foundation and give specific guidelines as to what information should be included in an appraisal, how an appraiser should approach an appraisal, and what an appraiser should do in specific situations. The guidelines also establish requirements for impartiality, independence, objectivity, and competency; seek to protect collectors from an appraiser's fraudulent behavior or other malpractice; and set out very specific guidelines for analyzing works of art and other personal property. Appraisers who are compliant are viewed as unbiased professionals whose work is worthy of the public's trust, and the guidelines state that, implicit in the notion of "trust" is the assurance of the appraisers' professional skills and expertise and their moral obligations to act in an "ethical and competent manner" and also to act on behalf of the public interest and not out of self-interest.

The guidelines are extensive, but the following are some of the particularly significant rules, all of which have important implications in the art market:

❏ The *competency rule* states that, prior to accepting any assignment, an appraiser must disclose any lack of familiarity with a specific type of property. This is important in helping to ensure that before hiring an appraiser, you can establish that he or she is expert not only in works of art generally, but also in your item's particular genre, medium, sector of the market, or even geographical location, if relevant.

❏ The *ethics rule* includes language that states an appraiser must perform an appraisal with independence, impartiality, and objectivity and without advocating the cause of any particular party or interest.

❏ The *objectivity rule* states that when a collector is enlisting an appraiser, the appraiser cannot be told or coerced into reporting what the value a work of art "should" be, and the appraiser's compensation cannot be tied in any way to the value of the outcome of the appraisal such that the appraiser would have any incentive to overstate its value.

❏ The *definition and analysis rule* states that an appraiser must define and analyze the appropriate market consistent with the type and definition of value of the item being appraised. The value of a work of art sometimes depends on where it is likely to be sold, for example, whether through auction, private sale, or retail dealer sale. An appraiser should also analyze the relevant economic conditions at the time of the valuation, supply and demand in the market, and the perceived or real scarcity or rarity of the item in question.

It is also crucial that your chosen appraiser follow IRS regulations, whether for a donation situation or for other tax purposes.[6] Since the weight the IRS gives to the appraisal will often depend on the IRS Art Panel's and state tax authority's assessment of an appraiser's competence and knowledge about the work of art and its market, the agency is inclined to credit the appraisal of an appraiser who

❏ specializes in the particular genre or category of art in question. For a tax-donation appraisal, the appraiser must fill out and sign Form 8283[7] and must either be certified or have many years of experience in the field in which the work of art falls. Among other details, the appraiser must state that he or she understands the penalties of over- or undervaluing the work of art, and confirm his or her relationship with the donor.

❏ is objective. The AAA Code of Ethics stipulates that all items appraised should be analyzed "independent of outside influences and without any other motive or purpose than stated in said appraisal." Having an objective appraiser eliminates any conflicts of interest in assigning value, and ensures that the appraiser is not motivated by any other factors, such as adjusting values in order to obtain works of art for sale.

Figures 2.1 and 2.2 below highlight the importance of expertise. In the case of two paintings by William Trost Richards, because they appear quite similar, it is easy to assume that they would have about the

FIGURE **2.1**   William Trost Richards, *Breaking Waves (Photograph Courtesy of Sotheby's Inc. © 2006)*

FIGURE **2.2**   William Trost Richards, *Crashing Waves (Photograph Courtesy of Sotheby's Inc. © 2006)*

same value. An expert, however, would be able to determine that one would bring far more than the other at a sale. In this instance, the works were of the same size, in the same medium, and by the same artist. At auction, they sold only two lots apart. Nevertheless, Figure 2.1, depicts the crashing waves that collectors of this artist seek, and brought a hammer price of $240,000[8] at Sotheby's New York, in the May 24, 2006 auction, while Figure 2.2 is considered too calm to be ranked among the painter's most desirable works, and was hammered down at $42,500[9] two lots later.

Approaches and Methodology of Appraisals

Finding an appraiser who is USPAP certified means that not only will she follow specific regulations regarding the information and organization of the appraisal, but she also will likely derive her values from what is termed the "comparative-market-data approach." Comparative market data are based on comparable sales from the same artist or, if no comparable sales from the same artist exist, from works by an artist of the same period, style, and value. This method reflects the current market trends for a particular artist or type of work, takes the venue of sale into account, and allows for flexibility in adjusting values for a work, as no two comparable works of art are exactly the same. Based on comparable market data, the appraiser can offer different types of appraisals on different sales:

❏ For a fair market value (FMV),[10] the appraiser will generally look at recent auction prices.

❏ For a retail replacement value (RRV), the appraiser will look at current gallery prices.

Using all the criteria mentioned, if similar works have been sold at prices within a limited range, and the market has continued to be steady overall for this type of work, the valuation will likely fall within the range noted. If similar works have fetched prices that vary widely, an appraiser needs to examine the causes of the variations. They must consider such factors as the following:

❏ *The location of the sale:* For example, were any of the auctions in a geographic area outside the normal location for selling a work by this artist?

❏ *The type of sale:* Were any of the comparables sold in types of auctions not compatible with the particular type of work? (For example, a work normally purchased by collectors of European paintings offered instead in an American paintings sale.)

❏ *The content of the sale:* For example, were other, more-commercial works by the artist placed in the same auction, thereby causing a particular comparable to fare poorly because it seemed less desirable?

❏ *The catalogue estimates:* For example, were some of the comparables overestimated, scaring potential buyers from bidding?

❏ *The condition of the work:* Were there condition issues in some of the comparables that caused collectors to shun those examples? (Since condition issues are rarely noted in online price databases, an appraiser must check the condition of the comparables by contacting the auction house or dealer for additional information prior to using the data.)

❏ *The composition of the work:* Were all the subjects of the comparables equally desirable to the market? (For example, see the William Trost Richards paintings described above.)

❏ *The provenance:* Was one of the comparables from a particularly noteworthy or desirable collection? You have only to review the staggering prices realized in the famous Andy Warhol sale, or in the Jacqueline Kennedy sale, to see the premium achieved for works sold from a well-known collector. Prices in these single-owner sales can be many multiples of the presale estimates because of the excitement generated by a particular collector. These prices are often not sustainable in future sales of the same works (as evidenced by works purchased for large sums in the Warhol sale and subsequently reoffered and sold for fractions of the original sale price).

❏ *The date of work within an artist's oeuvre:* Works that may appear to the appraiser to be similar but fetch widely disparate prices may well be from different periods of an artist's work, and discerning collectors often assign widely disparate values to them, resulting in widely disparate sales prices.

The value of a work of art can change over time, depending on the state of the art market, the state of the national and global economy, and current tastes and trends. With all of these factors in mind, it is recommended that you have an appraisal carried out every three to four years. However, for higher-value items, namely works of fine art above $1 million, or works of decorative art above $500,000, a yearly appraisal is ideal. The actual fluctuations of value of higher-priced works tend to be greater than those of lesser-value works, because their prices increase faster.[11]

Similarly, a more-frequent annual appraisal is recommended for items in volatile or changing markets, such as twentieth-century design or Contemporary art. For example, a Marshmallow sofa, by George Nelson & Associates, valued at $10,000 in 2004, quadrupled in value over the next few years and was valued at $40,000 in 2008. The value of the sofa increased as collecting trends shifted toward twentieth-century design. Similarly, comparing the Spot paintings of Damien Hirst sold over the past five years shows that a Damien Hirst Spot painting valued at $450,000 in 2003 would likely have fetched over $1.5 million in 2007, because the Contemporary art market flourished over those years. Shifts in taste and in the economy can result in drastic changes in value, as these two examples demonstrate. This is why revisiting your appraised items and updating their assigned values at appropriate intervals is a cornerstone of effective management of your art assets.

Appraisals before Buying or Selling Art

If you are considering either buying new works or deaccessioning part of your collection, having an accurate and up-to-date valuation of works of art is crucial in helping you make decisions. Buying new works to add to your collection and selling works that you own is nothing more than moving your assets from one class into another, converting financial assets into tangible items and back again. While the concept is simple, the process of buying and selling art can be quite daunting, making objectivity vital. Just as it does in an appraisal situation, objective advice can help protect against conflicts of interest, allowing the buyer to buy, and the seller to sell, works of art most advantageously.

BUYING

The decision to buy a work of art can seem overwhelming. To protect yourself from deciding unwisely, you should be fully aware of all the elements that can influence the value of a work of art. If they are not addressed, the buyer or owner can find himself at the center of a complicated legal situation or in some other great difficulty. For any work of art you are considering purchasing, you need specific information about these elements:

- ❑ Title
- ❑ Authenticity
- ❑ Condition
- ❑ Quality
- ❑ Rarity
- ❑ Provenance
- ❑ Value

Title.   Title issues in art arise more frequently than one might expect. A Picasso painting, for example, *Portrait of Angel Fernandez de Soto*, estimated to sell for between $40 million and $60 million, was withdrawn from a 2006 Christie's auction, apparently because of an ownership claim.

Authenticity.   Authenticity issues are frequently encountered and often pose unique and frustrating challenges. Works by the artist Dan Flavin offer a good case study of authenticity in art, particularly because Contemporary art introduces new challenges to authenticating works. If a collector owns a Dan Flavin light installation and has the certificate of authenticity, the Flavin Foundation will approve the replacement of the light bulbs in the installation should they burn out. If, however, the owner loses the certificate, or if the certificate is accidentally destroyed, the Flavin Foundation may not replace the certificate, and the work may no longer be salable in the market. This circumstance demonstrates how the future value of the art can sometimes exist as much in the certificate as in the work of art itself. It also demonstrates how, when you buy a work of art, it is important to make sure that you obtain the appropriate documentation and that you maintain the certificate in a safe place.

Condition.   A condition report is another important piece of documentation you should request when you are buying a work of art, because maintaining the condition of your art is simply effective asset management. Condition reports are readily available when you are buying at auction, and they provide important information about any areas of the work that are in need of cleaning, repair, or restoration or that have been previously restored, because this information can affect the value of the work. Since the reports provided by auction houses may be too brief in some circumstances and might not fully describe any previous restoration, inpainting, or damages, it is wise for a buyer to have her own conservator examine a work if she has any doubts. If a work in your collection is in need of restoration, you should consult a recognized expert in the field, since a restoration carried out by an unqualified person can do more harm than good. Suppose, for example, the original finish on an item of American eighteenth-century furniture is removed or retouched. To an untrained eye, the piece may look aesthetically flawless—but often the value of the item will have been significantly and irreversibly compromised. Conversely, since a high-quality restoration can increase the value of a work, it is always worthwhile to put in the time and effort to find a respected and expert restorer (Chapter 11 discusses art preservation and restoration in detail.).

Once you have made the decision to purchase a work of art at auction, it is important to read the "conditions of sale" printed in the auction catalogues. These describe the limited warranties of the auction house and should be reviewed by an attorney to ensure that you know your rights in the event of any controversy over title, condition, or any other factor noted above. Similarly, if you buy a work of art from a dealer, be sure to note what guarantees of authenticity, title, and condition you are getting.

Although there are many complexities of management—whether you are buying, selling, or maintaining a work of art—a crucial first step that can save you an exorbitant amount of stress is to have a professional, objective appraisal conducted. Once an appraisal has established value, you are equipped to make appropriate decisions about taxes, insurance, protection, buying or selling, and caring for works of art in your personal collection.

Quality. Without considering emotional ties to a particular work, from a financial standpoint it is prudent to find a work of art that is of the highest quality you can afford. Rather than choosing a secondary or lesser work by a major artist, it may be financially beneficial to find the highest-quality work by an artist even if it may be considered "less important" in the current market. These quality works will tend to maintain their value and desirability over time.

Rarity. Along with quality, it is important to be informed of the rarity of a particular work of art. If an artist has created a relatively small number of works, and that artist is considered of major importance, each individual work will likely be highly sought after and consequently expensive. Barring changes in taste, that artist's works are likely to increase in value over time. For these less-prolific artists, condition often plays a smaller role in the desirability of the work. For artists whose works are relatively abundant on the other hand, condition will be a more important factor, as there will presumably be many works in excellent condition available, and one in lesser condition should be avoided.

Provenance.   As noted earlier, provenance may have a distinct impact on the current and future value of a work of art. "Celebrity" provenance, for example, may greatly increase the current value of a work, and it may therefore be priced at multiples of its true value, but the sustainability of this price inflation may not be guaranteed in the long run. By contrast, provenance of a great collector may lead to the long-term maintenance of an increase in the value of a particular work. For example, a book by a famous author inscribed to a well-known person, a piece of silver engraved with a royal coat of arms, and a painting once in the collection of a highly regarded collector are all examples of works that will likely maintain a premium of value in the long term as a result of their provenance.

Value.   Having considered title, authenticity, condition, quality, rarity, and provenance, a potential purchaser can be better informed as to a reasonable price for a work of art. Value is always a relative concept and may vary among buyers and contexts. The emotional impact of a work on any buyer is also often incalculable but adds to the value of the purchase. Despite the complexity of the concept, it is important to consider value, and taking account of the various factors above should help buyers avoid costly mistakes.

SELLING

If you are considering selling any of your art, the first step is to determine the sale venue that will help you maximize your revenue and fulfill your intentions. The main choices include the following:

❏ A major auction house is a very public venue, with separate departments that can offer the advantage of marketing directly to buyers looking for works in a particular collecting area. The downside is that each collecting category is auctioned only at certain times of the year so there may be a time delay between the decision to sell and the availability of a particular category of auction.

❏ A local auction house might be preferable for lower-value items, such as general furniture and decorative objects, because its buyers may include younger collectors furnishing houses or dealers trying to build up their stock.

❏ A fine art dealer or private-treaty[12] sale might be able to offer discretion where it is sought and might offer more flexibility in terms of execution time.

❏ A specialized dealer might be able to offer higher prices for very specialized items, such as sports memorabilia.

Selling Costs and Fees

Selling costs vary according to venue and may be considerable, but they can sometimes be negotiated according to the value and desirability of the consignment.

The fees at major and secondary auction houses might include the following:

❏ Standard sellers' commissions

❏ Insurance fees (1.5–2 percent of the hammer price)

❏ Illustration fees for images in the catalogues (up to $900 per photograph at the major auction houses)

❏ Shipping charges to and from the auction houses

❏ Buy-in fees (fees charged on items that fail to sell at auction)

❏ Minimum commissions (minimum fees per lot charged by most auction houses)

❏ Authentication charges (if the attribution of a work needs to be confirmed by the recognized external expert)

❏ Restoration charges (if a particular work needs to be conserved)

❏ Title insurance (a more recent phenomenon, which sellers may wish to buy prior to consigning a work to insure that, should there be any future questions regarding the ownership or provenance, they will be covered for the amount derived from the sale of the item)

Private-treaty fees, on the other hand, normally consist of a commission to the agent or intermediary. The seller and the purchaser of an item may have a mutual intermediary who negotiates a fee from either or both of them. Alternatively, the seller and purchaser may have their own agents, each receiving a commission from their respective clients.

Time Until Payment Is Realized

The amount of time needed between consigning the work and receiving payment varies depending on the sales route chosen.

At the major auction houses, the deadline to consign is normally approximately two to three months prior to each sale. This allows the auction house adequate time to prepare the catalogue and to market the work. Following the sale, payment is normally made thirty-five days after each sale. The total time from consignment to payment is at least three to four months.

In a secondary or specialized auction house the time may be somewhat compressed, as the catalogues are generally less elaborate and take less time to produce. The time from consignment to payment can also be as short as two months.

The timing for private-treaty sales is generally more prolonged. These deals can take up to six months or more to finalize because potential buyers must be identified and contacted, the sale negotiated, payment terms agreed, and payment finalized. If the buyer is an institution, the acquisition process can take many months, because often the funds must be raised to complete the deal.

Reserves and Guarantees

To protect the seller, auction houses normally agree to a reserve, which is the confidential minimum price below which the work will not be sold. This protects the seller against a sale below true market value, but there are no guarantees that the work will reach or surpass that minimum price. Dealers also may agree to a minimum price with their clients, but, again, a successful sale is not guaranteed.

If a client wishes to have a sale guaranteed, and the consignment is important enough to merit it, the auction houses sometimes provide that guarantee, with a subsequent split between the seller and the auction house of the price realized above that guarantee. In times of art market fluctuations and uncertainty, however, such as in 2009, guarantees have become a risky proposition for the auction house or third-party guarantor to finance and have an item taken off the table.

Timing and Location of Sale

In addition to determining the best sale venue, the timing and location of the sale can also affect the sale revenues. To determine the best place to sell a work of art, you should examine the current and past sales results in different geographic locations and auction houses for the type of item that you wish to sell, and also look at what comparable works are coming up in the future sales, to ensure that there are no directly competing works. For example, one collector sold a private collection of Modern and Impressionist works at auction in London in June 2008. There were a number of factors he took into account:

❏ The dollar, at that time, was weak, and the British pound very strong.

❏ London sales at times attract a more international group of interested bidders than New York sales.

❏ The deadlines for the New York sales would have made adequate marketing difficult in the time allowed.

❏ Works by the artists represented in this collection traditionally fared well in the London market.

After considering all these factors, the collector decided to sell the works in London, with the result that he received record-breaking prices for some of the pieces and an extraordinary result for the collection overall.

Determining Art Prices:
Objective and Subjective Valuations
Clare McAndrew

Because of their unique nature, the factors that contribute to the price of a work of art can be difficult to analyze. Objective and quantifiable factors contribute to the financial value, but there is also a significant subjective aesthetic "taste" element that is much more difficult to measure or predict with definitive accuracy, and this element greatly affects the price a particular investor or collector will be willing to pay for a work.

Objective Drivers of Art Prices

There are a number of recognizable and objective drivers of value in the art market that center on features of the work, the artist, and the place and time of sale. These drivers are measurable, researchable, and part of the input into a valuation of a particular work at a point in time, and include these factors:

❑ The artist's reputation and standing
❑ Characteristics of the work itself
❑ Characteristics of the sale

The Artist's Reputation and Standing

One of the key determinants of the price of a work of fine art relates to the reputation of the artist who created it:

❑ What is his relative fame among his artistic peers?
❑ What was his role in the history of his particular genre?
❑ What was his role in the broader art market?

The more famous the artist, the greater his importance and innovativeness within his genre or school (and within the history of art generally) and the higher priced his works tend to be—although it is important to note that, even within one artist's body of work, different periods can be more or less valuable, depending on the desirability of that particular period in the collecting market.

A painting by a well-known artist will often have an established price history in the market, will offer its owner a degree of prestige, and generally will be a much less risky investment than a relatively unknown artist. All these factors (along with the rarity of the work of art) will be reflected in the price. For example, there is a group of what could be called blue-chip artists, whose works are commonly associated with prices at auction of over $1 million. Such artists as Picasso, Warhol, Cézanne, and van Gogh are instantly recognizable in the top price tiers in the market, and they also rank among the highest within their particular genres (e.g., twentieth century, Pop art, or Impressionism).

Each artist's road to fame is different, but it could be argued that there is a certain path that many artists follow that can also predict a rise in their work's potential value. The former director of the Tate Gallery Sir Alan Bowness believed the art market has a clear and linear progression of artists to fame (and high prices), with four successive "circles to fame":

1. The artist's peers recognize her (the Impressionist painters, for example, were often one another's first patrons).
2. The artist is recognized by key critics in the market, and these critics serve as interpreters who explain the artist's innovations to a wider audience.
3. Art dealers become interested and take on the artist, promoting her to their clients.
4. The public acknowledges the greatness of an artist (and, at this stage, the artist has an auction-sales basis).

These circles to fame suggest how an artist's fame leads to the rise in prices of her works over time and could imply potential strategies for selecting art to invest in: young artists, early in their career, who are innovative, popular, and purchased by other artists in their peer group.

Predicting how a particular artist's works will rise in value, however, is not an easy task, and even professional dealers put much time and research into finding the very few potentially successful artists among masses of unknowns. In addition, because achieving fame can take some artists years or even a lifetime to achieve, it takes a lot of patience to wait what could be a decade or more for the value of the artist's early works to start to rise in value. Also, once the artist has reached circle 3 or 4, her fame is already likely to be included in her sales prices, and, by then, it is too late to "beat the market."

Range in valuations for a single artist.   Fame alone, however, is not the only determinant of price, and this is clearly evidenced by the existence of an often very wide disparity of prices of works by the same artist. One of the most prolific of the blue-chip artists, Spanish painter Pablo Picasso, provides a useful example. In 2005 and 2006, Picasso had the highest aggregate auction sales of all artists but was number two in 2007, with approximately $319 million in total sales, when *Femme Accroupie au Costume Turc (Jacqueline)*, his highest-priced work, sold for a hammer price of $27.5 million, at Christie's, in New York.[13]

At Sotheby's, in New York, a bronze sculpture by Picasso, *Tête de Femme, Dora Maar,* was sold for $26 million, making it the most expensive sculpture ever sold at auction, and he had a total of forty-five auction sales that exceeded the $1 million mark. If, however, you look more closely at all of Picasso's works at auction that year, the range of prices is staggering. Seventy-two oil paintings by Picasso were brought to auction in 2007. Although the average price was just over $4 million, that figure does not begin to tell the story, because prices started at $2,146, and about one-third of the fifty-eight successful sales were hammered down at less than $1 million. In addition, 20 percent of the total of seventy-two paintings were "bought in," because they failed to meet their reserve price. Even though the record-breaking bronze pushed the average for the artist's sculptures up to $682,185, the median auction price was only $30,555, 44 percent of the successful sculpture sales for that year were $10,000 or under, and one of the five hundred or so Picasso ceramics sold at auction in 2007 for only $71.

Picasso was a particularly prolific artist, which makes his work a good example of the range of valuations for works by an artist who is globally recognized. Prices for lesser-known artists may vary less, and, for emerging artists especially, works may remain below a particular price ceiling for a period. All this only serves to illustrate that distribution patterns of prices vary widely among artists at all levels, and while an artist's name is an important contributing factor, it is not sufficient, in isolation, to explain price.

Characteristics of the Work Itself

With countless examples of the works of a given artist varying widely in price, it is clear that there are other factors at work in the valuation process besides the artist's fame and importance. Characteristics of the individual work itself can also enhance or detract from its sale price.

Size. The size of a work of art may affect its price. Although the dimensions of a work of art within a fairly mainstream range would not be expected to have a significant effect on its price, and art is not "priced per square meter" like many other goods, there are nevertheless instances when size does affect price. Sometimes larger works will reach higher prices than smaller examples by the same artist. A number of studies have shown that while price does increase with size, it does so at a decreasing marginal rate. The logic behind this is fairly straightforward: although the artist's production costs increase with size, which should drive prices up, many collectors prefer smaller paintings, because the smaller size permits them to exhibit them or hang on their walls at home. An average collector will have less desire for very large works that are expensive to exhibit, store, and maintain, a situation that can work toward reducing prices for large works. For this reason, museums and other such institutions, often the main purchasers of large works, have considerable negotiation power, because not only do they have the facilities to display works of great size, but they will also display the work publicly to the benefit of the artist.

Medium. Prices of artists' works vary from one medium to another. Oil paintings, for example, are generally more expensive than works on paper, because of their higher production costs and greater durability. If we look at Picasso's works in 2007 again, we can see that the average hammer price for an oil painting at auction was just over $4 million. Compare that with the average hammer price of $200,662 for works on paper.[12] The exact price effect of other media, such as sculptures, collages, or tapestries, is less straightforward, but often, if an artist has specialized in a particular medium or created some of his best-known work in one particular medium, a work executed in that medium will tend to be priced higher than his works in another medium.

Period. When a work was created can also affect its price. Artists' work can often be divided into early, transitional, and mature works, with periods often used as approximations for quality. Higher prices will often be paid once an artist has established his own form or style; yet, sometimes, the discovery of an early work by an established or famous artist can also drive prices up, especially if the work is of a particularly rare genre for that artist.

Going back to our previous example, we see that historians distinguish eight distinct working periods in Picasso's life, and the quality, number, and significance of the works he produced during these periods vary considerably. Works from the Blue and Rose periods (1902 to 1906), command the highest prices in all of Picasso's work, in part at least because they are thought to signify the end of his stylistic training and the beginnings of his own true form as a painter. During the Blue period, his paintings reflected death, loneliness, poverty, and age. In the Rose years, there was a decisive change of subject matter, with themes that included harlequins, acrobats, actors, and clowns that shifted his portraits' emphasis to youth. *Garçon à la Pipe*, thought to be one of Picasso's most beautiful Rose paintings, was created in 1905, when the artist was twenty-four, and sold at Sotheby's in New York in May 2004, for a world record price of $93 million.[13] *Les Noces de Pierrette,* another painting created in 1905 (although classified as still in transition from his Blue period), also sold for a record high of $48.2 million, at Binoche-Godeau, in Paris, in 1989. All of that notwithstanding, drawing any firm conclusions about how the period in an artist's life when a work was created affects price is a tenuous endeavor at best, since there are also several examples of artists creating numerous works in any one year that now vary dramatically in price.

Subject.   The subject matter of a given work is also a factor that can influence price, but, as with size, trying to distinguish a single rule that applies across different buyers and contexts is very difficult. Some studies, for example, have shown that men are said to prefer the female form in representational work and will pay more for it than for a male form. Other research shows that artists' favorite subjects or recurrent themes have been shown to sell at much higher prices than atypical works, because an artist's familiar themes act as a recognizable trademark. Still other studies have tied higher valuations to subjects of historical significance, content, and even color. As with all statistical studies, however, some of these correlations may be spurious, and it is certainly arguable that subject matter has lost some of its financial weight and artistic supremacy in genres such as Contemporary art.

Condition.   Condition is one factor in determining valuation that is unarguable. The condition of a work of art is of critical importance to its valuation, and, as noted in the previous section, most auction houses and some dealers will provide a condition report upon request, which should detail such factors as tears, cracked canvas or *craquelure*,[16] paint losses, or even evidence of poor attempts at restoration—all of which will detract from the price. For decorative art, works with their original surfaces and parts, and without faults and repairs, will also be valued at higher prices.

Provenance.   Like condition, provenance is also a clear and definitive indicator in valuation and pricing. Provenance is simply the origin or source from which a particular work has come to the market, and refers to the work's ownership history, various auction records, conservation records, certificates, and bills of sale. A record of provenance gives buyers reassurance regarding its value and provides a verifiable public certification of authenticity. Authentic, signed works with a well-established ownership history will generally earn higher prices. Unless the authenticity of a work can be established and it can be guaranteed as original, no matter what the work's size, subject, or sale venue, the work is arguably next to worthless. Documentation such as registration in established sales catalogues, proof of previous ownership, and other guarantees and assurances of authenticity will all, therefore, tend to also increase price. Obviously, the older the work, the longer and sometimes more difficult it becomes to track its provenance, which is one reason why Contemporary art is popular with investors—because ownership and authenticity are usually easily established, directly via the artist herself, if necessary.

A record of a work's previous owners is also part of its provenance, and this ownership history can have a marked effect on its value. Apart from revealing that the work is authentic and legally acquired, this element of provenance also contains an element of emotional and prestige appeal: if there have been any famous or notable previous owners, for example, this celebrity can add another layer of value and perceived quality that elevates the price.

Along with its provenance, a record of a work's exhibitions is often recorded in auction and sales catalogues. As a general rule, those works that have been exhibited will be more expensive, but this is presumably because their higher quality allowed them to have been accepted for exhibition, rather than because the process of exhibiting has itself driven up value. Also, when a work has been hidden from the market and public view for a long time, its being offered for sale can spark great publicity and enthusiasm, which can drive up prices.

Characteristics of the Sale

The characteristics of the sale in which the work of art is offered can influence the price, through its venue, its timing, or external economic conditions.

Venue. The location and characteristics of a particular transaction's venue may also influence the price of a work of art. The reputation of an auction house or dealer not only ensures it is consigned the best-quality and highest-value works but also, via its multidimensional role in buying, selling, financing, promoting, marketing, valuing, and essentially guaranteeing works of art, it acts as a market maker for artists and can actively alter their sales prices. The best-known auction houses and galleries can often charge more for works of art and can also raise their value through a greater capacity to get them catalogued and exhibited and in front of the "right" buyers. Many market experts would argue that the auction price on a given day can even be affected by the skills and characteristics of an individual auctioneer, since it is he who is responsible for creating the sale's suspense and anticipation, which can drive prices well beyond estimates.

The location of a sale also has an influence on price, and there has been a distinct trend in the last five to ten years of higher prices in the United States than in Europe[17] and in larger art centers like New York, London, or Hong Kong than in smaller, regional art markets. Larger centers tend to attract buyers with deeper pockets, and different tax rates and regulations will also undoubtedly influence the price and location of final exchanges.

Timing. Finally, the timing of a sale can influence the price achieved. The art market tends to be seasonal, with the largest auctions for fine art, for example, held during spring and autumn. Auction houses and galleries definitely use timing strategies to help push up prices, whether to arrange for sales to coincide with other events in the market or wider economy, to meet more-specific buyer schedules, or to tie in publicity and events related to the artwork or artist. Even the time of day a work of art sells at has been shown to affect prices. Researchers have found evidence of an "afternoon effect" in some auctions, whereby final bids relative to auction estimates decline throughout the course of the sale. An opposite effect has also been discovered using data from different art auctions called the "morning effect," whereby a sequential rise in auction prices relative to their estimates has been evidenced.

External economic trends. Works of art are luxury goods, which means that demand is positively affected by income, and many sectors of the art market can shadow economic conditions, albeit with a variable lag. Booms in particular sectors of art markets have often coincided with periods of prosperity in different sectors of financial markets or different geographical regions. The Japanese bubble economy of the late 1980s was undoubtedly one of the major instigators of the art boom of that period, with nouveau connoisseurs of the art world buying a lot of art without particular regard for quality or price. The downturn in the global economy that really got under way in 2008 has also been cited as having some dampening effects on the unprecedented bull run of Contemporary art.

Overall, the objective part of the valuation equation is complex but would conceivably be the estimate derived from appraising and researching all the different elements discussed above regarding the artist, his past sales, and the sales of others in his peer group. It should be similar to a measure an auction expert might use to set the reserve price for a work coming to auction, or the best estimate at a market price, based on the evaluation of an expert appraiser. In summary, therefore, it is possible to use the "objective" characteristics of a work of art only to estimate a *range* of prices it should fall within. When it comes to an actual sale at auction however, the hammer price includes some other subjective determinants.

Subjective Determinants of Art Prices

All of the objective, mostly quantifiable features of a work of art can go a long way in explaining how prices are established, and although they are useful in establishing a valuation range for works of art, since even very similar works from the same artist can sell for vastly different amounts, a combination of objective determinants can never be guaranteed to fully explain prices.

Looking again at Picasso's works, we can see another example of inconsistent sales results. (See *Table 2.1.*) Because every work of art is unique, it is impossible to say that the subject matter, size, or quality did not in some small way influence the prices paid for the two Picassos in May 2006. The *Tête de Femme, Dora Maar* was smaller, painted four years earlier, and sold a day earlier, in a different salesroom from the *Dora Maar au Chat*. Nevertheless, these differences cannot fully explain the $80 million difference in the price, or why, for example, a smaller painting with the same title sold for just under three times the price at auction in 2007.

We see, therefore, that, although the price of a work of art *appears* to be a function of all its objective and mostly measurable characteristics (the artist, the characteristics of the individual work itself, the

TABLE 2.1   Four Recent Picasso Auction Sales

Painting	Dora Maar au Chat	Tête de Femme, Dora Maar	Tête de Femme, Dora Maar	Buste de Femme, Dora Maar
Hammer price	$85MM	$5MM	$14.5MM	$4.5MM
Year of creation	1941	1937	1941	1942
Medium	Oil	Oil	Oil	Oil
Date of sale	3 May 2006	2 May 2006	6 Nov. 2007	2 Feb. 2004
Auction house	Sotheby's New York	Christie's New York	Christie's New York	Christie's London
Dimensions (inches)	51 × 38	22 × 18	16 × 13	28¾ × 23½

Source: *Arts Economics* (2008)

characteristics of the sale), certain prices also carry some unexplained premium that seems to derive from the emotional, subjective, and often-irrational process peculiarly attached to the purchase of art.

Once the objective range of value is determined for a particular work of art, there is often still an unexplained or irrational element to the prices actually paid at auction (and through private sales) that causes prices to fall out of these anticipated parameters. This unexplained premium is most noticeable in headline-grabbing sales, where prices paid at auction seem abnormally higher than anticipated, but it exists to some degree in all tiers of the market. Therefore, while you might be able to predict what is perceived as a fair price in the market based on well-informed research and expertise, it is impossible to predict the actual market price a work will earn with certainty.

What the *actual* sales price turns out to be depends on this irrational premium, which is itself a function in part of how skilled the seller or her intermediary is at driving up the emotional appeal of the work or finding buyers with the greatest "emotional potential." The premium above the reserve or fair value of the work represents the given work's emotional and aesthetic appeal to a particular buyer at a given sale or point in time, and is a unique feature of trading in the art market. This premium is not necessarily specific to particular buyers or particular works, and different individual buyers will have different premiums attached to different works at different times.

The "emotional premium."   Some of the top-selling works that have dominated media headlines in recent years offer the best examples of this "irrational" component. The record-breaking sale of van Gogh's *Portrait of Dr. Gachet* sold in 1990, at Christie's New York, for a hammer price of $75 million,[18] still one of the highest prices in the market in real terms. The work was purchased by the wealthy Japanese paper-industry tycoon Ryoei Saito. The bidder working on his behalf in New York doubled the prevailing bid to hammer down the winning price at auction, under instructions from Saito to pay whatever was necessary for the painting, whose melancholy portrayal of Dr. Gachet, Saito claimed, reminded him of himself.[19] Whatever his motivations, it is obvious that there was a large and emotional content to the final winning bid paid for the work, and Saito's intent was to hold for the long term rather than to try to resell it quickly for profit. Once such a record price is paid—with a high irrationality premium embedded in the price—it is very unlikely, if the work is brought to market again in the short or medium term, that the seller would find another buyer with both the same emotional attachment to the work and the same financial means to buy it, even at the same price—never mind trying to profit from its resale. In other words, despite grabbing all the media headlines, record-breaking works of art like this will often make the poorest financial investments, since they may be very difficult to resell and profit from.

Reference price effects.   Another important feature of the art market is that there are often strong "reference price effects" evidenced in sales over time. A work that sells for a very high price at a particular point in time is likely to result in a higher estimate being set for it in future when the painting is next put on the market and subsequently may sell for a higher price (with a symmetric effect for losses). Therefore, while works of art are generally resold very infrequently, the past price achieved for a work is important in establishing the next price paid. When a price jump is sudden and dramatic, it is easy to distinguish the irrational component of the premium, but if these premiums are embedded in sales over time they may become more difficult to establish or recognize. This is another reason why the Contemporary sector with a short history for the sales of a particular artist can offer a more comfortable choice for new investors.

Art prices, like all asset prices, are driven by the participants in the marketplace, whose combined preferences and demands exert an influence on how a work is valued over time. However, within this marketplace there is a unique combination of subjective elements alongside imperfect and asymmetric flows of information between participants. These features produce a heavy reliance on experts on the part of buyers and also allow various price anomalies to form and persist over time, which in other markets might disappear quickly as transactions take place and information is exchanged. Understanding some of these inefficiencies and anomalies in art prices not only helps in understanding the market but also opens up the possibility of positive abnormal returns, at least in the short term.

Chapter Notes

1. Clare McAndrew, *The International Art Market: A Survey of Europe in a Global Context* (Helvoirt: TEFAF, 2008).

2. Don Thompson, *The $12 Million Stuffed Shark: The Curious Economics of Contemporary Art* (New York: Palgrave Macmillan, 2008).

3. "A Pollock is Sold, Possibly for a Record Price," *New York Times*, November 2, 2006.

4. "Landmark de Kooning Crowns Collection," *New York Times*, November 18, 2006.

5. The Code of Ethics of the Appraisers Association of America can be found at http://www.appraisersassoc.org/personal-property-appraiser/fine-art-appraisals/find-an-appraiser/PageId/1/LId/0,1,3/Id/3/Code-of-Ethics.html.

6. See Chapter 9 for a further discussion of valuation and appraisal issues and the IRS.

7. If a person or an estate makes a noncash charitable contribution greater than $500, IRS Form 8283 must be included with his tax return. The appraisal must be made within sixty days of the gift.

8. Or $284,800 with premium.

9. $51,000 with premium.

10. For example, if an appraiser were attempting to place a fair market value on a Lucien Freud oil-on-canvas portrait of a woman, she would reference the recent auction records for similar works by the artist and would determine an appropriate value based on those auction records and on other factors that could increase or decrease the price, such as condition, composition, date of work, size, and provenance.

11. For example, a Jeff Koons *Balloon Dog (Blue)*, which is metallic varnish on porcelain, from an edition of 2,300, sold on average in the range of $3,500 to $4,000 in 2006 at auction, and on average in the range of $6,000 to $6,250 in 2008 at auction—overall not a significant change. To compare, a *New Hoover Convertibles, Green, Red, Brown, New Hoover Deluxe Shampoo Polishers Yellow, Brown, Double-Decker*, 1981–87, sold for $5,280,000 at Sotheby's New York in May 2006, while *New Hoover Convertibles, New Shelton Wet/Drys 5-Gallon, Double-Decker*, 1981–86, sold for $11,801,000 at Christie's New York in 2008. While not exactly comparable, the results show the exponential increase in major works by Koons over the same two years.

12. A transaction from a private or institutional seller to private or institutional buyer not in the open market.

13. The highest-selling artist in 2007, in terms of aggregate auction sales, was Andy Warhol, with sales of $420 million. Data from Artprice, *Trends 2007* (2008).

14. Drawings or watercolors.

15. $104 million, with the buyer's premium.

16. Fine cracks that appear over time, from drying or ageing.

17. In many cases, as a result of some of the regulatory regimes in place.

18. With the buyer's premium, the price was $82.5 million.

19. Saito's emotional attachment to this work was so strong that he reportedly once told a colleague that he wanted to have it cremated with him when he died. Retracting the statement, Saito claimed in various press articles that he had only been using a figure of speech and that what he had really wanted to express was his wish to preserve the painting forever. Many more cynical market pundits claimed that his incentive was more likely to be the avoidance of millions in inheritance taxes than his attachment to the piece. According to reports in the *Wall Street Journal* and other press, the painting was sold by Saito in 1998 to Austrian-born investment fund manager Wolfgang Flöttl for over $65 million. Flöttl is then reported to have sold the painting to Sotheby's to pay down part of a line of credit he had gained from the auction house of over $200 million. The current owner of the portrait is unknown, but a matter of much speculation in the art market.

3

Art Price Indices

Dr. Roman Kräussl

EDITOR'S NOTE: As with any other asset, when you are deciding whether or not to invest in art, one of the first things to consider is the financial returns on investment over time. Assessing returns over a given period is problematic, however, for this asset as works of art are unique, heterogeneous products that turn over extremely slowly compared with transactions on financial markets.

When looking at company stocks or money market instruments, it is possible to track returns by developing indices based on the prices of identical shares trading in. the market. For art, there are no daily closing and opening prices, and transactions even by the same artist can be relatively infrequent, with an average market turnover term of more than thirty years for an individual work. Economists have developed a number of methods to try to overcome these joint problems of heterogeneity and infrequent trading, but these each have their own sets of issues and complexities.

Although potential investors in the art market may not necessarily need to know how to construct an art price index, it is very useful to have a broad understanding of how such indices have been developed and—perhaps more important for the individual collector—an appreciation of how they can be used. Learning how to read indices and interpret their prices and returns over time can be a very important first step in evaluating the risk and return potential of an investment in art.

This chapter introduces many of the relevant questions regarding art market research. The first section discusses the advantages and disadvantages of several price index methodologies, such as repeat sales, hedonic indices, and hybrid models that have been used to construct art price indices. The cornerstone of any research into the art market is price data, and all price indices suffer bias because of the inherent problems in the data available on art sales. The only data readily available and made publicly accessible are art auction data. Several commercial data providers and the auction houses themselves offer access to past auctioning data, mainly through online or print channels. The most important sources, which vary in their coverage, are examined in the second section. Research on art finance and art investment has been fairly minimal, but there has been a growing body of academic papers in recent years. The third section takes a closer look at some of these studies, most of which take an investment perspective, focusing mainly on the return art generates and whether art provides an attractive alternative in a well-diversified portfolio, along with common stocks and bonds.

Art Price Indices

One of the seminal papers on art prices and investment returns was "Unnatural Value, or Art Investment as a Floating Crap Game,"[1] which was written in 1986, by economist William Baumol. Baumol argued that it is not possible to compute the true value of art, since an investment in art does not pay a cash dividend that can be discounted. Despite this, research papers and studies have proliferated in the field of what has become known as "cultural economics" that profess to do just that. In order to analyze art prices within the context of asset-pricing theory, information is needed on the distribution of the asset's returns. To facilitate the comparison of art market returns with stock, bond, and other financial market returns, numerous art price indices have been constructed.

Some economists argue that an art market index should outline general market trends, much the way the Dow Jones Industrial Average describes the general direction of the U.S. stock market.[2] On that basis, we can say that the important attributes of an art index are

❑ representativeness, to have minimal constraints on the selection of data and give a good representation of the average art market;

❑ liquidity; and

❑ capacity, which is indicative of the potential and value of sales that are made on the art market.

The aim of constructing a price index is to measure the price appreciation of a particular asset or group of assets. The easiest way to measure a price change is to calculate an average or median sale price of a sample of these assets in at least two subsequent periods. However, when the quality of the assets included in the sample change from one period to the next, some problems arise, such as the following:

❏ If, for some reason, a disproportionate number of high-priced paintings have been sold in a given period, the median painting price would have risen even if none of the painting's prices changed at all.

❏ Variation in the quality of the works of art sold from period to period causes the index to vary more widely than the value of any given work.

❏ If there is a progressive change in the quality of works of art sold at different times, an index that tracks them will be biased over time.

Because of these issues, average-price indices are only useful in the art market when you are looking at a very narrow category of works, such as paintings by a particular artist, but even then do not overcome these issues entirely and serve only as an indicative or proxy measure of returns.

Most art indices are based on a model for which the price of a work at a particular time is the function of the fixed characteristics of the work (its quality) and elements that vary over time. Two basic approaches have been used in order to correct for the problem of changing quality.

The first, called the *repeat-sales approach*, is based on data for works that have sold more than once during the period in question. The second, the *hedonic modeling method*, is based on data that control for differences in the characteristics of assets in various samples.[3] Recently, some researchers have applied a third approach called *hybrid modeling*, which is a combination of the two.

The techniques used generally attempt to construct an index that either controls for the quality features of the works (hedonic indices) or tracks the actual repeated sales of the same works (repeat-sales indices). Both methods have their own merits but also suffer some potentially serious flaws when it comes to the real business of investing in art.

The Repeat-Sales Approach

The repeat-sales method controls for quality by measuring the price change of the same art asset between two periods.[4] With this method, none of the attributes of the work are assumed to have changed between transactions, and hence there is no need to include the assets' characteristics in the model. In other words, the repeat-sales method measures the sales-price difference of exactly the same work of art sold at one time and then resold later. This implies that the difference between transaction prices at two dates is a function solely of the intervening time period.

ADVANTAGES OF REPEAT-SALES INDICES

Repeat-sales indices are easy to understand: because returns are based on the relative returns of the same work of art, the index produced automatically controls the heterogeneity of the work. What is measured is the change in price over time, with the quality held constant. It requires neither the measurement nor the definition of quality, but only that the quality of the individual assets in the sample be constant over time.

DISADVANTAGES OF REPEAT-SALES INDICES

There are several major disadvantages to using the repeat-sales method:

❏ *An unrepresentative data sample.* It does not use any data on single sales and thus discards a large part of actual sales being made in the marketplace, which often makes it unrepresentative and requires coverage for such a long period that using it is impractical.

❏ *A biased sample.* Again as it disregards all the information in single-sales transactions[5] it can introduce a sample-selection bias, since relatively frequently transacted assets may not be representative of the larger population.[6]

❏ *Changes in characteristics.* It is inappropriate if the characteristics of the artwork itself or of the sale change between two sales transactions, which is often the case in the art market. (Characteristics of the potential buyers and sellers for example frequently change between sales, and the work of art itself can also change between sales dates.[7])

Hedonic Price Indices

Hedonic price indices overcome the data problems described above by including single sales, rather than just repeat transactions. A hedonic approach implies that the quality of a work of art can be regarded as a composite of a number of different attributes or characteristics, and it will be valued for the utility that these characteristics bear. Hedonic prices are defined as the implicit prices of a set of attributes concerning the artist, the painting, and characteristics of the sale and are estimated by regressing the product prices on these hedonic variables.[8]

These attributes can be subdivided into two categories: physical and nonphysical characteristics. Physical characteristics include the auction house where the sale takes place, the medium, and the size of the work, and nonphysical characteristics are variables presale auction estimates, whether the work contains the artist's signature, and the artist's reputation. In other words, the hedonic technique seeks to homogenize paintings by taking their quality changes into account through subtracting the implicit price of their different characteristics from their actual price. It identifies all of the measurable and identifiable characteristics of the work that contribute to its valuation and then extracts these from the price, so that what is left is the pure time trend (and the influence of random elements) or a "quality-characteristic-free" index of homogenized art prices.

The most important advantage of hedonic regressions is that they avoid the problem of having to select items of the same quality for comparison at different times. Furthermore, unlike the repeat-sales method, it does not discard data of artworks that only have one recorded price, which often results in a larger sample size available for research. However, the hedonic method has the widely criticized disadvantage that it constrains the prices and influence of the different characteristics that are selected to be the same in every period the regression is covering. Moreover, neither the set of hedonic variables nor the functional form of the relationship is known with certainty, and it is up to the researcher or investor to define and estimate the entire set of characteristics that will affect prices over time. This problem can result in inconsistent estimates of the implicit prices of the attributes, which can have a strong influence on predictions formed using the hedonic price index.

Hybrid Models

Both the repeat-sales approach and the hedonic model have some strengths but also a number of deficiencies. Some hybrid models have been developed to try to mitigate these problems by using the hedonic information of paintings and the repeat-sales information of individual paintings simultaneously. These models combine information in repeat sales and on single sales in one model. However, the problem of model specification and functional form in the hedonic part leave room for error. Moreover, sample selection bias still exists if there are systematic differences between transacting assets and nontransacting properties.

Art Price Databases

All price indices for the art market suffer bias because of inherent problems in the available data on art sales. The only data readily available and made public are auction data, as dealers transactions are made in the private sector and are not published or generally made publicly available. Auction data can be retrieved from various specialized companies and also directly from some of the auction houses via printed catalogues and Web sites. Several commercial data providers offer access to past auction data, although they range in quality and coverage and each has their own advantages and disadvantages. *Table 3.1* shows a summary of some of the characteristics of a selection of the main, currently functioning databases.

Table 3.1 indicates that Artfact and Artprice are among the strongest in terms of the number of artists in their database, which is reported as 500,000 and 405,000 respectively. The range of art sales they cover is different however: Artfact covers both fine and decorative art from 1986 to the present; whereas Artprice covers fine art only, which means it has a stronger coverage of certain artists with transactions from 1960 to the present.

Artnet and Art Sales Index find themselves somewhere in the middle of these providers. Art Sales Index has the advantage of being free of charge, whereas Artnet is one of the most expensive databases, although one of the most aesthetically appealing and easy to navigate. AMR is unique in that it offers ready-made indices that can be customized to some degree and are supplied along with the aggregated data on which the indices are based. AMR does however not supply raw price data, only averages and indices based on averages that are subject to some of the methodological issues mentioned above. All of these databases have their own unique traits, advantages, and drawbacks, and the option chosen should depend on the goal you are trying to reach.

TABLE 3.1 A Selection of Art Data Sources

Auction Data	Artnet	Artprice	Art Sales Index	AMR	Artfact
No. artists	182,000	405,000	200,000	Dependent on index	>500,000
No. auction houses	>500	2,900	>500	N/A	>2,000
Coverage	Fine art only/ (3.8MM results) and some decorative art	Fine art only/20MM+ results	Fine art only/ 3.5MM results	Limited fine and decorative art	Fine and decorative art/53MM results
Range	1985– present	1960– present	1920– present	1975– present	1986– present
Search engine	Advanced	Moderate	Advanced	N/A	Moderate
Related activities	Gallery database/ online auctions	Market analysis/art indices	Market analysis/ art magazines	Art index building/ customization	Online auctions
Annual subscription	$99–$2,000	$148–$565	Free	Varied	$200– $1,995

Artnet

Artnet (www.artnet.com) is an online art database, based in New York, that offers an archive of auction prices along with a variety of other art-related services. Users at the Web site can access articles on art events and particular artists as well as trends in the art market via the publication *Market Performance Reports*. These reports compile yearly auction market information on over 4,300 of the most important artists driving the global public auction market and offer readers information on market trends such as liquidity, volatility, sales volume, and pricing. The reports range in price from $50 to $3,000.

Artnet focuses mainly on fine art but launched a smaller decorative art database in February 2009. The art database covers a wide range of art auctions that have already occurred and is constantly updated for changes and new events. The fine art database covers auctions of over 182,000 artists covering auction sales from 1985 to the present and includes a wide range of nationalities and styles. The database is accessible through a search engine where users can specify the name, type of art and medium, size of work, year of work, sales price range, and title and sales number. Based on the specified criteria, the database will offer all of the artists it estimates could belong to a search term. When there is only one or when the correct artist is chosen from the lot, sales transactions from that artist can be viewed. Before showing the search results, users can specify the sorting method, including chronological order (ascending/descending), work date, and price. All artworks are vertically sorted in the prespecified order, with one hundred paintings on each page. As is the case with most of the databases, information cannot be downloaded in a spreadsheet, and images are available for many works in thumbnail form, depending on the type of subscription. The art price database requires a paid subscription, which ranges in price from around $15 for a one-day pass (without images) up to $2,000 for specialist, unlimited subscriptions.

What sets Artnet apart from other databases is that it not only provides data on auction houses but also has a gallery database. This allows users to search galleries for works of fine and decorative art currently on sale. The Web site also offers the possibility to participate in online auctions, albeit on a relatively small scale.

Artprice

Artprice is a French-based database that has been in operation since 1987, and is currently one of the most comprehensive in terms of the number of fine art auctions and artists it covers. Accessible at www.artprice.com, the database covers 290,000 art catalogues covering over twenty million auction sales transactions that are accessible with a subscription.

The database includes 405,000 artists and allows users to search by artist only (however, they can also scroll through catalogues that are archived from 1960 to the present). Once the correct artist is chosen, an overview of the artist's available data is offered, including available auction records, images, presale estimates, price levels, indices, and in many cases an artist biography. Within the auction records, works of art are vertically sorted in chronological order. The search can be refined by various criteria such as title, sales price, size, medium, and date created.

Artprice provides a variety of subscription levels, which range from a basic starter package with unlimited searches at an annual fee of $148 to other, more-expensive options with access to other Artprice publications.

It also offers the ability to buy and sell artworks on the Web site. This is different from Artnet in the sense that they are offering access not to online auctions but to a classified listing service of works that are up for sale. Artists or collectors can post an ad on the Artprice site to which members have access. Interested members can then respond to the ad and purchase a work of art of choice.

Artprice publishes reports and articles concerning developments on the art market and provides an annual summary of fine art auctions through the publication *Trends*. Some of these reports are accessible without a subscription. Artprice also offers an art market confidence index along with other value indices under its Artprice Indicator service.

Art Sales Index

Art Sales Index is one of the oldest of the databases listed in Table 3.1, although it was relatively recently purchased by Louise Blouin Media and relaunched via their Artinfo portal (www.artinfo.com). The Louise Blouin Media group includes Web sites and print publications such as *Art + Auction, Modern Painters, Culture + Travel, Gallery Guide,* and *Museums New York*. It also offers an e-mail service to keep the reader up to date with a weekly newsletter.

The art price database Art Sales Index covers over 3.5 million auction results, for more than 200,000 artists, and 500 different auction houses. The data run from 1970 to the present, and catalogues by Christie's and Sotheby's supplement data from 1920 onward.

The search engine for Art Sales Index offers the option to specify the artist's name, type of art or medium (sculpture, painting, photograph), title of the work, year of work, size of work, price range (and the possibility to exclude unsold items), currency, auction house, and sale date. Auction results can be sorted by a range of parameters such as title, artist, price, and date of sale. Auction results are available to a limited extent for nonsubscribers, and the full package is also available for free through the creation of an account. Auction results are available on the Web site only and are not downloadable into a spreadsheet.

AMR

AMR, or Art Market Research, is different from the previous three providers in that it does not provide access to an online database of auctions prices but specializes in the development of art indices. AMR provides its subscribers with access to a variety of art indices based on genre or artist, which can be changed to some extent to user needs. Since 1985, AMR has developed 500 indices but also allows online creation of over 100,000 indices through custom development. The underlying averages on which the indices are based are supplied along with a chart of the index and data range from 1975 to the present. In addition AMR has its own investment vehicle that specializes in art investments and also offers an art consultancy service.

The AMR database through which indices are established covers fine art, decorative art and collectibles, and a variety of other markets. The market most frequently analyzed is the paintings market, which is subdivided into predetermined categories, which represent several nationalities covering European countries, America, and the painting market in general. Within these categories, users can also select different movements or styles of painters, such as Old Masters or Modern and Contemporary. The decorative and collectibles data encompass items such as jewelry, ceramics, and furniture, with more specific sectors available in some categories. Finally the "other markets" category offers indices from a selection of markets, including precious metals and stones, real estate, wine and the stock market.

A variety of indices are therefore available to users; however, the sectors offered by the database do not cover the entire fine and decorative market or all artists and genres. For paintings, for example, each index is based on the artists that are categorized within the specific sector by the database. (It is not possible to add or delete artists or items from the selection or view the underlying transactions data for the index.) The index can be specified in U.S. dollar, pound sterling, yen, euro, and other European currencies (current and historical) and filtered to a certain layer (say, the top 10 percent or central 50 percent) of the particular art market segment. The method used to establish the index is a rather naive average-price index method. As stated earlier, the application of this method can lead to substantial bias: the price level can be strongly biased upward due to the sale of one or few very highly priced works in one year, while in other years this is not the case.

The average-price index method can show a strong increase or decrease in an aggregate index because of outlier prices that are not necessarily representative of the market. The way AMR tries to get around the aggregation issues to some extent is through the careful choice of which artists to include, though this very process itself brings along its own selection biases. Pricing information is not given on the company website and there is no way to subscribe directly online. According to their list of clients, the service appears to be directed at specific public and institutional users rather than individual collectors and investors.

Artfact

Artfact is a U.S.-based art price database that provides coverage of the fine art and decorative art markets as well as collectibles such as books and coins. The database covers a vast 50 million transactions from 2,000 auction houses.

Artfact distinguishes three main sections in its database: Fine Art, Auction Advisor, and Past Auction Prices. The first covers over 500,000 artists, their biographies, over two million fine art price results, and full catalogue descriptions for paintings, sculptures, photography, drawings, and prints. The Auction Advisor is an alert system notifying the subscriber of upcoming sales according to the subscriber's preference. The Past Auction Prices database has over 50 million auction price results from thirty-five countries since 1986, including fine and decorative art, antiques, and collectibles.

The search engine allows a moderate amount of refining specifications such as sale date, price, auction house, and auction location. Access to the database and other Artfact services is available for a fee and requires a subscription. The cheapest subscription, called Artfact Basic, offers auction data for the previous year only for a fee of $200 annually. Artfact Premium provides coverage of the previous five years and a larger part of the quantity of auction sales records for $450 annually. The full database, covering the previous fifteen years and the total quantity of records, costs $1,995 annually. The smaller fine art database gives unlimited access for $350 annually.

There are a few other databases apart from these mentioned, notably Artvalue (a smaller, free auction price database), Findartinfo.com, icollector.com and some others. Auction price data are also available directly and free from the Web sites of many of the larger auction houses, such as Christie's, Sotheby's, Bonham's, and Phillips de Pury. A problem with all of the databases at present is that they all have limited search parameters and, as a rule, do not sell data in bulk in spreadsheet format. To study art prices over time, therefore, these Web sites provide easy access to the same information that is available in printed catalogues with the ability to sort the data but not extract it.

Art Market Performance

Investors are constantly on a hunt for assets that can improve the risk-adjusted return of their financial portfolios. In times when the economy is performing poorly, there is a demand for assets that have a low correlation with such traditional asset classes as stocks and bonds. Articles in the financial press that report on the record prices paid for paintings give rise to the idea that art might be an asset that can be used to make large returns. However, it is important to remember that works of art are very different from stocks and bonds. First, unlike stocks and bonds, which offer returns in the form of dividends or interest, art can be classified a consumer good that provides its owner with aesthetic pleasure and social status. Second, stocks and bonds are traded almost continually, while the time between a sale and resale of a particular painting can take more than a century. Finally, compared with owning a stock, owning art has additional risks such as theft, forgery, and possible physical damage. In order to tell whether reported high returns on art are consistent or just the result of plain speculative luck, it is important to investigate whether investing in art yields a competitive risk-adjusted return in comparison with other, more-traditional asset classes and can be used to diversify a financial portfolio.

There have been a number of studies carried out to compare the returns on art with the returns on financial assets, and the results are mixed. Some studies showed that in some periods art is not a competitive alternative investment. Baumol (1986), for example, found that paintings had a lower return when compared to that of risk-free assets.[9] Mei and Moses (2002) found that the returns on works of art is higher than returns on fixed-income assets and equivalent to returns on equities, but the returns are accompanied by a high volatility.[10] The high volatility of the returns can hinder the assimilation of art in the portfolio of an asset manager. Other studies have shown more positive results, with returns on art beating inflation and many financial indices during some periods. And several have shown art to have a low correlation with other financial assets, making it suitable for diversifying risk in a portfolio of assets.

Throughout the research on art investment, different measures have been applied to determine the relationship between the art market and stock markets such as correlation analysis, optimal portfolio allocation, and causality and co-integration analysis. All empirical studies have been applied to auction house data only (available via the databases discussed in the previous section), thus excluding the dealer and gallery markets. Moreover, all art research is highly subject to researcher specification and sample selection, which means that results vary quite strongly when it comes to matters such as returns and risk.

As there is a large degree of diversity in the data sets used, the art markets studied (e.g., which genres, regions, or countries are analyzed), and different art index methodologies applied, there is also a great variation in the returns that have been found in previous research. *Table 3.2* summarizes some of the major studies on art market performance to date, along with their characteristics.

Some of the early works on the rate of return on investing in paintings were by Anderson (1974)[11] and Stein (1977).[12] Anderson applied both the hedonic price regression and the repeat-sales regression methodology. The hedonic price regression was done for paintings in general auctioned between 1780 and 1970, which found a nominal return of 3.3 percent per year. Anderson also used repeat sales between 1780 and 1970 to construct a rate of return, which resulted in an average nominal return of 3.7 percent per year. The different results in the two methods could be attributed to sample-selection bias. As repeat-sales analysis only includes those sold twice or more, it potentially includes more-popular and well-performing paintings, thus creating an upward bias. Moreover, the period chosen also differs. Anderson attributed the spread between paintings and stocks to the psychical effects of art consumption.

Stein (1977) delivered the second study on the rate of return on paintings. Using U.S. and U.K. auction prices for paintings in general sold between 1946 and 1968, he found a nominal return of 10.5 percent per year for that period. The annual nominal return on stocks was 14.3 percent for the same period. Stein also argued that paintings have two types of returns. The first is the financial return resulting from a work's price appreciation, while the second is the nonfinancial return resulting from the pleasure of viewing the paintings.

TABLE 3.2 Summary of a Selection of Art Price Research

Researcher	Data source	Type of Paintings	Time Period	Nationality	Method	Nominal %	Real %
Anderson (1974)	Reitlinger and Mayer's Compendia	General/popular	1780–1960	No distinction	Hedonic	3.30	2.60
—	—	General/popular	1780–1970	—	Resales	3.70	3.00
Stein (1977)	Art Prices Current	General/popular	1946–1968	No distinction	Random sampling	10.5	—
Baumol (1986)	Reitlinger	General/popular	1652–1961	No distinction	Resales	—	0.55
Buelens and Ginsburgh (1993)[13]	Reitlinger	General/popular	1652–1961	English/Dutch/Italian	Hedonic	0.90	—
—	—	Impressionist	—	English/Dutch/Italian	Hedonic	3.00	—
—	—	English	—	English	Hedonic	0.60	—
Goetzmann (1993)[14]	Reitlinger and Mayer's Compendia	General/popular	1855–1991	No distinction	Resales	3.20	2.00
Mok et al. (1993)[15]	Christie's and Sotheby's auctions	Modern Chinese	1980–1990	Chinese	Hedonic	52.90	—
Pesando (1993)[16]	Gordon's Print Price Annual	Modern prints	1977–1992	No distinction	Resales	—	1.51
—	—	Other Impressionists	—	—	—	8.00	1.00

Study	Source	Subject	Period	Nationality	Method		
Chanel (1995)[17]	Mayer's Compendia	General/popular	1963–1993	No distinction	Hedonic	Only graphs	—
Ginsburgh and Jeanfils (1995)[18]	Mayer's Compendia	General/popular	1963–1992	European/American	Hedonic	—	—
Agnello and Pierce (1996)[19]	Annual Art Sales Index	General/popular	1971–1992	American	Hedonic	9.30	3.00
Chanel et al. (1996)[20]	Reitlinger	Impressionist paintings	1855–1970	No distinction	Hedonic	—	4.90
—	—	—	—	—	Resales	—	5.00
Candela and Scorcu (1997)[21]	Finarte Casa D'Aste	Italian paintings	1983–1994	Italian	Average painting	3.84	—
Czujack (1997)[22]	Mayer's Compendia	Picasso	1964–1995	Italian	Hedonic	—	8.30
Mei and Moses (2002)	New York Public and Watson Libraries	Several schools	1875–2000	No distinction	Resales	—	4.90
De la Barre et al. (1994)[23]	Mayer's Compendia	Great Impressionists	1962–1991	European born after 1830	Hedonic	12.00	5.00
Renneboog and Van Houtte (2002)[24]	ArtQuest	Belgian paintings	1970–1997	Belgian	Hedonic	5.60	—
Hodgson and Vorkink (2003)[25]	Campbell, Sotheby's, and Westbridge	Canadian painters	1968–2001	Canadian	Hedonic	8.5	—

(Continued)

TABLE **3.2** Summary of a Selection of Art Price Research

Researcher	Data source	Type of Paintings	Time Period	Nationality	Method	Nominal %	Real %
Worthington and Higgs (2004)[26]	AMR	Several schools	1976–2001	European/ American	Provided by AMR	3.03	—
Higgs and Worthington (2005)[27]	Australian Art Auction Records	Australian fine art	1973–2003	Australian	Hedonic	7.00	—
Worthington and Higgs (2006)[28]	Australian Art Auction Records	Australian contemporary and modern art	1973–2003	Australian	Hedonic	4.82	—
Kraeussl and Roelofs (2008)[29]	Art Price Index	General/popular	1957–2006	No distinction	Hedonic	—	—
Kraeussl and Elsland (2008)[30]	Artnet price data-base	German artists	1985–2007	German	Hedonic	3.8	—

Despite the fact that Anderson (1974) and Stein (1977) already conducted research on the rate of return on paintings, the study done by Baumol (1986) opened the way to a large number of studies about the subject. In that study, Baumol analyzed 640 repeat-sales transactions between 1652 and 1961 and found a real average return of 0.55 percent per year. This return is much lower than the 2 percent that a risk-averse investor could have made on bonds over the same time period. According to Baumol, the 1.5 percent difference can be attributed to the utility derived from the aesthetic pleasure. Like Anderson and Stein, Baumol concluded that the financial rate of return on paintings is lower in comparison with an investment in financial assets, because paintings also provide a psychical return from owning and viewing the paintings.

After Baumol, a number of other studies about the return on paintings followed. Buelens and Ginsburgh (1993), Goetzmann (1993) and Pesando (1993) found a number of different rates of return on art investments. Buelens and Ginsburgh (1993) found that there are large time intervals when art investments perform better than other financial assets. They also used the repeat-sales regression and found an average real return of 0.65 percent per year between 1700 and 1961. However, returns were quite diverse when the entire time period was broken down into smaller time periods and schools. Between 1950 and 1961, for example, the Dutch painters had an impressive return of 32.68 percent, while the Impressionists lost 19.48 percent between 1914 and 1949.

Goetzmann (1993) found a real return of 2 percent using the repeat-sales method. In that study, he also investigated the relation between stock and art markets and concluded that booms in stock markets could create booms in art markets (but not the reverse).

Pesando (1993) was one of the first researchers not to use paintings in general for his analysis. Instead he used a portfolio of modern prints from artists such as Picasso, Miró, and Chagall and found an average real rate of return of 1.51 percent for a modern print portfolio using the repeat-sales technique.

The studies by De la Barre et al. (1994) and Chanel et al. (1995, 1996) used the alternative hedonic regression technique. De la Barre et al. (1994) produced results with higher returns for his Impressionist data set in comparison with previous studies using repeat-sales regression methodology and paintings in general. This particular study also focused on relatively shorter time periods and specific styles, finding a nominal return of 12 percent per year for sales of paintings of Great Impressionists between 1962 and 1991. For other Impressionists, a return of 8 percent for the same period was found. Substantial price increases in the last years of the 1980s contributed partly to these higher returns. Chanel et al. (1995 and 1996) also used the hedonic price regression to calculate a return for a selection of major painters. In the first study, the eighty major painters had to fulfill the criterion of having spent part of their life in France. Sales between 1960 and 1988 were collected, and this resulted in a real return of 6.7 percent. The second study (1996) used only forty-six painters (Impressionists) and a larger period, namely between 1855 and 1970. This resulted in a real return of 4.9 percent.

Mei and Moses (2002) selected paintings from New York auction houses between 1950 and 2000 that were sold more than once. These data were then backfilled to get all the paintings that were sold before 1950 and all their previous sales going back to 1875. They found that the return on art did not differ that much from that of stocks. For the period between 1950 and 1999, where the data were the most accurate, art yielded 8.2 percent, compared with 8.9 percent for the Standard & Poor's 500 Index. The risk of the art investment was higher with a difference of 5.2 percent. The low correlation between the markets suggests that it could be beneficial to assimilate art in a mean-variance efficient portfolio. (An efficient portfolio is where the trade-off between risk and return is most optimal.) In contrast to the previous literature, they also showed that art outperformed bonds, but again its volatility was also substantially higher. The single-market model (capital asset pricing model) has also indicated that art investments have less systematic (market) risk than the market portfolio and thus yield less then the equity market and more than bonds.

More recent performance studies using the hedonic regression model have focused more on sales of paintings of specific painters and those from a specific country. Renneboog and Van Houtte (2002) used hedonic regression as well as a market basket of artists. Their study was carried out for sales of works by Belgian painters between 1970 and 1997. This resulted in an average nominal return of 5.6 percent for all paintings, while the basket of paintings gave a slightly higher return of 8.6 percent between 1980 and 1997. Hodgson and Vorkink (2004) used a data set of sales of paintings by major Canadian artists between 1968 and

2001 to analyze the rate of return and found a real return of 2.3 percent. Higgs and Worthington (2005) studied auction results of 60 major Australian artists who sold between 1973 and 2003 and found an average nominal return of 6.98 percent.

A more recent study from Kraeussl and Elsland (2008) presents a novel two-step hedonic regression approach, which is used to construct a price index for the German art market. Their approach enables the researcher to use every single auction record, instead of only those auction records that belong to a subsample of selected artists. This results in a substantially larger sample available, and it lowers the selection bias that is inherent in the traditional hedonic and repeat-sales approaches. Using a unique sample of 61,135 auction records for German paintings created by 5,115 individual artists over the period 1985 to 2007, they create the *German Art All* index with an annual return of 3.8 percent and substantial volatility (of 17.8 percent).

Kraeussl and Logher (2008) analyze the performance and risk-return characteristics of three major emerging art markets: Russia, China, and India.[31] According to three national art market indices, built by hedonic regressions based on auction sales prices, the geometric annual returns are 10.0 percent, 5.7 percent, and 42.2 percent for Russia (1985–2008), China (1990–2008), and India (2002–2008), respectively. *Figures 3.1–3.3*

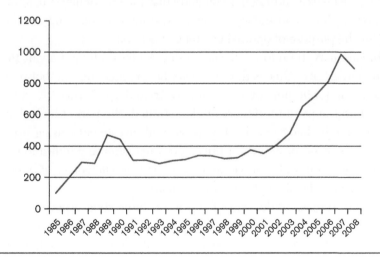

FIGURE 3.1 Russian Art Market Index (1985–2008)

Source: *Kraeussl and Logher* (2008)

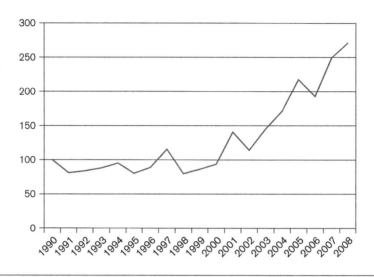

FIGURE 3.2   Chinese Art Market Index (1990–2008)

Source: *Kraeussl and Logher* (2008)

display the resulting art indices for Russia, China, and India, using end-of-year index values (January to December), though the 2008 index values are based only on January through April. Based on their empirical findings, Kraeussl and Logher conclude that the emerging art markets of Russia, China, and India provide interesting investment opportunities for the purpose of optimal portfolio allocation.

In summary, therefore, all that can be conclusively said about the returns to art over time is that they vary between genres and between periods, and whether art outperforms or underperforms the stock market will depend on the art market studied, the period looked at, and the methodology used. Also, as with all investments, using price indices based on past auction prices does not offer any indication of future prices, but rather serves as a useful first step in looking at trends that have already taken place in the art market.

Setting returns aside, one of the more interesting aspects of art investments is their relation to other markets. In the research to date, there is conflicting evidence about the profitability of investing in art and its prospects for portfolio diversification. Worthington and Higgs (2004) found a correlation between art and small-company stocks of –0.31. This varying degree of correlation can strongly influence the

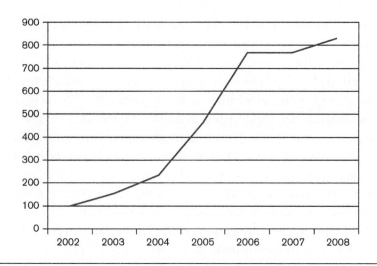

3.3 Indian Art Market Index (2002–2008)

Source: *Kraeussl and Logher* (2008)

optimal investment portfolio chosen. Other studies have found that art has a positive market beta, which indicates its relation to the general stock market (as the S&P 500 well represents). This varied from 0.25, 0.36 and 0.82 according to research by Kraeussl and Elsland (2008), Hodgson and Vorkink (2003) and Renneboog and Van Houtte (2002) respectively.

Mei and Moses (2002) concluded that art has a lower volatility and a lower correlation with other financial assets than previously thought, making art an attractive investment for portfolio diversification. Campbell (2007) obtained very low and even negative correlation with other asset classes, indicating that art is a highly beneficial investment vehicle for an investor's portfolio.[32] (Risk issues and correlation are discussed in Chapter 4.)

Art and the Economy

Art is a luxury good. If aggregate levels of wealth are high, the demand for art may also be expected to be high, as investors may spend part of this excess of wealth in the arts. Changes in income are therefore likely to have a significant effect on the demand for art and the prices paid for works of art. At times when the rates of return for alternative investments are high, the demand and prices paid for art are likely to be low. Investors hedge against inflation, and material assets such as commodities, real estate, and works of art serve this purpose well. Thus, when rates of inflation are high, demand for these material assets is likely to increase. Financial markets are highly integrated with the economy and react quickly to economic shocks. This is normally expected to be different for the art market. Therefore, it is likely that financial markets and (to a somewhat lesser extent) economic indicators will function as advance indicators that predict what will happen in the art market. In reality, however, the art market often functions independently of financial markets, making it a less straightforward and more complex market to base any forecasts and predictions on.

Studies on the returns on art investment have produced very mixed results. Some that focused on returns in certain periods have put art in a bad light, while others have been positive, with results strongly subject to the specifications that the researcher applies: what stream of artists, what period, what country, and a host of other assumptions. As with stocks, the results of a particular investment in art are also highly dependent on the timing of investment and disinvestment. It is safe to say that when investing in art, it is essential that one also evaluate the current market tastes and fashion. Just as the stock market is affected by certain investor sentiment, the art market is affected in the same way by aesthetic preferences, and certain sectors will come in and out of favor at different times.

Chapter Notes

1. W. Baumol, "Unnatural Value, Or Art Investment as Floating Crap Game," *American Economic Review* 76, no. 2 (1986): 10–14.

2. See, for example, V. Ginsburgh and D. Throsby, *Handbook of the Economics of Art and Culture* (Amsterdam: Elsevier 2006).

3. The key difference between repeat-sales regressions and hedonic regressions is whether the fixed component of the return is determined by a number of hedonic characteristics or is treated explicitly by tracking only works of identical quality.

4. Repeat sales are expressed as a regression with its dependent variable being the ratio of the new/old price. Then, to take into account the changes for each time period, so-called time dummy variables are added as independent variables.

5. For example, very-high-quality paintings that are sold to museums are excluded, even though their prices embed significant information and are relevant to analysis of the art market.

6. For example, Old Masters may have a higher chance of being sold repeatedly than artworks of the twenty-first century.

7. For example, the physical condition of the work or the perception of its relative quality might be altered by changes in its physical surroundings or scholarly assessment.

8. These implicit prices are used to correct the quality change of a certain sales mix. The hedonic regression method requires the specification of quality-characteristic variables, in addition to time dummy variables, to build an art market index.

9. W. Baumol, "Unnatural Value: or Art Investment as a Floating Crap Game," *American Economic Review* 76, no. 2 (1986): 10–14.

10. J. Mei and M. Moses, "Art as an Investment and the Underperformance of Masterpieces," *American Economic Review* 92, no. 5 (2002): 1656–1668.

11. R. C. Anderson, "Paintings as an Investment," *Economic Inquiry* 12, no. 1 (1974): 13–26.

12. J. P. Stein, "The Monetary Appreciation of Paintings," *The Journal of Political Economy* 85 (1977): 1021–1036.

13. N. Buelens and V. Ginsburgh, Revisiting Baumol's "Art as a Floating Crap Game," *European Economic Review* 37 (1993): 1351–1371.

14. W. N. Goetzmann, "Accounting for Taste: Art and the Financial Markets Over Three Centuries," *American Economic Review* 83, no. 5 (1993): 1370–1376.

15. H. Mok, V. Ko, S. Woo, and K. Kwok, "Modern Chinese Paintings: An Investment Alternative," *Southern Economic Journal* 59, no. 4 (1993): 808–816.

16. J. E. Pesando, "Art as an Investment: The Market for Modern Prints," *American Economic Review* 83, no. 5 (1993): 1075–1089.

17. O. Chanel, "Is Art Market Behaviour Predictable?" *European Economic Review* 39 (1995): 519–527.

18. V. Ginsburgh and P. Jeanfils, "Long-Term Comovements in International Markets for Paintings," *European Economic Review* 38 (1995): 538–548.

19. R. J. Agnello and R. K. Pierce, "Financial Returns, Price Determinants, and Genre Effects in American Art Investment," *Journal of Cultural Economics* 20 (1996): 359–383.

20. O. Chanel, L. Gerard-Varet, and V. Ginsburgh, "The Relevance of Hedonic Price Indices," *Journal of Cultural Economics* 20 (1996): 1–24.

21. G. Candela, P. Figini, and A. Scorcu, "Price Indices for Artists-a Proposal," *Journal of Cultural Economics* 28 (2004): 285–302.

22. C. Czujack, "Picasso Paintings at Auction, 1963–1994," *Journal of Cultural Economics* 21, no. 3 (1997): 229–247.

23. M. De la Barre, S. Docclo, and V. Ginsburgh, "Returns of Impressionist, Modern and Contemporary Modern Paintings," *Annales d'Economie et de Statistique*, 35 (1994): 143–181.

24. L. Renneboog and T. van Houtte, "The Monetary Appreciation of Paintings: From Realism to Magritte," *Cambridge Journal of Economics* 26 (2002): 331–357.

25. D. J. Hodgson and K. P. Vorkink, "Asset Pricing Theory and the Valuation of Canadian Paintings," *Canadian Journal of Economics* 37, no. 3 (2004): 629–655.

26. A. C. Worthington and H. Higgs, "Art as an Investment: Short and Long-Term Comovements in Major Painting Markets," *Empirical Economics* 28 (2004): 649–668.

27. A. C. Worthington and H. Higgs, Australian Fine Art as an Alternative Investment, Accounting & Finance Working Paper 05/02, School of Accounting & Finance, University of Wollongong (2005): 1–30.

28. A. C. Worthington and H. Higgs, "A Note on Financial Risk, Return and Asset Pricing in Australian Modern and Contemporary Art," *Journal of Cultural Economics* 30 (2006): 73–84.

29. R. Kraeussl and J. Roelofs, Long and Short Term Relationships between Art Investments and Financial Markets. Working Paper, VU University Amsterdam (2008), available at www.art-finance.com.

30. R. Kraeussl and N. van Esland, Constructing the True Art Market. Working Paper, VU University Amsterdam (2008), available at www.art-finance.com and at SSRN: #1104667.

31. R. Kraussl and R. Logher, Emerging Art Markets, VU Amsterdam Working Paper (2008), available at SSRN#1304856.

32. R. Campbell, Art as a Financial Investment, Maastricht University Working Paper (2007), available at SSRN#978467.

4

Art Risk

Dr. Clare McAndrew and Dr. Rachel Campbell

EDITOR'S NOTE: Risk is an important feature of any investment. The basic financial risk of investing is caused by uncertainty concerning the rate of return, and returns to art can vary considerably between different sectors, artists, periods, and places. One of the most important features for investors to remember about the art market is that there is essentially no such thing as "the art market." It is the de facto name given to the aggregation of many independently moving and unique submarkets that are defined by artists and genres, and that often behave in significantly different ways. This is fundamental to understanding investment in the market: art can be a good investment because it trades on markets that have different risks. Careful quantification of those risks and unique trading patterns can lead to the development of hedges against specific anticipated risks in other investments. The markets for various subspecies of art can, for example, show low correlation to markets for specific fungible assets, which makes it a suitable asset for portfolio diversification.

Although the application of standard financial risk metrics to the art market has been limited up to quite recently, understanding the risk-related advantages of art is key to realizing the greatest benefits from an investment in this asset class. Also, in addition to some of the standard financial benchmarks, the unique nature of the art auction process and expert presale valuations also provide an additional method of analyzing the downside risks for investing in art, which while still in its infancy, lends much credence to the possibility of fully underwriting art as collateral.

Although there are a few examples of successful speculation, art investing will invariably be a more successful longer-term investment. Significant positive returns are much more likely over the longer term but, as will be seen in some of the subsequent chapters, costs of the investment, such as insurance, storage, restoration, and maintenance, also pile up over a longer horizon. What maintains the attractiveness of the asset class over time therefore centers on some of its risk characteristics, which are highlighted in the discussion that follows. The first section reviews some of the basics concerning the measurement of risk in the art market. It introduces the concepts of risk and correlation, and shows how art can act as a suitable asset for portfolio diversification. It also looks at presale auction estimates, showing how they can be used to help assess the downside risk of an investment in art. In the second section, Rachel Campbell revisits the debate on risk versus return in art investment. The discussion first defines art price or financial risk and then looks at the developing sector of art risk management and art banking. It introduces the innovative concept of "art credit default swaps" which have the potential to be used to hedge against certain risks in the art market and enable banks to remove the risks from lending on art from their balance sheets.

Risk Basics
Clare McAndrew

The basic financial risk of any investment is the uncertainty concerning the rate of return. When making an investment, to estimate the return due over a specific holding period, you need to know the price of the asset at the end of the period. The estimation of that end price is always the subject of uncertainty and volatility, and the presence of risk means that more than one outcome is possible. The risk of returns on an investment in art therefore arise from fluctuations in the price between purchase and sale. As with all assets, the objective of investing is to minimize the downside risk for a given level of return or to maximize the returns for a given level of risk. Another aim for an investor is to hold a balanced portfolio of assets such that the constituent parts, when considered as a whole, sum together to minimize overall portfolio risk.

To measure risk for a single asset, various statistical measures of dispersion and volatility are used. In statistics, volatility is calculated as the variance or as the standard deviation of returns, which both measure how the actual return you achieve deviates from the expected or mean return. Standard deviation measures the dispersion of prices around their average, and if prices were the same throughout the period it would equate to zero.[1] In the art market, as there are no option prices available as yet, risk must be analyzed using historical measures of volatility. By looking at returns and prices over time, the average return can be estimated and then the standard deviation of that return is one measure of risk. The reward for the investment is then measured as the expected excess return over the holding period above a risk-free investment, or what is called the risk premium. In other words, the risk premium is the rate of return over the period minus the risk-free rate, i.e., the premium you would need to invest in a risky asset such as art rather than hold an asset that had a stable constant return over time. This risk-free rate is defined as the return on an investment that has no risk of default, but in practice instruments such as U.S. Treasury bills or Euribor rates are often used, as these instruments are the closest to being virtually risk-free from default.

It is possible to create a risk and return picture of a given investment by looking at the past rates of return and their standard deviations over different holding periods. More often, however, investors will want to look at not only the risk of an individual investment over time, but also its risk relative to alternative assets, asset classes, or markets. For example, a buyer considering the purchase of Monet's *Dans La Prairie* (which sold at auction for $16 million in February 2009 at Christie's in London) might wish to compare the risk and performance of

❑ *Dans La Prairie* relative to the rest of Monet's works;

❑ Monet relative to the rest of the French Impressionist cohort;

❑ Monet relative to the rest of the entire cohort of Impressionist painters;

❑ Monet, or French Impressionists, relative to an index of stocks, bonds, or commodities; or

❑ any combination of these.

One of the most common ways to assess *relative* risk is to determine the beta of an asset. Beta (β) is a measure of the systematic risk of an asset or the tendency of a particular asset's returns to respond to swings in the broader market. Beta measures the covariance of a particular asset in relation to the rest of the market or whatever the chosen asset base is. For example, if returns to Monet are R_m and returns to the French Impressionist cohort are R_{FI}, then the beta for Monet (β_m) is:

$$\beta_m = cov(R_m R_{FI})/\sigma(R_{FI})$$

where $cov(R_m R_{FI})$ is the covariance between the returns in the Monet market and the larger French Impressionist market and σ is the standard deviation of returns in the wider (French Impressionist) market. Covariance simply measures how two variables move or vary together, or their correlation with each other.

The base represents the wider market as a whole (in this case, French Impressionists), and its beta will have an assigned value of 1. The beta of the asset being compared to the market (Monet's works), will then have a value of greater or less than 1, as it is measuring how sensitive prices of the specific asset are in relation to prices in the market. If it is greater than 1, this indicates that prices are more volatile than the market and can be expected to rise and fall more quickly and to a greater extreme than the market. If the beta is less than 1, the asset will tend to move more slowly or to a lesser extent than the market. A beta of +0.33, for example, would indicate that, on average, prices for Monet's works move one-third as much as the French Impressionist market does and in the same direction. In other words, this submarket is around three times less risky or less volatile. If the market rose by 10 percent, Monet's works would be expected to rise by 3.3 percent. On the other hand, if the market fell by 10 percent, they would fall by only 3.3 percent. So they vary less, or are less risky, than the overall market. Similarly a beta of –0.10 would indicate that on average, the prices of the asset in question move one tenth as much as the market's, but this time in the opposite direction. Negative betas are less common but imply that if the market rose by 10 percent, this investment would be expected to fall by 1 percent. So it is still less risky, but moves in the opposite direction to the wider market's movements. If the beta is greater than one, this means that the investment's returns will move, on average, in the same direction as the market's returns but to a greater extent (meaning greater downside risk and volatility than the market but also greater returns in an upswing).

Investors can use analysis of betas to alter the content of their portfolios over time as the market changes. If the market is rising (a bull market), the logic would follow that investors should hold stocks with high positive betas, as they would outperform the market. Beta has no upper or lower bound, and betas as large as 3 or 4 will occur with highly volatile stocks. However, in bear markets, investors should be targeting low beta stocks as they should outperform the falling market or make a safer and less risky investment.[2]

In many financial markets, it is rare to find negative beta assets, since equities and other assets, for example, will tend to go against the trend of the overall market index, particularly in the longer term. However, various sectors of the art market often throw up negative betas when compared with an equity index or other benchmark, as they do not always follow or lead trends in financial markets. A negative beta simply means that the asset is inversely correlated with the market, and some sectors of the art market have been found to be beta negative in different periods as their value tends to increase when the stock market is down and vice versa. Artists within segments of the art market may also behave independently of trends in their sector or the aggregated art market.

Selecting individual art objects to include in a portfolio can therefore be based on trying to find the maximum return while achieving the appropriate (minimum possible) risk level, and there are a number of statistical methods to measure risk, at least in the short run. Risk and return will always go hand in hand, however: riskier assets will have the potential to generate higher returns.

Relative risk measures such as beta are useful in helping investors compare assets and can even aid in deciding the most appropriate time to hold more or less risky assets. A problem with relying on betas and other statistical measures of risk is that they all rely on historical data and are therefore giving a picture of what *has* happened in the market, without any guarantees about future events or trends. They are also best used for short-term decision making, which is not often appropriate in the context of investment in the art market. Because of the low liquidity and the supply-driven nature of the market, it is not possible to make the same short-term buy and sell decisions that investors may use in other asset markets. What these measures are useful for is to help build a picture of how markets and assets have interacted in the past and to help suggest ways to combine art and other assets to reduce risk in a more long-term portfolio of assets.

Correlation and Diversification

All modern forms of risk quantification originate in the seminal work of U.S. economist Harry Markowitz, who formalized the concept of "not putting all your eggs in one basket" and applied it to financial instruments in a portfolio. Three simple concepts summarize the crux of portfolio theory and are important to understanding how art can help achieve Markowitzian diversification:

1. A portfolio's return is simply the weighted average of the returns on the individual assets, but a portfolio's risk will typically be less than the weighted average of the individual asset's risks.
2. The lower the correlations between the constituent assets' returns, the lower the portfolio's risk (the "diversification principle").
3. The risk of each asset can therefore be thought of as having two components:
   a. The specific, unsystematic or "diversifiable" risk—that is, the risk of a price change because of unique circumstances associated with that particular asset, as opposed to overall risk in the market. Specific risk arises from market events that affect a particular company, industry, market, or country or, in this case, artist or genre. This risk can be virtually eliminated from a portfolio through efficient diversification.
   b. Unspecific or market risk, which is common to an entire class of assets or relates to general market movements. This risk is measured by the beta of an asset and must be borne by investors.

The main principle of portfolio management is efficient diversification. Through finding assets that have low correlation with each other, it is possible to obtain a portfolio risk that is less than that of the component assets considered in isolation. Diversification is simply a strategy designed to reduce exposure to risk by combining a variety of investments such as different types of equities, bonds, property, and alternative assets (e.g., art and commodities), which are unlikely to all move in the same direction at the same time. The goal is to combine these assets in a portfolio to reduce its overall risk, with the rationale that different kinds of investments will, on average, yield higher returns and pose a lower risk than any individual investment in isolation, as not all asset classes, sectors, or individual companies within industries, or artists within genres, move up and down in value at the same time or at the same rate.

Diversification aims to smooth out the effects of unsystematic risk events in a portfolio so that the positive performance of some investments will neutralize the negative performance of others. These risks can be diversified within a portfolio by holding securities that are not perfectly correlated. The diversification benefits from investing in art are among its strongest selling points and are apparent not only in portfolios that mix various assets with art but also through strategically combinations of different categories of art, with each other to hedge against risk within the single asset class. Much of the research has shown that not only do many genres of art have low or even negative correlation with stocks, bonds, and other assets over the long term but also that particular genres are similarly uncorrelated with each other.

A correlation matrix can be used to show the various correlation coefficients between pairs of different asset classes. This coefficient measures the degree to which the pairs of assets move together, and translates the measure of combined variance into a scale from −1 (or −100 percent) to +1 (or +100 percent). In considering correlation, there are three different possibilities. The two assets may show a positive correlation: when values in one market rises, the values in the other market also tend to rise as well. Alternatively, the assets may display a negative correlation: when prices are higher in one market they tend to be lower in the other. Or, finally, there may be no correlation: the two assets do not appear to have any relationship and prices are independent of each other.

Correlations can also be weak or strong, meaning the relationship between the prices of the assets may be very significant or very slight. The closer the coefficient approaches zero from either direction, the smaller the relationship between the asset classes. Absolute or perfect independence is indicated by a zero coefficient.[3] Investors will attempt to find assets that have negative, zero, or low positive correlations with each other to enhance the potential benefits of diversification. The judgment of what constitutes acceptable independence can be highly subjective. Among professional money managers, as gross a standard as less than 50 percent correlation can define a suitable level of acceptable independence, although a more useful benchmark for low correlation would be somewhere less than 25 percent.

Table 4.1 below shows a sample correlation matrix between art and various different financial and commodity markets. This data uses three different art sectors and compares them to the Standard & Poor's 500 Index of stocks as well as the gold spot price index and the consumer price index (a measure of inflation).

The table offers an example of how art prices can be shown in different periods to have a low and negative correlation with many financial indices. The index for Dutch Old Master paintings, for instance, has a significantly negative correlation (moves in the opposite direction) with both the S&P 500 and the gold index in this period. In other words, these figures show that at a time when Dutch Old Master prices rose 1 percent, the S&P 500 fell 0.77 percent, and gold prices fell 0.70 percent. Or taking another example, when Italian Contemporary art prices doubled (rose 100 percent), gold prices also rose, but only by around 40 percent. These results indicate that there are possibilities where including art in a portfolio of other assets could bring significant diversification benefits.

TABLE 4.1   Correlation Matrix, 2008–2009

	Dutch Old Masters	American Pop Art	Italian Contemporary	S&P 500	CPI YOY	Gold Spot $/Oz.
Dutch Old Masters	1.00	0.70	–0.82	–0.77	–0.37	–0.70
American Pop Art	0.70	1.00	–0.31	–0.21	0.30	–0.62
Italian Contemporary	–0.82	–0.31	1.00	0.96	0.73	0.40
S&P 500	–0.77	–0.21	0.96	1.00	0.81	0.41
CPI YOY	–0.37	0.30	0.73	0.81	1.00	0.08
Gold Spot $/oz.	–0.70	–0.62	0.40	0.41	0.08	1.00

Source: *Arts Economics* (2009)

It is important to remember that these correlation statistics indicate the direction and extent of the association between pairs of price movements, but they do not reveal anything about causality. So, for example, the correlation between Dutch Old Masters and the S&P 500 is a large and negative one at –0.77, but this does not indicate what effect, say, a 10 percent rise in the S&P 500 would have on the prices of a Jan Davidsz de Heem painting or even on the entire Dutch Old Master market. The correlation matrix only shows how the patterns have played out over time in history. It also does not imply in any way that a 1 percent rise in the S&P 500 *causes* these art prices to drop by 0.77 percent. The direction of causality can be tested for with specialized diagnostic tests and regressions of lagged variables over time. However, as with all of these metrics, the basis for the interpretation of any results should come from basic intuitive economic theory *supported by* empirical findings, and not vice versa.

Some studies have shown that art prices follow equity prices, with a lag. The intuition offered is that as equity prices rise, investors become richer and therefore buy more art, driving prices up. Although this has been shown to be true in some sectors of the market, such as Contemporary art, there are a number of flaws in applying this across the board, and the most reliable conclusion when much of this research is extended is that, in most instances, the markets for art and equities are often simply unrelated.

Diversification across asset classes (or what is sometimes called asset allocation) is the foundation of any prudent and successful long-term investment strategy. By diversifying among different asset classes, the risk of being exposed to the specific risk of any one asset class is reduced. Diversification is also possible within an asset class through reducing exposure to the unsystematic risk of different individual assets. In the equity market, for example, company-specific risk can be diversified away by investing in a range of companies across different sectors, industries, or countries. The same is true within the art market. It is possible to diversify risk within an all-art portfolio by choosing different artists, genres, segments of different markets, and subsectors that have favorable risk and return characteristics. For example, Table 4.1 shows that Dutch Old Master paintings have a high correlation with American Pop Art during this period but also a large negative correlation with Italian Contemporary paintings, suggesting a possible hedge. The art market can be divided into genres, categories within genres, subcategories within those categories, and further by individual artists. Also within genres and categories of art, the market can be divided into bands of value, such as the top 5 percent, bottom quintile, or middle 60 percent range. All of these divisions can provide opportunities for achieving diversification within a portfolio of art.

The low correlation between many of the different genres has provided the impetus for the development of art mutual funds for investors, which raise significant amounts of capital to invest across several genres of art in the hope of creating a diversified portfolio. (The success and other aspects of these funds are discussed in Chapter 6.) It can be more difficult for individual investors to diversify successfully to an optimal level within their own art collections, and it is also important to balance risk objectives with collecting goals, such as amassing a sequence of works in a collection by a particular artist or group of artists that may also enhance value versus a more diverse and diversified selection. For many individual investors, therefore, the more important risk dimension that art offers is its low correlation with other asset holdings. Just as holding one company in an equity portfolio would not achieve an optimal level of diversification, having most or all of an investor's net worth in one or two asset classes—even if these individual portfolios are diversified—still does not achieve the most favorable risk position. Although this strategy avoids unsystematic risk, it still leaves investors exposed to market risk. By investing in a number of different asset classes, however, including art, the exposure to market risk or the systemic risk of any one asset class, can be very successfully reduced.

Downside Risk and Presale Estimates

While correlation analysis, betas, and various other risk analytics can be used across a range of different assets, the daily functioning of the auction sector of the art economy provides an additional and unique platform for risk analysis through presale estimates. Prior to each art auction, auction houses will publish a presale catalogue containing various details of forthcoming works to be sold alongside their presale high and low estimates. Instead of experts deriving a single-point estimate of what they expect the work to sell for at auction, the convention at most auction houses is to derive a valuation range within which they expect the winning bid at auction to fall; that is, within the low and high estimate.

The auction houses do not publish the seller's reserve price but commonly observe the custom of setting it at or below the presale low estimate. The process of setting the estimate involves some degree of negotiation between the seller and the auction house experts, but the reserve generally lies at about 75 percent of the lower estimate range. Reserve-setting policies do vary between auction houses and sales, however, within certain guidelines. Christie's stated policy, for example, is that the reserve price must be set at or below the low estimate and advises that it is usually between 70 percent and 80 percent of the low estimate for paintings. The stipulation for Sotheby's is also that "no reserve should exceed the low estimate," and it reports a range between 50 percent and 100 percent of the low estimate, depending on the value of the item and seller's preferences.[4]

Looking at the relationship between the market prices achieved for works of art and these contemporaneous presale estimates provides an opportunity for assessing risk in relation to an investment in art. In this case, risk can be measured through assessing the deviation of actual market prices from the presale valuation range, or in other words how the price achieved at auction deviates from the price it was expected to achieve. If the price the work sells for is above the estimated range, that is obviously an unexpected upside benefit, so in terms of assessing risk, the focus is on the downside—that is, if the price achieved at auction falls short of its expectation.

Are Presale Estimates Unbiased?

Before discussing the issues surrounding the measurement of this downside risk of art investment using these methods, it is important to establish that the estimates that auction house produce are, on the whole, both accurate and unbiased. There have been some suggestions that, for example, auction house experts may deliberately push estimates higher in the hopes of achieving higher bidding at auction and a higher eventual hammer price (and hence a higher commission for the auction house). Jianping Mei and Michael Moses (2002)[5] investigated art auction price estimates, building on their earlier analysis of the "masterpiece effect," where investors seem to overpay for masterpieces. They found that while, in general, estimates are highly correlated with prices paid, there was an apparent upward bias in estimates for very-high-priced paintings. They suggest that this is because auction houses try to maintain an overall unbiasedness but tilt estimates upward for expensive paintings to enable auctioneers to receive higher commissions on these sales. Mei and Moses read further into their evidence as supporting the notion that investors are significantly influenced by price estimates and also tend to pay more when the spread of the upper and lower estimates is larger.

Another argument might be that there is an incentive for experts to keep estimates low to encourage more potential buyers to attend an auction, and some studies have shown a downward bias in estimates over time in auctions of items such as English antique silver.[6] Some of these studies have also found that there may be under- or overestimation depending on the specific auction house, circumstances of the sale, or art genre.

Despite the rationales offered for estimate bias and some of the evidence supporting biases of different kinds, intuitively and empirically the strongest case by far is that experts are unbiased. First, given that any intentional bias would be revealed in the marketplace over time, it would be both detrimental and illogical for experts to attempt to be anything but as accurate and as truthful as possible. A number of empirical studies have also borne this out in practice. Economists Paul Milgrom and Robert J. Weber (1982),[7] for example, argued that in most auction models, including the English variety, "honesty is the best policy" for sellers. Noted cultural economist Orley Ashenfelter's (1989)[8] empirical work reiterates these conclusions, showing that auction houses are generally truthful since estimates are highly correlated with prices achieved. One important empirical study in this area by McAndrew, Smith, and Thompson (2009)[9] showed that bias did not exist as long as works of art that are bought in at auction (buy-ins) are included in the sample. This research directly refuted some of the previous studies, explaining that their reasons for finding bias were due to the fact that data were being modeled incorrectly by confining the conclusions of their analysis exclusively to works sold; in other words, bias was measured inappropriately.

Another simple reason for the bias found in some samples of auction data may arise out of expert's errors, even systematic ones in some cases. On balance, however, it appears that presale high and low estimates are generally reliable and often accurate guides to the value of works of art and can therefore provide a unique and very useful tool in risk analysis. As any strategic biases up or down on the part of experts would be revealed at auction over time, it seems safe to presume for the most part that their estimates are also unbiased, and this is backed up by the strongest academic research. Apart from a significant body of empirical evidence, there is also substantial anecdotal evidence from those working within the market that this should hold for the most part. Even the disgraced ex-CEO of Sotheby's, Dede Brooks, claimed that experts at auction houses were both "honest and unfaltering." In her testimony at the Christie's–Sotheby's price-fixing trial, Brooks claimed that her boss, Alfred Taubman, had proposed that auction houses should collude in providing their clients with similar estimates of the value of works of art they wished to auction. Brooks stated that she had told Taubman that to do so would be impossible, as it would not be possible to tell the departmental experts at Sotheby's and Christie's who produce the estimates to do a dishonest job.

Measuring Bias: The Hammer Ratio

The conclusion from all of this is simply that if estimates are generally good estimators of the expected price of a work of art, the deviation of actual prices from this expectation can be a useful measure for downside risk. McAndrew and Thompson (2007)[10] have come up with the term *hammer ratio* as the focus of this risk analysis. The hammer ratio is simply the ratio of hammer prices for works of art to the average of their estimates, or

$$HR = P/M$$

where the hammer ratio (HR) is equal to hammer price (P) divided by the mean of the high and low estimate (M).[11] Instead of looking at prices over time, investors can look at this hammer ratio or the "error distribution" of prices from their estimates. *Figure 4.1* shows an example of such a distribution taken from a sample of French Impressionist paintings. It is clear from the figure that the distribution of the hammer ratio (P/M) is not symmetric but is highly skewed to the right. This is to be expected, as prices cannot be negative, and it actually conforms to the distribution of many other equities and financial assets, in what is called a "lognormal distribution."

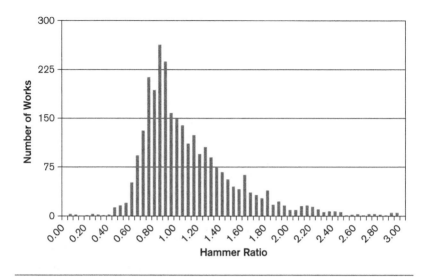

FIGURE **4.1**   Hammer Ratio for French Impressionist Paintings

Source: *McAndrew and Thompson* (2007)

Value-at-risk, or *VaR, analysis* is used in financial markets to provide an estimate of how much value can be lost by a portfolio over a given time horizon. Standard practice would be to measure the left side of the distribution, where the HRs are less than 1, or in other words where prices turned out lower than expected. From the distribution, an analyst can derive a whole host of important downside risk metrics related to art investment. Even for an individual investor, such a distribution shows a very clear risk picture of the particular segment of the art market in the given period. Looking at Figure 4.1, investors can see that the HR distribution is mainly skewed to the right. That is, most of the HRs were greater than 1, which means prices were greater than average estimates: when a work was brought to auction, the price it was hammered down at was greater than the average of the high and low estimates, which is obviously attractive to investors. Those HRs that fall below 1 represent the downside risk of the investment, where the hammer price at auction turns out less than estimated.

However, Figure 4.1 only tells part of the risk story. Looking only at hammer prices versus presale estimates is in fact insufficient when measuring downside risk. One important feature of the art market that is neglected in this figure, but is crucial in measuring and understanding the downside risk of art investment, is the inclusion of buy-ins at auction. As already explained, some works that are offered for sale at auction do not attain the seller's reserve price and are therefore bought in-house by the auctioneer. These works may be returned to the seller, sold privately with the assent of the consignor within a day or two of the failed auction, or offered at auction again at a later date. In the sample of French Impressionist paintings taken from the McAndrew and Thompson (2007) research, for example, about 30 percent of the works offered for sale at auction did not find buyers. As these works must be valued at below their seller's reserve prices, they would have fallen into the lower or left portion of the HR frequency distribution. In evaluating risk therefore, if the analysis only focuses on the valuations of the works actually sold, it will completely omit the risk that a work, once purchased, might not sell at a later date. Therefore the distribution in Figure 4.1 is incomplete or "censored" on the left side.

The data for auction sales that exclude buy-ins contain a bias: in order to purchase the work, buyers will have to pay more than the reserve price, but when they go to sell the painting in the future, there is no guarantee that the painting will exceed that same reserve. In other words, in Figure 4.1, there is a truncation in the distribution: to be included in the data of voluntary sales at auction in the first place, it has to be a successful sale. However, in that set of French Impressionist sales, one-third were bought in, and as this group of transactions did not have a hammer price, they aren't featured in Figure 4.1. They *are* important transactions, however, particularly when measuring downside risk, and they have an implicit price (their final unsuccessful bid or some price below the reserve).

In *Figure 4.2*, the HR distribution including buy-ins is provided (superimposed over the original distribution).[12] This shows the full distribution that must be considered when estimating the downside risk of an art investment, recognizing that works that do not sell at auction also present a downside risk to potential investors, alongside works that sell for less than estimated. It is clear from the figure that when buy-ins are considered, there is a greater downside risk (left portion of the distribution) than when only successful sales are considered.

Art as Collateral

The application of risk analysis to the art market is still very much in its infancy, with pioneering research such as this opening up the

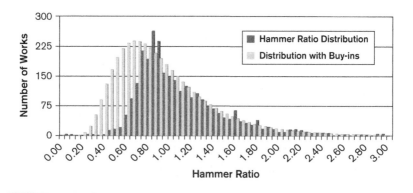

FIGURE **4.2**   Hammer Spread and Fitted Lognormal, Recognizing Buy-ins

Source: *McAndrew and Thompson* (2007)

possibility for assessment of downside risks in similar terms and measures as other financial assets. One area that has emerged from the recent research discussed above is the possibility of using art as collateral for lending. Using these distributions, it is possible to determine the appropriate loan loss calculations using standard VaR analysis. A bank can figure out, for example, what the probability would be of a collateral shortfall for a loan on 60 percent of the value of a work of art or collection (called a "loan-to-value" percentage of 60 percent); or how much it should lend on art (what loan-to-value percentage it should extend), if it wants to hold the probability of a loss at, say, 1 percent; or how much of the loan it might expect to lose if the work or portfolio was forced to be liquidated (or the "loss given default"). In other words, banks and other financial institutions could formally underwrite art, and art could validly be used as collateral for lending, just like other more traditional assets such as property.[13]

Some of the larger auction houses have occasionally offered loans using artworks as collateral, with loan-to-value ratios of about 40 percent. A small number of banks such as Citi and Bank of America (Private Bank) offer art services that include forms of lending. These practices are discussed in Chapter 5. In practice, however, all of this lending is carried out based on rules of thumb for loan-to-value ratios, and either explicitly or in reality with recourse to other assets besides art, as these services are only offered to very-high-net-worth clients with substantial wealth portfolios in other assets. However, using the analysis emerging from the recent research on risk analysis in the art market, it is possible to formalize this process and accurately underwrite the art-based lending process.

A key issue is that ignoring buy-ins, or in other words ignoring the liquidity issues in art investing, can significantly understate downside risk. The buy-in phenomenon is critical for potential lending institutions as they will want to know what the downside looks like for works sold without reserve. In the French Impressionist data set analyzed by McAndrew and Thompson (2007), for example, the authors found that implied loan-to-value ratios are twice as high as when buy-ins are not accounted for. Their paper also shows that the risk in relation to lending on art seemed higher than with other asset categories such as property. It is significant, though, that these risks are measurable given the appropriate data. Banks need to be comfortable with the kind of coverage a piece of collateral provides in the event that collateral has to be sold to cover the loan. They want to be able to assess downside risk in terms they are familiar with. And the downside risk of art investing is a quantifiable and manageable process.

Financing is badly needed in the market and would have the added benefit of bringing additional stability to the market for several reasons. If buyers can finance purchases, they can take advantage of good prices that they see, and this adds depth to the market. Sellers will also have an additional tool to help them smooth the sale of works of art. Rather than being forced to sell works because of temporary financial needs, sellers can borrow against a collection. Thus, both buyers and sellers should benefit, and the flow of available capital should both smooth prices and, by reducing risk, increase average prices, which will also benefit artists.

Art Price Risk

Rachel Campbell

Risk Versus Returns to Art

In financial economics, there is always some degree of trade-off between the return from increase in an asset's price and the degree of risk involved with holding the asset. Assets with small increases in price and low financial return are low risk. Treasury bonds, for example, offer lower rates of return than corporate bonds. In turn, bonds tend to have lower price increases than equities. Very risky financial products such as commodity futures, hedge funds, and private equity have, in the past, reaped the highest returns with large price rises over time. The justification is simple: for an investor to hold a risky asset, a large financial return is required as compensation for that risk. If we take art as a financial asset, then what is the risk to the investor from holding art? Can we look at art in a similar manner as other financial assets, or as other real assets such as real estate or commodities like gold and silver? The financial return that art prices reap can be measured from art indices using repeat sales or average price increases, and this financial return indeed appears in some research studies to be moderate—higher than inflation but at times not as high as many other traditional or alternative financial assets in at least some periods and some sectors of the art market. In some studies of the aggregate art market, it has been shown that often the risk, as measured by price fluctuations (or variance) appears to be too high to warrant such low returns, especially given the high transaction costs involved in investing in this market place.

Two lines of thought can be drawn from these empirical observations. One possibility is that the returns from holding art are lower to the investor or collector than they should otherwise be. Or alternatively, the risk from holding art is not correctly captured from looking simply at price variation alone. However, neither of these two lines of thought can alone cover the story completely. By measuring returns from a purely financial perspective, the consumptive value of the work of art is not captured. Stocks may be bought purely for their future expected value, with their value derived by the discounted value of future payoffs. Works of art are desired, by both investors and collectors, for very different motives. Prices paid can reflect a value placed on a desire for a work, which can be highly emotive and irrational. Auction houses, collectors, museums, dealers, gallerists, and the media all play a vital role in establishing prices, with a higher-than-expected price representing not only a higher desire for holding a piece of work but also the value reflected in the buyer's own ability to judge the work of art as worthy of attracting a higher price.

Returns from holding art are therefore twofold: financial and consumptive. Although it is possible to generalize about the amount of utility that is gained from holding homogenous assets—"More is better, but the additional bite is never as satisfying as the initial bite"—this need not be the case for heterogeneous work of arts. Little is known about the preferences and utility functions of art collectors and investors. The marginal or extra utility from holding a second or third Picasso, Goya, or Warhol, in your art collection may not decrease by as much as owning the second or third piece of real estate in your favorite holiday destinations, which can only be used sporadically and not viewed on a daily basis.

This observation would lead one to believe that the consumptive returns are relatively high for such goods. Moreover, the risks inherent in the asset are not captured by price variance alone. The perceived risk-return trade-off is therefore underestimated when using only financial returns (ignoring consumption values) and underestimates risks. What investors would ideally like to capture is the illiquidity risk and downside risk from investing in art, which when large, would result in an additional return premium from investors and collectors holding this additional type of risk.

Defining Art Risk

Defining the risk of holding or buying art depends very much on the motivations for holding or buying that work of art in the first place. If the work of art is bought as an indirect investment and purely for monetary price appreciation, then the risk to the investor is the potential fluctuation in price occurring from a realized sale and hence a change in the artwork's value, as determined by the price reached at the point of sale. Alternatively, if the artwork is not sold and an appraisal-based valuation is made, the valuation is determined on the estimated price that would be reached at auction. Many art price indices that are used to measure returns are based on auction prices achieved in the market. If appraisal-based valuations are included in the art price data, however, as is often the case with the average price methodology, the result is a much smoother index and low volatility associated with the return distribution of prices.

Due to the lack of depth in some art markets, illiquidity is a large risk for investors and collectors. Individuals considering investment in art must realize that it may be difficult to sell or realize their investment due to a lack of liquidity in the market. This risk can be highly significant during downturns in the economy, when markets dry up, cash for purchases is short, and it becomes more difficult to realize sales.

However, if the work of art is bought for direct investment (and also for its consumption value), then the risk to the investor is not only monetary fluctuation but also the risks attributed to the characteristics of the art itself, many of which do not exist for other financial assets. For example, a number of physical risks related to investors or collectors holding the work of art need to be covered for insurance purposes. There is a risk that the collector will no longer find the piece attractive or in keeping with the rest of his collection. There are also risks in relation to moving or selling works overseas, such as export licensing requirements or other government approval and requirements in countries in which art is located, which can often take a period of time to process before you can purchase or transport art. There are a range of risks related to advisers and vendors and possible conflicts of interest they may have with an investor. A further risk is the risk related to having the correct title to the work and regarding its authenticity and provenance. Sellers of works of art are not always the rightful or legitimate owners of the works in their possession, and in some cases may be unaware that their right of ownership is impaired. The investor or collector can purchase title insurance to cover this type of risk which can therefore be hedged at a price to them.

All of these risks are relevant in a decision to invest in a work of art; however, for the purpose of this chapter, we define risk purely in terms of financial risk, captured by the monetary change in value or the uncertainty of the outcome of the realized price when selling a work of art. This financial or art price risk can be measured and estimated using an art market index, which is important for both individual investors and institutions. Banks are unwilling to hold art price risk on their books; therefore, risk-management tools can be used to address the pricing and transfer of art price risk for such institutions. The methodology also applies to investors who would like to reduce their exposure to art risk and can, on the reverse side of the coin, be adapted to collectors, funds, and museums that are potentially willing to increase their individual exposure to art risk.

Art Risk Management

Banks provide loans backed by art for two main reasons: first, to provide dealers with greater working capital; and second, to provide collectors with greater liquidity. Banks holding art as collateral are therefore concerned about fluctuations in the value of the art being lent against, as negative changes in art prices are a market risk that banks need to be able to correctly estimate and manage.

Currently, of the few banks that offer art-related services, most charge relatively high interest to lend against any form of art. Also, only a small percentage of a work of art or collection's value is used typically as a guarantee for a loan against art. (See Chapter 5 for an overview of historical and current practices on art banking.) Additionally, banks lending against art face credit risk from a borrower potentially defaulting on the loan payments. Banks therefore justify these high rates because they may not be able to recover the full value of the loan if forced to sell a work of art at an inopportune time or during a depressed market. This is a risk that most mainstream banks are not willing to take and the reason for the relatively low percentage of the work of arts value being covered in the loan for those that do.

However, what is the actual likelihood that the work of art will fall to only 50 percent of its current value? And what is the chance that the value of a whole art collection will fall below 50 percent of its current value? These are typical financial questions that regulators ask banks when assessing the amount of capital they should hold against their liabilities. The lack of full and available art price data makes it difficult and complex to estimate these figures, especially if auction sales dry up during slumps in art markets. If artworks do not hit their reserve price and are bought in, it becomes more difficult to estimate their current market prices.

Given the highly volatile, illiquid global art market with low levels of transparency, the risk to banks is high. Apart from the licit trade in art, there is also a substantial underground market for work of arts, with both forgery and theft being serious factors that add to considerations in restricting current lending practices. All these risks have to be correctly accounted for by banks in their daily risk-management procedures and legal reporting requirements at a national and supranational level.

One possibility to help encourage lending against art is the development of derivative products designed to transfer art price risk onto third parties who are willing to carry this risk. Through the use of art credit default swap (ACDS) contracts, banks would be able to transfer undesirable art price risk off their balance sheets and onto candidates such as art funds, museums, or private collectors. An alternative way to provide greater liquidity to the market for art and improve the ability of banks to measure art price risk is through the securitization of art loans. The securitization of art can be broadly defined as the process through which works of art, which are highly illiquid assets, could be packaged into an interest-bearing security with investment characteristics that are marketable. If banks in the future held a large amount of art loans on their books, or if auction houses such as Sotheby's or Christie's decide to securitize their art lending practices, then this could become common practice as in other areas of lending, where financial institutions are able to create assets suitable for resale from loans, such as consumer installment contracts (credit cards), leases, or receivables. The purpose for the financial institution is to hold assets that are more liquid than the underlying loan.

The recent credit crunch has forced banks to seriously rethink the amount of risk involved with the securitization of assets. A safer mechanism in relation to art, therefore, is for banks to sell art credit default swaps, transferring all of the art price risk from banks to third parties that are willing to hold the risk, because it falls under their own business risk or because they hold an offsetting position. Although these strategies are not common in this market, they are similar in nature to what occurs regularly in the insurance industry.

Art Credit Default Swaps

In finance, a swap is an agreement between two parties to exchange future cash flows according to a prearranged formula. The cash flows that will be exchanged are calculated over a notional principal amount, which is usually not actually exchanged between counterparties. Swaps can therefore be used to create unfunded exposures to an underlying asset such as art, since the counterparties can earn the profit or loss from movements in prices without actually having to post the notional amount in cash or collateral. These derivative contracts can be used to hedge certain risks, such as changes in the interest rate, or to speculate on changes in the underlying prices of the assets.

In an art credit default swap (ACDS), a contract is written to provide protection on the par value of a specified reference asset (in this case, the artwork or the collection held as collateral on a loan to a collector from a bank), where a *protection buyer* pays a periodic fixed fee or a one-off premium to a *protection seller*, in return for which the seller will make a payment on the occurrence of a specified credit event.[14] In this particular case, the bank is the protection buyer and a third party that has an interest in buying the reference art asset is the protection seller. The third party, such as a fund, is willing to accept the art price risk for a premium and enters into a contract with the bank that also entitles it to buy the reference asset at a set price if a credit event is triggered. A credit event in this case is triggered if the reference entity (the art collector) defaults on the loan. When this occurs, the swap contract is terminated and the protection seller makes a settlement payment to the protection buyer. The settlement payment in this case is the exchange of the work of art for a set termination price from the art fund to the bank as specified in the contract.

Since the collector has covered the loan with the artwork as collateral, the credit event being triggered is also contingent on the price of the artwork falling below the outstanding loan payments. At the beginning of the loan agreement, the value of the artwork to the bank used as a guarantee is the current value of the loan, which is likely to be set as a percentage of the current market valuation of the artwork. Only if the artwork falls below this guaranteed price and the lender defaults on the loan is the credit event triggered, and the protection seller is obligated to buy the artwork at the set price. Since the value of the loan must be less than the market price for the artwork in order for the credit event to be triggered, the bank with the long position (that is, who owns the asset) in the ACDS is necessarily out of the money or at a point where the contract has no intrinsic value. This is a necessary requirement for the third party to be obliged to fulfill its obligation on the contract and buy the artwork for the guaranteed price. The risk is transferred from the bank as long as the termination price for the artwork is set at least equal to the outstanding value of the loan.

An ACDS can be used to enable banks to transfer unwanted credit risk exposure to a third party. In this case, the use of risk-management techniques transfers the default risk from the loan backed by art off the bank's balance sheet. Since the art is held as collateral, the bank's assets are subject to changes in the value of the work of art, and the bank carries the art price risk. The benefit is that the bank can make a loan using the art as collateral but can transfer the risk from holding the art as collateral. By writing a credit default swap on the loan, the bank removes the risk of carrying the art price change on its books if default occurs. The bank is not required to monitor the underlying value of the art and, importantly, is not required to be tracked under risk-management regulations (as stipulated in the Basel Accords for capital requirements).

One of the key factors for all of this to work, however, is that the bank has to be able to find a counterparty for the ACDS. At present, parties who might be willing to hold such a derivatives contract could be art funds, art museums, or more speculative parties such as hedge funds, institutional investors, or wealthy individuals that are willing to expose themselves to art price risk and are willing to pay a low premium for the small probability of being able to buy an attractive work of art or collection at a fraction of the cost.

To review, the main steps for the financing structure introduced here are as follows:

1. The bank issues a loan to the art collector, with the artwork as collateral. The value of the artwork is estimated, and as is currently the practice, a price is guaranteed on the art as a percentage of the current value. The bank carries the art risk on its books in lieu for giving the loan. Commonly the uncertainty in the value of the art would be reflected in a high interest rate on the loan, manifesting itself in an inefficient market for asset-backed lending.

2. The bank, not wanting to hold the risk of art price fluctuations on its books, issues an ACDS to a third party, such as an art fund. If the art collector defaults on the loan, the bank has the right to deliver the artwork to the seller in exchange for its face value. This is set at the face value of the loan.

    The bank buys protection by taking a long position in the ACDS but actually shorts the artwork. The bank therefore transfers the risk of holding the art as collateral in exchange for the credit risk on the ACDS. If the third party is not sufficiently rated, the bank may want to enter into a funded credit agreement and therefore mitigate all risk on the bank's books. Otherwise, if the party is creditworthy, it is likely that the bank will be willing to carry the credit default risk of the ACDS.

3. When the credit event is triggered, the ACDS is terminated and the protection seller (third party) makes a payment to the protection buyer. In this case, the bank sells the artwork at the termination value, calculated at the time the contract was specified, to the third party. *Figure 4.3* gives an example of the art finance structure showing

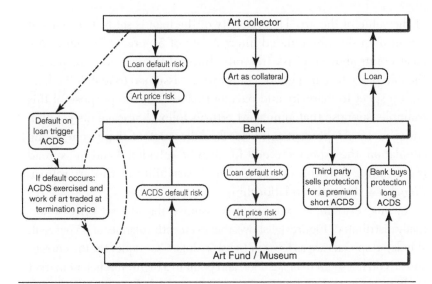

FIGURE 4.3 Relationship Between the Parties Involved in an ACDS and the Transfer of Risk

the relationships between the different parties. The default occurring is contingent on the market price of the artwork falling below the amount of outstanding loan payments. If this does not happen, the bank uses the artwork in its primary role as collateral, with its market price able to cover the value of the outstanding loan.

Another premise for this structure to work is that the ACDS is priced correctly. A risk to the bank will be the correct pricing of the ACDS, which is substantially lower than the risk from holding the artwork on the bank's books.

In order to correctly price the ACDS, the credit spread must be determined so that the present value of the total fee payments made by the bank is equal to the expected credit loss in today's terms. Assuming that default probabilities and interest rates are independent, the expected loss is a function of the default probability at a given time and the amount by which the face value of the loan exceeds the value of the collateral at that time, calculated in present terms.[15] An example of how this is priced is given in the appendix to this chapter.

Taking a numerical example, say the initial value of the work of art is assumed to be 125,000 euros and the loan granted is set at 80 percent of the value of the art. The maturity of the loan is set to five years at a continuously compounded interest rate of 5 percent, which is 200 basis points above the risk-free rate. Interest is assumed to be paid at the end of each year. The ACDS is further assumed to match the loan with respect to maturity and payment dates. For the purpose of this example, suppose that annual art returns follow a normal distribution with a mean of 6 percent and a standard deviation of 15 percent. Using simulation, the expected credit loss can be calculated and the spread is a positive function of the assumed variability of the art return. *Figure 4.4* shows this relationship.

In this very simple example, it is assumed that the art price is normally distributed. Figure 4.4 shows that even with volatility at 25 percent, simulated spreads are as low as 71 basis points. Consequently, the current spreads do not seem to be justified and point to a highly inefficient market for both banks and borrowers. To reconcile modeled credit spreads with market spreads, it is clear that the liquidity premium used is substantial.

Art lending and art finance are still in their infancy. However, the growing availability of loans backed by art and the potential to develop derivatives in the art arena should lead to continued growth in the market for lending against art. If banks are able to transfer the art price risk, the rates

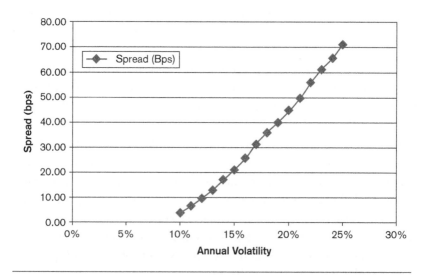

FIGURE 4.4   Credit Spread as a Function of Art Price Volatility

Source: Campbell and Wiehenkamp (2000)

for loans using art as collateral will also be reduced. This depends on the willingness of a creditworthy third party to carry this art price risk. The emergence of art funds, museums, and other collectors who may be willing to carry this risk means that banks may be able to develop such products.

Moreover, the derivatives market for art may bring the necessary liquidity to the art market, which would deregulate the market and, in turn, fuel the move toward greater investment in art as an alternative asset class. New developments occur more quickly in the art market than expected, and they parallel developments that have already taken place in other asset markets. It was not so long ago that derivatives were introduced on real estate markets, and it is likely that the near future will see synthetic trading on art markets.

Appendix
Pricing Art Credit Default Swaps

As an example, consider a loan whose face value is initially set to x percent of the value of the work of art. Currently, the common practice is to use a maximum of 50 percent of the current market price of the work of art to back the loan. The idea of this financing structure using the ACDS is to mitigate the risk of the art price falling below the loan value. Therefore, a much higher percentage x, even up to the full value of the work of art, can be used if the collector is of high credit quality. Equation (1) shows this relation as

$$P_{t=0}^{Loan} = x\% P_{t=0}^{Art} , \tag{1}$$

where $P_{t=0}^{Loan}$ and $P_{t=0}^{Art}$ are the prices of the loan and artwork, respectively, at $t = 0$. Default is contingent on the full price of the work of art at time t falling below the outstanding value of the loan at time t as shown in equation (2):

$$P_t^{Art} \leq P_t^{Loan} . \tag{2}$$

From equation (1) the price of the work of art is simply equal to the guaranteed percentage on the initial value of the work of art, assuming bullet repayment, shown in equation (3):

$$P_t^{Art} \leq x\% P_{t=0}^{Art} . \tag{3}$$

The probability density function of default at time t required for the expected loss determination is the probability that the price of the work of art falls below the percentage of the work of art guaranteed at the initial market value of the work of art at $t = 0$. Formally this distribution function is expressed in equation (4) as $q(t)$:

$$q(t) = \text{Prob}\left(P_t^{Art} \leq x\% P_{t=0}^{Art}\right). \tag{4}$$

In case of default, the protection seller will be required to pay the difference between the face value of the loan and current market value of the collateral plus any accrued interest to the bank. Assuming (4) to represent a risk-neutral probability density function, this can be discounted at the risk-free rate. Setting

$$v(t) = \begin{cases} e^{-r_f t}\left((x\% P_{t=0}^{Art} - P_t^{Art}) + y \cdot \delta_t \cdot P_{t=0}^{Loan}\right) & \text{if } P_t^{Art} \leq x\% P_{t=0}^{Art} \\ 0 & \text{if } P_t^{Art} > x\% P_{t=0}^{Art} \end{cases}, \tag{5}$$

where δ_t is the year expressed as a fraction of time between 0 and 1, since the last interest payment and y is the interest rate charged on the loan to the art collector, the expected credit loss (ECL) can be expressed by equation (6):

$$\text{ECL} = \int_0^T q(t) \cdot v(t) dt. \tag{6}$$

As noted above, the ECL should equal the present value of the fee payments. With payments being made until default or maturity of the ACDS, whichever occurs earlier, the cost of default can be expressed as a weighted average of the two. For a maturity of T years and ω payments per year, it is straightforward to see that, in the case of no default, the present value of these payments is

$$s \cdot u(K) = \sum_{k=1}^{K} s \cdot \frac{1}{\omega} \cdot (x\% \cdot P_{t=0}^{Art}) \cdot e^{-r_f T_k}, \tag{7}$$

where s is the credit spread quoted on an annual basis, and $T_1,...,T_K$ are the fee payment dates. The probability weight corresponding to no credit event is 1 minus the probability of the art price falling below the face value of the loan during the duration of the ACDS and is given as π in equation (8):

$$\tag{8}$$

$$\pi = 1 - \int_0^T q(t) dt.$$

If default occurs before maturity at time τ, the present value of the payments is the sum of the fees paid at payment dates before default and the accrued value since the last payment date T_n and the time of default:

$$s \cdot g(\tau) = \sum_{k=1}^{n(\tau)} s \cdot \frac{1}{\omega} \cdot (x\% \cdot P_{t=0}^{Art}) \cdot e^{-r_f T_k} + s \cdot \delta_t' \cdot (x\% \cdot P_{t=0}^{Art}) \cdot e^{-r_f \tau}, \qquad (9)$$

with δ_t' being the year fraction since T_n.

Putting the equations together, we obtain the value of the fee payments:

$$s \cdot \left(\int_0^T q(t)g(t)dt + \pi \cdot u(K) \right) \qquad (10)$$

which gives, after equating fee payments in (10) and expected credit loss in (6), the credit spread of the ACDS,

$$s = \frac{\int_0^T q(t) \cdot v(t)dt}{\int_0^T q(t)g(t)dt + \pi \cdot u(K)}. \qquad (11)$$

Chapter Notes

1. Standard deviation is simply the square root of the variance. To calculate variance, you compute the difference between each pair of numbers, square the differences, compute the mean of these squares, and multiply by 0.5. The squaring is done to eliminate the potential negative signs of some of the differences, and the multiplication by 0.5 is used because, if you consider all pairs, then you see each difference twice.

2. Beta can be 0. Some 0-beta securities are risk free, such as Treasury bonds and cash and assets with zero correlation with the market.

3. A correlation can also be perfect, that is, every change in one set of prices or values may show an exact corresponding change in the second set.

4. Certain lots may be sold without a reserve price at a seller's special request and these will be marked without reserve in the auction presale catalogue.

5. J. Mei and M. Moses, "Art as an Investment and the Underperformance of Masterpieces," *American Economic Review* vol. 92, no. 5 (2002): 1656–1668.

6. See O. Chanel, L. Gérard-Varet, and S. Vincent, "Auction Theory and Practice: Evidence from the Market for Jewelry," in *Economics of the Arts: Selected Essays*, ed. V. Ginsburgh and P. Menger (Amsterdam: Elsevier 1996); and L. Bauwens and V. Ginsburgh, "Art Experts and Art Auctions: Are Presale Estimates Fully Informative?" *Louvain Economic Review* vol. 66, no. 1 (2000): 131–144.

7. P. Milgrom and R. J. Weber, "A Theory of Auctions and Competitive Bidding," *Econometrica* vol. 50, no. 2 (1982): 1089–1122.

8. O. Ashenfelter, "How Auctions Work for Wine and Art," *Journal of Economic Perspectives* vol. 3, no. 3 (1989): 22–36.

9. C. McAndrew, J. Smith, and R. Thompson, "The Impact of Reservation Prices on the Perceived Bias in Expert Appraisals of Fine Art: Controlling for Latent Censoring of Transaction Prices" (January 12, 2009), Social Science Research Network, http://ssrn.com/abstract=1327026.

10. C. McAndrew and R. Thompson, "The Collateral Value of Fine Art," *Journal of Banking and Finance* vol. 31, no. 3 (2007): 589–607.

11. In this equation, M = the *geometric mean* of the upper (U) and lower (L) presale estimates, or $M = (U \times L)^{0.5}$ (rather than the arithmetic mean, $[U + L]/2$). McAndrew and Thompson (2007) explain in their paper why price is divided by the geometric mean of the high and low estimate. They show that an (unbiased) expert first establishes an expected hammer price and then selects a pair of estimates whose geometric mean is equal to this value.

12. How buy-ins are valued is explained fully in McAndrew and Thompson (2007), but the values are set at approximately 0.75 of the mean estimate (or 0.87 of the low estimate).

13. The methodology for underwriting art is discussed fully in McAndrew and Thompson (2007), although it is not yet used by any bank at the time of writing. It is very likely that as art is increasingly accepted as a valid investment asset class, this service will be offered by some of the more progressive international banks.

14. The concept of an ACDS was introduced by R. Campbell and C. Weihenkamp in "Art as Collateral" (working paper, Maastricht University, 2009).

15. This follows J. C. Hull and A. White, "Valuing Credit Default Swaps I: No Counterparty Default Risk," *Journal of Derivatives* vol. 8, no. 1 (Fall 2000): 29–40.

5

Art Banking

Suzanne Gyorgy, Citi
Dr. Clare McAndrew

EDITOR'S NOTE: Driven by a need to offer wealthy clients new products and the demand for banks to securitize loans using alternative assets, a number of private banks now include art-related financing among their offerings. The art trade itself has also provided a significant impetus for the development of art banking in an effort to bring stability and lower levels of risk to the market. On the buy side, with access to financing, dealers, collectors, and institutions can take advantage of good prices they see, which adds depth to the market. Sellers can also use art as collateral to borrow money against rather than be forced to sell a work or collection at an inopportune time. Therefore, both sides of the market benefit and the flow of available financing and liquidity helps to smooth prices and reduce risk.

Art-based lending started in the booming art market of the late 1980s, when a number of finance companies began offering loans to investors seeking to borrow against the works of art in which they were investing. Art loans were used by collectors who wished to leverage their existing art collections to fund new purchases (in the art market or other markets) or to cover existing debts, as well as by art dealers and other vendors needing funds to acquire new stock. There were also a number of tax-friendly arrangements devised for lenders that work in a manner similar to reverse mortgages, whereby borrowers receive monthly payments against the value of their art instead of selling the work outright and being charged capital gains tax. When the market bottomed out in the 1990s, however, many of the loans were defaulted on as the rush for liquidity drove a large number of speculators out of the market. This downturn led to a significantly lower level of supply and demand for art-based loans until relatively recently, when the boom of the last five years has seen growth in lending by auction houses, specialty lenders, and traditional banks.

This chapter looks at origins of art finance, from the early days of art patronage to the more formal art-based lending structures and art banking of the present. It summarizes the state of art banking today and takes a look at how the valuation process works, how lending offers different individuals and institutions the opportunity to access greater liquidity through their art collections, and how it can be used to monetize art assets and promote tax efficiencies.

The Origins of Art Finance
Suzanne Gyorgy

As modern civilization emerged from the Dark Ages, patrons of the arts were unquestionably the essential factor for the success of many art projects and often, to a lesser degree, the success of the artists. Charlemagne's first efforts to achieve architectural grandeur at the Palace Chapel at Aachen in the eighth century are an early example of such patronage. Later, Abbot Suger played a similar role in bringing to fruition the basic ideas of Gothic architecture. Kings, prominent churchmen, and aristocrats were engaged in nurturing artists throughout the Middle Ages and Renaissance. The disparity in wealth at these times, when the rich were infinitely richer than the poor, meant that works requiring sustained labor could only be made through patronage. This could be good or bad: while patrons gave early artists the chance to survive and flourish, some who only sought their own glory in art often made life miserable for their protégés (with the Archbishop of Salzburg and Mozart providing a case in point). Some patrons, however, delighted in new creations as much as their artists did: Jean, Duc de Berry, and Cosimo de' Medici, for example.

By the nineteenth century, the financial landscape had changed in important ways. The Church had split into large fragments, none of which had the means or vision to play a part in the artistic expression of the age. The various royal and aristocratic families (e.g., the Fabergés), with a few exceptions, helped create art only to adorn and amuse themselves.

However, toward the end of the nineteenth century, it was art dealers who began to play the more direct role in offering financial aid to artistic enterprises, taking the place of former grand patrons. The famous dealers of Duret and Vollard are the best known of these. In the post–World War II era, the role played by art dealers and individual and corporate patrons of the arts who encouraged visionary artists was critical in supporting the artists and introducing their work to the world. This relatively simple system laid the groundwork for today's more complex art market.

Today, the fact that many gallery owners are also the present-day patrons has had interesting consequences in that the dealer is financially tied to the successful sale of the product and not just its creation, as in the Renaissance. Additionally, the enhanced role of auction houses in both the secondary and, more recently, the primary market has made the monetary values (past, present, and future) a much more prominent aspect of the visual arts. This has enabled art objects to have more exact valuations and become more marketable commodities, which encouraged the creation of art funds and the emergence of buyers acquiring art as investment and as a tool for asset allocation. The resulting monetization of art also caused a new financial avenue: collectors looking to use their art as collateral for loans.

Using art as commodity has a long history, beginning with artists in need trading their creations for food and rent and arriving at the complex loan structures issued today by banks for their high-net-worth clients seeking liquidity for other investments. The terms of the lending programs that banks currently offer has been largely shaped by lessons learned in past art market fluctuations. The art lending programs offered today are more stable and better structured as a result of the difficulties many banks endured when the boom market of the 1980s collapsed in the early 1990s. A very significant factor in the feasibility of lending based on art values has also been the greater transparency that has arisen in the art market through the arrival of the Internet, price databases and other Web-based information. A great wealth of previously hidden or difficult-to-unearth information about provenance and the past sales history of an artist's work has become readily available to just about anyone who is interested, making it much easier for financial institutions to judge value.

The last great art market boom, preceding the current market adjustment, was in the late 1980s. Impressed by the prices paid by rich Japanese collectors for European Impressionist and Post Impressionist paintings, banks joined in the excitement and quickly built large loan portfolios, secured by the high prices being achieved. The record of the price of the transaction became the most salient feature of works of art at the time—as opposed to, say, the opinions expressed by art historians and critics—in determining the overall valuation. The monetary figures and their apparently rosy futures transformed formerly staid art galleries and auction rooms into market arenas where prices were liable to double in a year's time, and older collectors had to stand aside. All sorts of people suddenly became art dealers, art consultants, and experts, all hoping to pry away some of the quick money some collectors were spending on art transactions. The excitement grew and prices reached unprecedented levels. Skeptics were reminded of the tulip-bulb boom in seventeenth-century Holland: tulips are exquisitely beautiful but not worth the net value of a small town.

After the Asian markets crashed in the 1990s, most of the direct liability associated with the loan defaults had to be absorbed by Japanese lenders and, ultimately, the Japanese government. Works that reappeared at auction on behalf of the lending institutions did not perform as well as they had a few years before, and the monetary values assigned to them turned out to have been a matter of overenthusiasm. An interesting aspect of this boom and bust was that spending exorbitant amounts of money on iconic European masterpieces was to a certain extent an assertion of pride on the part of the Japanese collectors who got caught up in it. The prices themselves were trophies in an undeclared nationalistic competition. This added to the boom mentality, in which caution was abandoned to satisfy emotional impulses.

The increased interaction between art and financial markets had both good and bad effects. One positive result can be illustrated in a classic art finance story that may not be entirely factual but is telling nonetheless. It is the story of Ryoei Saito, then chairman of Daishowa Paper Manufacturing. In 1990, Saito bought the *Portrait of Dr. Gachet* by Vincent van Gogh for $82.5 million at Christie's in New York, along with *Au Moulin de la Galette* by Pierre-Auguste Renoir for a record price of $78.1 million, also in New York at Sotheby's. According to the tale, Saito placed the paintings in a storage vault where he allowed them to be viewed by a very select few and only when he wished.

He also declared, as was his right, that upon his death he would be cremated along with the van Gogh and Renoir. This caused understandable outrage in the art world, which was not put to rest until after Saito's funeral in 1996, when it was reported that the paintings had in fact been pledged as loan collateral and were in the possession of a Japanese bank and were thus saved from destruction and later sold on.

In any event, the Japanese foray into the Impressionist market demonstrated clearly that valuation is an essential question and caution is a critical attribute for would-be lenders. A sound valuation requires an element of intuitive understanding that transcends an actuarial-type predictability. Tastes change. Some art keeps its fascination and allure, while some does not. Artists go in and out of fashion. While these trends are not completely arbitrary and unpredictable, they require expertise and a deep familiarity with the art world in order to attempt to predict them.

Art Banking Today

Art-based lending can currently be broken down into two main categories: loans to galleries and loans to individuals. Within these two categories are a myriad of loan structures and business models. Loans structured within banking institutions house the majority of art financing by value at present and are the main focus of this discussion; however, there are also a number of boutique lenders and auction houses that carry out art financing activities.

The majority of loans to galleries are structured as business finance loans in the consumer or commercial divisions of major banks, or from nonbanking boutique lending businesses. The purpose of these loans is to give dealers an available lien of working capital. With this type of loan, the bank will consider both the value of a dealer's art inventory and the gallery's cash flow and receivables. The advance rates can be flexible but typically are in the range of a 50 percent loan to value for the art inventory, with the valuation based on an appraisal or cost and a 75 percent advance rate on the galleries receivables of 90 days or less. Most of these loans are also guaranteed by the gallery owner. While many banks will leave the artworks in situ, with nonbanking boutique lending businesses, the artworks or art collection is sometimes surrendered for available liquidity and returned when the loan is paid back with little financial reporting required. For example, Art Capital

Group requires that the art used as collateral is stored in one of their storage facilities in New York City or displayed in its Madison Avenue gallery space. Other specialist institutions and most of the banks that offer art-based lending allow clients to retain possession of their art and antiques.

Loans secured by art to individuals come from private banks or, again, from nonbanking boutique lenders and the major auction houses. Individuals seeking loans secured by their art collections typically come in two categories: people who are art rich and cash poor and need the money for a particular purpose or people who are both art rich and cash rich and want to monetize their art holdings, a typically illiquid asset, to use the resulting liquidity for other investment.

The types of lending available for art rich and cash poor lenders include the nonbanking entities discussed above, which lend on the basis of an assessment they have either done themselves or based on research done by a relevant auction house. The lenders may be offered a recourse or nonrecourse loan depending on this assessment. A recourse loan is secured by the art assets but also guaranteed by the borrower, which implies that the borrower's full credit essentially backs the loan. A nonrecourse loan, on the other hand, is secured solely by the art assets underlying it. Because this is a higher-risk loan, it will typically incur a higher interest rate, as the art is not undersigned by the lender and acts as the only source of collateral for the loan. (Some of the issues with using art as collateral are discussed in Chapter 4.) Although terms vary based on the particular client, rates for bridge loans are reported at 8–12 percent versus in the mid-teens when the artwork is the only collateral.[1]

Typical art-rich, cash-poor borrowers would be people of more modest means who have inherited an art collection, which they plan to sell, but on which they need to raise money quickly to pay the estate or other inheritance taxes that are due within a relatively short period of time. Waiting for the appropriate auction, a gallery consignment or other private sale may not be viable or suit the requirements of their situation. The funds are often needed in a relatively shorter time horizon, and an art loan is often a quick, effective solution. After the estate is settled, the art is then sold and the loan is repaid.

In other cases, people have art that they do not want to lose but need money for some unforeseen reasons. Again, as a method of raising money quickly, boutique lenders can be a solution. These lenders can offer lines of credit to fund short-term cash needs (usually for a period of less than five years) or term loans with accrued interest that can range in structure from interest only, partially amortizing, or fully amortizing facilities. Loans from these institutions are not without risk however, and borrowers need to be fully aware that they are entering into an agreement that may force the sale of their art. It often seems unlikely when entering these agreements that they will default, optimism prevailing, but fortunes and finances can change, and it does happen that unlucky debtors have to go through the heartbreak and embarrassment of a forced sale of a family treasure. As noted earlier, some of these nonbanking entities typically take possession of the art and charge the borrower rates on par with most charge card rates.

Some of the major auction houses also offer art-based financing and loans to assist prospective consignors in need of liquidity by lending money prior to the sale of the art in the short- or longer-term future. These loans generally constitute an advance that is paid off with the proceeds of the eventual sale, making them essentially bridge loans. The loans are asset-based transactions in that the amount of the loan is determined by the value of the art itself and not by the borrower's creditworthiness, as is the case with many bank loans. The benefit to the auction house in a boom market is that if the borrower is unable to pay the loan back, the auction has the right to sell the art and realize the gain in sales commissions. In a more stagnant market, auction houses tend reduce their lending activities, since any upside in an eventual sale is greatly diminished. Loans from the major auction houses such as Christie's and Sotheby's are generally extended at a rate of 40 percent to 50 percent of the average or low presale auction estimates. Rates vary over time and between houses, but these are typically priced at prime plus 2 percent or 3 percent, there are often minimum amounts applied (such as a minimum loan of $1 million), and the services may only be selectively offered to long-term clients and those planning to sell at that particular auction house.

Several major banks offer loans secured by art to their best clients, including Citi, Bank of America (Private Bank), and Emigrant Bank Fine Art Finance. In most of these cases, the art offered as collateral for lending remains in the client's home or office. Citi was one of the first banks to offer art-based lending, with the Citi Art Advisory

Service established in 1979. This service was set up in response to the bank's recognition that art made up a substantial portion of many of its high-end clients' overall net worth, and that many clients needed help navigating the largely unregulated art world. Citi hired trained arts professionals to run the in-house service, advising clients on art acquisitions and sales and managing their art collections. The staff is qualified by training and experience to provide in-house valuations of art being used as collateral and to visit sites to ensure that the art is properly cared for in client's homes.

Within the banks there are a variety of offerings to lenders, with a standard model of structuring art loans as recourse loans that are personally guaranteed by the borrower with a purpose consistent with the client's business goals, and with the art generally remaining in the client's possession. Again, terms vary between banks and clients but there are generally minimum loan amounts—for example, the minimum loan is $5 million at Citi and the minimum value of each piece of collateral for most collectors is $200,000. Loans are typically priced at traditional bank rates, ranging from the London interbank offered rate (Libor) or prime plus a percent. Lines of credit or term loans range from one year to twenty years, and most of the banks lend up to 50 percent of the art's estimated value.

Generally, the financial due diligence bankers do for clients pursuing art loans is similar to what would be carried out to structure an unsecured loan. Bankers need to assess the financial health of the client along with the quality and marketability of the art. Unlike asset-backed lenders and auction houses, banks will avoid being put into the situation of having to sell art if the client cannot repay. For that reason, the client's cash flow and investments are relied upon for repayment, not the sale of the art. To underwrite the loan, therefore, bankers must assess the borrower's principal assets, liabilities, and contingent obligations. They are charged with determining unencumbered liquidity and evaluating the quality of recurring cash flow. The latter is important because, like raw land, art collections require maintenance (e,g., insurance, restorations, and storage), are not income producing, and may be illiquid.

Standard procedure to complete this analysis is to ask clients to provide a personal financial statement and copies of their tax returns. The financial information is assessed by the banker or credit team while the art collection is evaluated and individual values assigned for lending purposes. At Citi, for example, the art is valued in-house by Art Advisory specialists to ensure confidentiality. (This valuation is then carried out on an annual basis for the term of the loan.) The bank requires a minimum of four pieces of art from a diverse group of internationally marketable artists. Detailed information on the art to be pledged is requested, including photographs, bills of sale, and provenance information. The art specialist completes a comprehensive market-based fair market valuation for each piece of art selected for loan collateral. Other banks that do not have in-house art advisory services rely on third-party appraisals from auction houses or independent appraisal firms to value the art as collateral and weigh its marketability.

The Loan Valuation Process

Citi and some other lending institutions use fair market value for lending purposes. A fair market valuation is the value that an appraiser feels a piece of art would sell for in the open market in real time. It is a speculation based on as much relevant factual material as can be gathered. It is a comparative statement that endeavors to predict, on the basis of what has happened in the past, what will happen in the near future. These valuations are updated as needed and must be reviewed annually.

Both measurable, objective factors and subjective considerations must be taken into consideration when assigning value. Measurable factors include provenance (ownership, exhibition, and publication history), recent sales history, marketability, condition, subject matter, rarity, and medium. (Chapter 2 discusses the process of art valuation in greater detail.) The more subjective factors that influence value are opinions on quality, importance, and beauty. These are more emotional in character but carry equal (if not more) weight in the final analysis than the purely factual data. Subjective factors are numerous and often subconscious in nature. As noted earlier, there were factors in the Japanese Impressionist-buying frenzy that had nothing to do with the Impressionist vision per se. Subjective opinions range from exalted to popular. There are a number of academic opinions and "celebrity" opinions that can also play a role: a work of art that belonged to a famous collector or major museum, for example, enhances its objective market value considerably. Finally, why collectors "like" or "have to have" a particular work of art remains something of a mystery.

This is why an art expert has to be someone who knows two very different worlds: what makes great works of art and what makes the art market work.

At Citi, the in-house art specialists provide comprehensive valuation memoranda that include detailed descriptions of each piece of art with at least three supporting recent, comparable sales at auction and all the additional private sale information available. Auction sales records are used predominantly since sales data from auction is the only documented public record for art sales. Most appraisers use Internet sites like Artnet or Artprice to research comparable works recently sold, along with private sales data when verifiable. Again, the importance of art expertise cannot be overemphasized because of the multitude of factors involved in the pricing of an artist and where that pricing is likely to go.

Once a selection of works of art has been approved for use as collateral, its continued well-being must be monitored. The site where it is stored must be physically viewed to assess whether it has the appropriate conditions to maintain value such as proper installation, security, and climate control. Banks also need to have a sense of how well the client or lender cares for the art. Key questions to pursue when doing an on-site art inspection might include the following:

❑ How is the collection cared for?

❑ Are light-sensitive works kept well away from direct sunlight?

❑ Are fragile works safe from children, pets, or other potential threats to their integrity?

❑ Are the people who maintain or clean the premises familiar with security and climate control mechanisms?

Although art used as loan collateral is covered by insurance policies, the future value of a work of art is determined in part by how it is treated by its owner. This is why the character of the borrower, apart from creditworthiness, becomes a factor in the loan. The future value is contingent upon the willingness of the owner to take good care of the art that he or she is borrowing against.

When the art valuation and physical inspection is completed, the lending team typically structures the loan at 50 percent of the work's appraised value. These loans generally contain net-worth covenants, requirements for financial reporting on an assigned basis, and a requirement that the lender be notified before any piece of art collateral is moved or sold. To mitigate the risk of lending against movable loan collateral, banks in the United States first consider the character of the client and their reputation in business, the art world, or other relevant sector and gain further comfort by having a perfected security interest in the art consistent with Uniform Commercial Code (UCC) Article 9.

The UCC is a group of laws adopted by most U.S. states to ensure that there is consistency in commercial transactions throughout the country. Article 9 addresses "security interests" in real property, which are the partial or total claims to a piece of property being used to secure a debt. The law deals largely with priority of claims and the creditor's rights in regard to the property while it is in the borrower's possession. This group of laws is often referred to as the UCC-9s. A "chattel mortgage" covers similar issues in the United Kingdom; however, under British law, there are difficulties with perfecting a security interest when the collateral is owned by an individual. The resulting solution for art loans structured there is to ensure that the collateral is in the name of a legal entity or that the collateral itself is held by the bank in a secure fine art warehouse. In many countries, art collateral must be warehoused if there are no laws in place favoring the perfection of a bank's security interest. In all cases, when perfecting an interest in movable collateral, such as art, legal counsel must be obtained.

In the United States, the UCC-9s are widely used to allow collateralized art to remain in clients' homes and offices. The borrower must understand that moving, consigning, selling, or substituting art collateral requires prior approval and additional legal documentation. Clearly, if the art is moved to a third-party location, such as a fine art warehouse, museum exhibition, or gallery, the bank's security interest can be impaired, leaving the bank in a legally unsecured position. Therefore, a "bailment agreement" or "third-party agreement" must be made between the third party and lending bank with the pledgor consenting. The bailment agreement is an acknowledgment between the lender and the third party housing the art collateral that the bank (the lender) is the lien holder and recipient of any insurance claims.

The banks are further secured by requiring that each piece of art be insured by a comprehensive fine art insurance policy listing the bank named as joint insured or loss payee. The bank holds the original policies and is either empowered to pay the premiums directly or to receive documentation confirming that the premiums have been paid and the policy renewed. Many banks now require that the fine art insurance policy include coverage for acts of terrorism.

Historically, financial necessity has always been the prime motivator of those wishing to borrow against their art. However, an important question is, why are high-net-worth individuals with plenty of resources interested in obtaining loans secured by their art collections? There are in fact many reasons. First, it is a way of "cashing in" on the increased value of a work without selling it. The freed-up cash can be used for other investments. It is also a way to gain liquidity without realizing the capital gains tax that a sale would entail. In the United States, art is deemed a collectible and subject to a federal capital gains obligation of 28 percent. Add to this the city and state capital gains taxes and, depending on where you are, the capital gains tax alone can be as high as 40 percent. Ultimately, as Ben Franklin observed, death and taxes are inevitable, but using lending on art, these taxes at least can be deferred.

Some collectors may also like to isolate their art collecting from their other business activities by establishing a revolving line of credit secured by their existing art collection that is used exclusively to acquire additional art works. This provides collectors with ready money to act quickly when an art acquisition opportunity arises. This type of client views art collecting and the art market as similar to the real estate market, where using loans to purchase real estate is common practice. This rather dynamic art collecting approach is appropriate for collectors who know their area of the market well and watch it closely, almost instinctively identifying good possibilities.

In recent years also, hedge fund managers and private equity partners have successfully used their existing art collections as collateral for term loans, drawing down the full amount to invest back into their funds or investments. They are essentially creating an arbitrage, whereby they borrow from a bank at a relatively low rate and use the proceeds of the loan to gain a higher level of return. There are also tax benefits that defray the interest charges on the loan. For this group of investors, the prevailing mindset is that every asset should be an available source of liquidity for other investments. Art-collecting real estate developers similarly use the revolving lines of credit to invest in their real estate projects when necessary or useful.

As the financial markets declined during 2007 and 2008, some individuals with loans secured by equities of diminished value, who have unencumbered art collections, are now adding the art to the collateral pool to bring the loan to value ratio in line and avoid having their stock positions sold out in margin calls.

Most art dealers and gallery owners also use loans to grow and manage their businesses. Most of these loans are structured as business finance loans in the commercial lending area of the bank. Here, the bankers assess the gallery's cash flow and receivables along with the art inventory. Loans to high-net-worth, blue-chip art dealers are handled in the bank's private-banking lending area, where the art dealer's personal collection and high-end long-term hold inventory is used as collateral. These loans are usually the revolving lines of credit used by the financial types described above to purchase fine art inventory at auction or privately, as the opportunity arises. Typically, these loans are drawn on and then paid down when the work is sold. They are an important resource for gallery business, and a long-standing relationship frequently exists between banker and gallery owner.

Art loans allow bank and lending institutions the opportunity to offer their clients a unique opportunity to use a traditionally nonliquid asset as collateral for loans to reinvest in their business, acquire additional art or diversify assets, often while continuing to enjoy the work of art in their homes and offices. For the bank, a well-managed, properly valued art loan portfolio with smartly structured loan facilities is good business that enhances the client relationship. The risks associated with this business come from not understanding the mechanics and nature of the art market, improperly valuing the art, or not understanding a collector's true situation: his or her business model, cash flow, and character. In the end, rather than looking solely at the value of a work of art, a strong loan portfolio will rely on the three Cs of lending: character, cash flow, and collateral.

Motivations for Art-Based Lending

Clare McAndrew

Borrowing can be an attractive and tax-efficient way to buy art and to monetize existing art assets. The following are a few scenarios where borrowers could use art to free up capital from traditionally illiquid assets, minimize taxes, or facilitate estate planning.[2]

Estate-Planning Strategies

Say, for example, you own a collection worth $5 million on a nominal cost basis and want to raise cash. The choices you face in deciding whether to borrow versus sell are as follows:

1. *Sell the collection:* If you choose this route, the transaction costs of the sale at auction for example could range anywhere from 15 percent to 30 percent of the value of the items you sell. (Assume, for example, these work out at 20 percent; this amounts to $1 million.) You will also be liable to pay capital gains tax (CGT) on the net sales proceeds of around 40 percent[3] (assuming a federal tax of 28 percent and a state tax of 12 percent), which amounts to a further $1.6 million. The potential net postsale proceeds available for other investments would therefore be $2.4 million ($5 million less $1 million less $1.6 million). Assuming an estate tax of 50 percent, your heirs could then receive $1.2 million, which represents a total loss of 76 percent in value across one generation, as well as the loss of the ownership and possession of the art works themselves.

2. *Borrow against the collection:* An alternative would be to keep the art and borrow cash. For example, you could borrow $2.5 million and instead of paying selling costs, pay a closing fee of 1 percent ($25,000) to the lending institution as well as costs of the annual debt service.[4] If you defer the sale of the collection, you will benefit from a step-up in basis and avoid paying CGT, while having $2.475 million available to invest elsewhere. You could repay the loan over time with the earnings from the invested proceeds, with the proceeds from the sale of the art or other assets, or from another source. Alternatively, the estate can repay the loan with estate assets, including life insurance proceeds. (The estate may be subject to estate taxes of 50 percent on assets above a certain threshold, depending on their tax nexus.)

Divorce

Say, for example, a couple are divorcing and when dividing the marital assets, the husband would like to keep a collection of art but does not have the liquidity at that time to settle for it. Rather than being forced to sell the collection, he could borrow the funds from an art-based lending institution (secured against the works themselves), and then repay this loan over time from income or from a sale of art or other assets. The advantages of this solution are that he retains the art he loves, can fund the divorce settlement without decreasing his liquidity, and avoids both the CGT and selling costs incurred if he were to sell the art and antiques.

Asset Diversification

If you have a significant percentage of your wealth concentrated in works of art, you may want to diversify your portfolio and increase your personal liquidity. Say, for example, you own an art collection with a $1 million cost basis and a current appraised value of $3 million. Selling the collection will trigger the usual selling costs and CGTs, however borrowing against it will allow increased liquidity without these costs or the loss of the collection. If you defer the sale and have your estate sell the collection, you will also benefit from a step-up in basis and avoid payment of CGT.

Life Insurance Premium Financing

Many art owners have significant assets but are relatively illiquid in terms of their overall net worth. When planning your estate, you may want to transfer art across generations but might be concerned that there will be a lack of cash to pay estate taxes. One solution is to set up an irrevocable life insurance trust (ILIT) for the purposes of buying life insurance. The ILIT can borrow against your art collection and the cash surrender value of the life insurance policy to buy the insurance policy.

Say, for example, you have a collection worth $20 million. You set up an ILIT and the estimated premiums are $500,000 per year for ten years for $30 million of life insurance. Your income is $1 million per year from interest and dividends. An art-based lending institution could make a loan to the ILIT (secured against the art collection) in order to buy the insurance, and the ILIT can pledge the cash surrender value of the insurance (if any) as additional loan collateral. The ILIT can also borrow subsequent premium payments for the policy, and pay interest on the loans either on a current basis or by borrowing again from the art lending institution secured by the art. If, for example, you die in year nine, the life insurance policy will pay benefits to the ILIT, and the ILIT can repay the loan (estimated at $5.5 million in principal and accrued interest) and distribute the balance of the insurance proceeds in accordance with the ILIT trust agreement (i.e., $30 million in death benefit – $5.5 million loan payment = $24.5 million).

The advantages of this method of financing are that you get life insurance without depleting your liquidity or liquidating income-producing assets to pay the premiums. You also limit the gift tax you will pay, as the ILIT is funded with a loan rather than a gift from you.

Charitable Giving

There are several methods of using art for charitable giving. A common issue faced by art owners is that they wish to make charitable gifts but are worried about depleting their liquidity. An art collection can be used to secure a loan from which to make such contributions. In this case, you can retain ownership and possession of your art, you can make a charitable contribution without reducing your liquidity, and you may receive a current tax deduction.

Annual Exclusion Transfers

Parents and grandparents may wish to make annual exclusion gifts to their families but may be concerned about reducing their liquidity and not wish to sell or gift their art collection. Take an example of a husband and wife who each wish to give $13,000 ($26,000 for the couple) to their three grandchildren ($26,000 × 3 = $78,000). They also give the grandchildren tuition payments ($36,000) and health care payments ($12,000), amounting to a total gift from the couple of $126,000 for the year. To fund these payments, the couple organize a loan from an art-based lending institution that provides cash flow of $126,000 per year (using their art collection as collateral). The couple can arrange the interest on the loan so that they do not have to worry at present about the annual debt-service payments.

The couple could then repay the loan and accrued interest over time from other income or from the sale of the art assets or, alternatively, may defer the sale and have the estate of the second to die sell the collection. If they choose this option, they can keep the art collection for the remainder of their lives, benefit from a step-up in basis, and avoid the payment of CGT on the art. The estate can then repay the loan with proceeds from the sale of the estate assets, which have a stepped-up basis.

The advantages of this arrangement are that the couple retain ownership and possession of their art collection and can still transfer wealth to their heirs without having to pay gift taxes. They accomplish this without decreasing their liquidity or negatively impacting on their available annual cash flow. These grandparents also decrease the size of their taxable estate and therefore the estate taxes that will become due on death. They also avoid paying CGT plus the costs that would be incurred in a sale of their collection.

Chapter Notes

1. Rates reported for Art Capital Group in R. Campbell and C. Wiehenkamp, "Credit Default Swaps and an Application to the Art Market: A Proposal," in *Credit Risk*, ed. N. Wagner (Portland, OR: CRC Press, 2008).

2. I would like to thank Andy Augenblick from Emigrant Bank Fine Art Finance for his assistance in describing these strategies. The information used in them is based on the market as of 2008/2009. Tax rates change over time, as do selling costs. Individuals considering implementing any of these strategies should consult with their own attorney, tax adviser, accountant, and financial adviser prior to taking any action. Each individual's circumstances will vary.

3. Capital gains taxes vary depending on the individual's tax domicile and personal tax situation and may be as much as 40 percent. The long-term federal capital gains tax in 2009 is 28 percent and the New York state CGT is an additional 12 percent. Others in different tax domiciles pay different rates.

4. These fees are based on rates available with Emigrant Bank Fine Art Finance.

6

Art Funds

Jeremy Eckstein and Randall Willette

EDITOR'S NOTE: Like the rest of the global economy since the turn of the century, the art market was beset with a number of disruptions, some providing valuable opportunities for investors, others causing significant destabilization. An important impetus for change, however, was that for the first time since the development of the modern art trade, investors were increasingly able to use well-established analytical models and financial metrics to make sound investment decisions about the art economy.

An important trend in the years just preceding the financial crisis of 2007–2009 and one that is expected to continue long after the crisis has run its course the heightened sophistication of the art sector regarding financial services. In addition, the erratic and poor performance of international equity markets had been a key driver in financial investors' search for greater diversification into alternative asset classes. These features combined to provide significant opportunities for profitable innovation in the art sector and offered new scope for vehicles like art funds to meet the emerging requirements of art investors. The key benefits these new "informed investors" were seeking related to increased overall risk-adjusted returns from diversification into assets that offered low or negative correlation with equities, bonds, or whatever other assets they already held in their investment portfolios.

Traditional alternative investments, like commodities and hedge funds, have seen significant growth in the previous two decades, but more recently, a number of funds specializing in art investment have emerged, offering slightly different versions of some highly beneficial diversification strategies. The main selling point of these funds is that they offered investors the opportunity to use their money to purchase a wider selection of high-quality works of art. These funds allowed investors to

❑ achieve a diversified art portfolio,
❑ take advantage of the portfolio's low correlation with traditional asset classes, and
❑ avail themselves of expertise in art purchasing and divestiture for a variable management fee.

Although the concept of an art fund was relatively new, there was one important historical example: the British Rail Pension Fund. This premier art fund and the lessons learned from it are discussed in Jeremy Eckstein's section. The second section, written by Randall Willette, looks at the different structures and objectives of art funds in the current market.

Art Funds as Asset Class
Jeremy Eckstein

Works of art have many characteristics that make them ideal for being treated as an investment asset, and an awareness of this has piqued the interest of the financial sector. Carefully selected works of art can have an international marketability that transcends many of the weaknesses in individual economies or currencies, and as an asset class, they generally have a limited downside potential and lower volatility than conventional equities. Commencing from around 2000, calculations based on the use of the Sharpe ratio,[1] have demonstrated repeatedly that a portfolio that includes art along with its more conventional assets offers risk-adjusted rates of return that are superior to portfolios without art.

Art Price Correlation With Other Asset Classes

Art and equities have shown a very low rate of short-term correlation. While global equity markets were falling sharply during 2008, the art market continued to perform strongly, beginning to show signs of weakness only in 2009, and then only in some sectors. As a result of this favorable asset profile, fine art has increasingly been viewed as a viable and attractive alternative asset by high-net-worth individuals and institutional investors within the context of a broader allocation strategy.

The art market thrived at the beginning of the twenty-first century, buoyed partly by flourishing economic and financial markets and partly by emerging-market economies. Global economic growth generated unprecedented individual prosperity, and the art market was one of many sectors that benefited from the massive increase in the number of high-net-worth individuals and ultra-high-net-worth individuals.[2] During 2008, however, as the global economic fabric began to unravel, all eyes turned to the art market to assess how art as an asset class and investment would be affected.

Looking at the history of the art market offers considerable insight into the current interest in art funds. The art market had shown exceptional resilience in the face of past economic crises, not least because the cultural consensus that underpins the value of most categories of art tends to hold strong through even the direst economic conditions. The art market survived the market crash of 1929 and the Great Depression that followed, fared reasonably well in the first oil crisis in the early 1970s, and turned itself around from recessionary forces in the early 1980s, early 1990s, and early 2000s.

One of the lessons we can learn from past recessions is that the art market tends to emerge from a downturn with a different focus from the one it had entering into it. Prior to the downturn of the early 1990s, for example, the principal focus of art market attention had been the Impressionist and Post-Impressionist sectors. As the art market recovered, the focus of collecting and speculative-investment attention began to shift toward Western (mainly American and European) Contemporary art. In turn, the Western Contemporary art sector was the principal art-market victim of the 2008–2009 economic crisis. Art in this category had increasingly been acquired by wealthy individuals whose speculative activities during the years preceding the downturn had sent prices to unprecedented—and ultimately unsustainable— levels. Since it was these buyers who were among the most prominent victims of the financial crisis, the impact on their disposable wealth quickly led to a downturn in the art market category they were no longer in a position to support.

Although it is impossible to predict how the art market will emerge from the 2008–2009 downturn, it seems unlikely that any of the Contemporary sectors will soon see the prices seen in recent years. Old Masters and nineteenth-century and Modern masters, on the other hand, which represent a much larger pool, might just continue on the path they had been on, in a steady, unspectacular fashion, over a very much longer time horizon.

To the extent that the current economic crisis might ultimately lead to a gradual global realignment of wealth in favor of the Eastern and emerging economies, it is also possible that the collecting tastes of these new high-net-worth individuals might dominate in the second decade of this century. Cumulatively, all these possibilities illustrate that a large, diversified portfolio of art has many financial advantages over collecting in one narrow genre.

The Evolution of the Art Fund

While art is likely to continue to hold interest for investors, those individuals who do not have the space, specialized knowledge, interest, or inclination to buy and hold actual individual works of art can still have access to art as an alternative investment through investing an art fund. Investing in art through a fund, rather than directly, holds a number of advantages, especially for the noncollector who appreciates the financial characteristics of art but has no interest in actually acquiring "the real thing." Benefits of fund investing include the advantage of pooled spending in acquiring higher-quality pieces, the ability to achieve wider diversification, and the prospect of active asset management.

The British Rail Pension Fund

Although there are some earlier examples, the modern history of art investment funds really began in 1974, when the British Rail Pension Fund (BRPF) put into effect a decision to diversify its investment portfolio by putting a portion of its assets into art. At that time, British Railways was a unified, state-controlled industry, responsible for all aspects of running national railway services throughout the United Kingdom. The BRPF, established for the benefit of its employees, had become one of the largest pension funds in the country. When the fund began investing in works of art at the end of 1974, the total value of its assets was almost £1 billion ($2.4 billion). At that time, the fund's pension liabilities were principally "final salary scheme" pensions (a form of defined-benefit pension) with inflation-linked postretirement increments. It was a growing fund, with its net annual income in the range of £50 million ($120 million), and its total of investment income and incoming active-employee contributions was well in excess of its pension payouts for retired employees.

The fund's original decision to purchase works of art was largely a result of the financial and economic conditions that prevailed in 1973–1974:

❏ The OPEC-led oil crisis of 1973 had had a devastating impact on the world's leading economies, leading many market observers, especially those in the United Kingdom, to seek a new paradigm for investment strategies.

❏ Stock markets had fallen dramatically, with the FT-Actuaries Index (the main U.K. equity index at that time) having fallen by more than 70 percent, and the U.S. Dow Jones Industrial Average having fallen by more than 40 percent.

❏ The rate of inflation was at unprecedented highs, with the annual U.K. figure at the end of 1974 only a little short of 30 percent and the annual U.S. rate higher than 12 percent.

❏ The pound sterling was depreciating strongly against other European currencies and the U.S dollar.

❏ The commercial property market, which had previously been a popular investment arena for pension funds, had dropped sharply.

If such a situation had occurred later, an acceptable investment strategy might have been to diversify into index-linked securities, but such investments were not available at that time.

Against this background, the fund's investment managers concluded that it would be advisable to diversify a portion of the fund's investments into a class of assets where there were reasonable prospects of achieving long-term growth at least equal to inflation. The tax regulations governing pension funds made it irrelevant whether the fund's value growth derived from long-term capital gains or income from dividends.

Fine art was identified as an asset-backed investment whose financial characteristics were ideally suited to the fund's requirements. The asset profile of fine art seemed to have a close inverse relationship with the liability profile of the fund, and it offered the further advantage of having international marketability, thereby providing a hedge against the vagaries of the U.K. economy or currency realignments. Works of art also provided a convenient means of taking advantage of nondomestic investment opportunities without attracting the premium that was levied on foreign-currency investment.[3]

In 1974, when the BRPF managers first decided to invest in works of art, it was agreed that in order to achieve their required long-term objective, up to 6 percent of the annual cash flow of the fund (amounting to approximately £3 million) should be allocated to works of art, subject to the availability of suitable (investment-quality) items. (As it turned out, the fund exceeded this limit during the peak of its buying activity.)

It was the end of 1974 by the time the fund made its first art purchases. (*Table 6.1* shows the amounts invested from 1974 through 1980.) From the outset, the diversification strategy had been intended to be a long-term exercise, covering the normal life of a collection of works of art, which was considered to be about twenty years. Although the fund was not precluded from taking advantage of short-term selling opportunities—subject, of course, to tax implications—it never expressed any intention of seeking short-term trading profits.

Initially, there was no time limit or predetermined ceiling on the total amount to be invested. By 1978, however, some £27 million had already been spent on works of art, and it was agreed that the program would have an overall expenditure limit of £40 million and that the fund would probably achieve this limit toward the end of 1980. That did, indeed, prove to be the case.

The fund bought widely from major auction houses and dealers, and occasionally privately, but at no time did the expenditure of the fund in any single category of art amount to being sufficient to push prices up against itself. At the conclusion of its acquisition program in 1980, the total amount invested in works of art represented no more than 2.9 percent of the total fund assets.

The original investment strategy was intended to achieve maximum protection against fluctuations in value arising from trends in taste and underlying market movements. To achieve this, the fund's managers had decided to diversify across a wide spectrum of key collecting areas but with one exception: they would not invest in Modern art, because of the perceived uncertainties and potentially high volatility of that sector of the market.

The intention was to concentrate on forming "well-rounded" collections that were representative of each of the agreed-upon collecting

TABLE 6.1 British Rail Pension Fund Expenditure

Year	Amount Invested in Art (£MM)
1974	0.5
1975	4.8
1976	7.4
1977	7.6
1978	8.2
1979	8.1
1980	3.4

Source: *Eckstein and Associates* (2009)

categories. The motive for this was both financial and esthetic, because collections were known to have a "financial synergy" that derived from carefully assembling works of art into well-balanced collections that were worth more in aggregate than as discrete works without a cohesive theme. Nevertheless, although the principal objective had been the formation of coherent collections of art, the fund also recognized the financial potential arising from opportune purchases of outstanding individual pieces. Whether the fund was purchasing a work of art as part of a key collection or as a "one-off" item, the investment strategy was to purchase the finest quality of works available on the market. It was also understood that because of the premium prices such works normally attracted, the fund would not, without an exceptionally compelling reason, purchase from major single-owner collections.

In 1978, the fund managers decided they would spend only a further £12–£13 million on the purchase of art and concentrate on rounding off their existing collections, whose works had already achieved a certain degree of cohesiveness and were recognized as forming an important nucleus. Reviewing the situation again early in 1980, they decided that although a number of collections were complete, others were still lacking in many respects. Even though there would be a significant advantage in spending a further £8–£10 million on carefully selected items to complete these collections,[4] in compliance with its investment strategy, the fund stopped buying art. Its holdings were deliberately spread over a large number of different collecting areas, but, as a result of the premature halt to the acquisition program, some holdings constituted effectively complete collections, while others were still relatively fragmented. A total of seven key collections accounted for approximately 76 percent by value of the whole portfolio, with the remaining 24 percent spread thinly across a wide range of other collecting categories (see *Table 6.2*). The total number of works of art acquired by the fund in its various collections, over its six years of active buying, amounted to approximately 2,400.

In order to gain access to expert advice, the BRPF worked closely with Sotheby's throughout what was, at the time, a highly innovative and controversial acquisition program. Were such an arrangement to be entered into today, it would undoubtedly raise criticism because of the potential conflicts of interest over whether Sotheby's could give investors objective advice on acquisitions it allowed, because its contractual obligations then, as now, were to the sellers, not the buyers, of works of art.

TABLE 6.2   Value Share of the BRPF by Sector

Collections	Share of the Fund (%)
Old Master paintings	18.8
Old Master drawings	11.1
Impressionist art	10.2
Chinese works of art	10.2
Books and manuscripts	10.0
Antiquities	8.3
Medieval/Renaissance works of art	6.9
Others	24.0
—Old Master prints	2.0
—Japanese art	1.0
—19th-century decorative art	2.0
—Continental pictures	2.0
—English pictures	2.0
—Furniture	3.0
—Vertu	4.0
—Silver	2.0
—Others	6.0

Source: *Eckstein and Associates* (2009)

Even though these risks were not so clearly identified then as they would be later, in order to keep the decision-making process and administration of the fund at arm's length, the actual management of selecting the purchases was undertaken by an independent intermediary company that was set up specifically for this purpose—an early example of a firewall. The intermediary company also employed its own general-ist art expert, whose function was to head a panel of experts drawn from Sotheby's and elsewhere, convened for the specific purpose of assessing purchase recommendations and recommending sales strategies.

Art experts from Sotheby's and elsewhere were invited to recommend purchases of suitable artworks to the panel, and the intermediary com-pany's employees and agents would then make confidential decisions, on the basis of the panel's advice, on whether or not they wanted to acquire a piece, and, if so, at what price. The company therefore acted as an efficient buffer between the recommendations made by Sotheby's experts and ultimate purchasing decisions. This not only effectively protected Sotheby's from potential conflicts of interest but also made it possible for the fund to draw on Sotheby's expert art advice while buying widely from other major auction houses in the United Kingdom, New York, Hong Kong, and Monaco; dealers; and private owners.

Once the fund ceased actively buying works of art, its ongoing curato-rial costs and insurance became its largest expenses. In order to minimize these, the fund lent works of art from its own collections to muse-ums in the United Kingdom and overseas. Through the 1980s, between 30 percent and 40 percent of the total collection by value was on loan at any given time to museums in the United Kingdom and the United States.[5] Only relatively minor or unpopular items, or those that were frag-ile or required special display conditions, were not lent out and instead were kept in a secure, environmentally controlled storage facility. The loans benefited the fund by substantially reducing insurance and storage costs, and they also had the advantage of giving the works exposure in prestigious international museum collections, which, it was hoped, would increase their potential value when they were ultimately offered for sale.

While works of art acquired by the fund had originally been intended to be long-term investments, the managers, upon reviewing the portfolio in 1983, decided they should sell a number of works that fell outside their key collecting areas.[6] When the fund's management changed in 1987, the trustees decided, in principle, to dispose of the entire portfolio of works of art and made plans for a carefully controlled program of sales to be implemented over a period of years.

The decision to sell was made somewhat earlier than had originally been envisaged, but it had been prompted in part by the belief that the late 1980s upward spiral in art market prices represented an ideal opportunity for achieving a significantly better return if the art was sold at that time than if they were to hold the works a few more years before selling them.

The decision turned out to be more than justified by the crash in the art market that soon followed in the early 1990s, and it was further reinforced by the new availability of investment-index-linked bonds, which had not been available when the fund had started buying art but were a far more appropriate investment for the fund. The fund managers were also mindful of art's relatively high maintenance costs (principally collection management, administration, storage, and insurance) and the perceived difficulties of valuing a portfolio covering so many different categories of art.

The first sale consisted of the fund's collection of Old Master prints. The delicate condition of this collection had made it difficult to display or lend, which made it an obvious candidate to test the waters for the gradual disposal of the fund's other collections. The print collection was sold at auction in June 1987. Its aggregate original cost had been £607,000, and the sale realized approximately £2 million. The collection had given the fund an internal rate of return (IRR) of about 11 percent a year, some 2.5 percent per year higher than the rate of inflation. The fund's investment in the collection had achieved the fund's principal objective: it had provided a real rate of return over and above the underlying rate of inflation.

The satisfactory outcome of this first sale prompted a number of subsequent sales from the fund's other collections during the latter part of the 1980s and into 1990 (see *Table 6.3*).

Toward the end of 1990, in light of rapidly deteriorating market conditions, the fund's selling program was suspended temporarily, and only a few minor sales were made over the next four years. In 1994, when the art market returned to its former strength, the fund began to work actively to dispose of the remainder of its holdings. By that time, the remaining art accounted for less than 1 percent by value of the pension fund as a whole and could no longer be justified by rational portfolio-management criteria.[7]

TABLE 6.3 Sales by the BRPF From 1987 to 1990

Sale	Date	Location	Returns (IRR per annum)
Old Master prints	June 87	London	Cash IRR 11% (2.5% after inflation)
English silver	Nov 87	London	Cash IRR 15.7% (2.5% after inflation)
Japanese prints	Dec 87	London	Sold for 3× original cost
Oceanic art	Jul 88	London	Sold below original cost
Books and manuscripts	Sep 88	London	Cash IRR 8.7% (0.9% after inflation)
Continental porcelain	Oct 88	London	Cash IRR 11.4%
Continental silver	Nov 88	Geneva	Cash IRR 14.1%
French furniture	Nov 88	London	Cash IRR 11.6%
Impressionist & Modern art	Apr 89	London	Cash IRR 21.3% (12.9% after inflation)
Chinese porcelain	May 89	Hong Kong	Cash IRR 15.4% (8.2% after inflation)
African tribal art	Jul 89	London	Cash IRR 4.1% (negative after inflation)
Early Chinese ceramics	Dec 89	London	Cash IRR 15.8% (8.2% after inflation)
Gold boxes & vertu	May 90	Geneva	Cash IRR 12.9% (4.5% after inflation)
19th-cent. Continental pictures	Jun 90	London	Cash IRR 14.6% (6.2% after inflation)
19th-cent. Victorian pictures	Jun 90	London	Cash IRR 17.6% (9.3% after inflation)

Source: *Eckstein and Associates* (2009)

By December 2000, the fund's art sales had been completed, and the total profit from the sales amounted to £168 million, an overall cash IRR of 11.3 percent, or 4 percent per year in real terms, allowing for inflation. The fund's formally stated investment objective for its art portfolio had never been to beat equities over the same period but simply to beat inflation over the holding period. Nevertheless, the large majority of the sales had not only achieved the primary objective but also amply demonstrated the validity of the thesis underlying the fund's diversification into works of art: that, over the long term, collections of mainstream works of art provide a more-than-satisfactory hedge against inflation.[8]

Although it must be said that, with some notable exceptions, the rates of return achieved by individual works of art were generally less than would have been realized in U.K. equities over the same period, allowing for the reinvestment of gross dividends, this needs to be seen in the context of the extraordinary growth in equities prices during that time. From a historically low starting point of 66 at the end of 1974, the United Kingdom's FT-Actuaries Index increased almost seventeen-fold to approximately 1,100 at the end of 1989. Had it not been for this extraordinary performance, it is likely, based on more-typical long-term returns achieved during the second half of the twentieth century, that the art holdings would also have yielded an even greater return than corresponding equity investments over the same period.

The exceptions that beat equities were found principally in the fund's collections of Impressionist art and Chinese ceramics and porcelain.[9] The extraordinary performance of the fund's Impressionist art collection was the result of several factors:

❏ Art's period of unprecedented, and ultimately unsustainable, growth through the late 1980s
❏ The careful selection of works at the time of purchase
❏ The sale's fortuitous timing at the sector's market peak

The fact that the fund's art holdings yielded less than did comparable equity market investments overall was not necessarily an indication that the other categories of art had performed poorly. In the unprecedented U.K. bull market during that period, it was unrealistic to expect an alternative-asset-backed class of investment that offered the level of security of fine art to provide the consistent returns that could have been achieved by an equity index fund over the same period.

In looking at the fund's achievement, it is apparent with hindsight that through lax management, inexperience, and the enthusiasm of the art experts making purchase recommendations, the fund did not always adhere to its original stringent purchasing criteria. By 1978, the fund's art holdings were already overdiversified, a problem that was exacerbated when a £13 million limit was placed on further expenditure for that year. It soon became evident that the amount was never going to be sufficient to complete all the collections that had been started, and it is doubtful that even the additional £8–£10 million suggested would have sufficed even if deployed. The resulting holding—2,400 individual works of art spread over seven major and many smaller collections—proved, from a purely administrative standpoint, to be a major problem and ultimately had a detrimental impact on investment performance. In addition, the fund's collection included a relatively small number of valuable works, together with a much larger number of less-valuable works. In the early 1980s, it was estimated that just fifty works out of the total of 2,400 were likely individually worth £250,000 or more and that together these works accounted for well over a third of the value of the whole art portfolio.

A "top 100" group of works was identified, which corresponded to one hundred of the works individually valued at £120,000 or more and included a small number of lower-value works that were preeminent examples of their kind. In aggregate, these one hundred works were estimated to account for approximately half the value of the fund's total art portfolio, and returns achieved on their sales tended to be superior to the returns achieved by the large number of lower-value works.[10]

That the fund's overall investment performance would have been markedly improved, and administrative expenses significantly reduced, if the holding had been limited to a much-smaller number of higher-value higher-quality works of art remains a valid conclusion for any art fund contemplating investing in works of art. There are two further practical reasons for following a more stringent buying policy:

1. A smaller number of pieces in a collection will incur considerably lower administrative and handling expenses than a larger number.
2. The better the quality of works purchased, the more likely it is that the fund will be able to lend them to eminent art galleries and other collections around the world, which can reduce the fund's insurance and holding costs as well as enhance the collection's eventual sale prices.

Lessons From British Rail: 30 Years On

Although the BRPF did not finally finish disposing of its art portfolio until 2000, the decision to invest in art and its main acquisition phase both occurred more than thirty years ago, which prompts the question of why the experience of the fund is so often cited and still relevant today. There are a number of answers to this:

1. To this day, the fund is the only available model of institutional-investment-fund performance about which significant information, even if incomplete, is available.
2. Many of the fund's structural details and operational considerations still stand as models of good practice for ongoing and prospective later funds.
3. Most important, the BRPF's original decision to invest in art had been prompted by the appalling state of the U.K. economy at that time and the realization that traditional equity investments were losing so much capital that they were failing to deliver the returns investors expected.

The economic scenario has changed over time, but some of the lessons of these broad economic weaknesses are still relevant. Investors with capital are now more determined than ever to find relatively secure asset-backed alternative investments. Many of the strengths of art as an asset class—the reduced volatility, resilience, and superior risk-adjusted rate of return—are encouraging wealth-management advisers to recommend a diversified asset-allocation strategy in a balanced portfolio, in which art has a place alongside equities and fixed-income investments.

Why Follow-On Funds Struggled

The relative attractiveness of art as an asset class, together with the many practical difficulties involved in acquiring and holding the underlying asset, provided fertile ground for the growth of art investment funds, but, after the BRPF's bold first attempt, many follow-on funds nevertheless struggled to achieve a firm foothold among asset classes. There were two main reasons for this:

❏ First and foremost, the workings of the art market remain a mystery to many who are not directly involved. The very lack of regulation and transparency that allow knowledgeable participants to achieve superior returns acts as a deterrent to many fund managers and wealth advisers, who see the art marketplace as hostile territory.

❑ Second, an art fund requires a mix of money-management skills and an intimate understanding of the unique mechanisms of the art market, a balance that is difficult to achieve. Many prospective art funds have failed to achieve funding because they were devised by art experts who had little understanding of the financial structure and mechanisms required by institutional or high-net-worth individual investors. Conversely, other prospective art funds have failed because they were devised by financial people who recognized that superior returns were available on art but thought the same disciplines could be applied to the art market as to financial markets. Quite simply, they failed to understand the unique practicalities of operating in the art marketplace.

What a Successful Art Fund Must Be Able to Accomplish

A successful art fund, in order to achieve coherence and avoid any potential conflicts of interest, needs to devise a strategy that will

❑ remunerate the advisers in some way that aligns their interests with investors';

❑ develop an achievable investment objective in terms of sourcing and acquisition policy;

❑ offer attractive prospective returns in the context of the historical risk-adjusted returns achieved by that category of art;

❑ devise an ongoing holding strategy that offers the prospect of genuine value-added content over and above the projected underlying growth in market value;

❑ devise a realistic exit strategy that can function even in an illiquid market;

❑ determine an optimal financial structure, whether open- or closed-ended, with consideration of the implications of the assets' interim and indicative valuations, without "mark-to-market" pricing; and

❑ market itself aggressively, overcoming the hurdles in investors' minds when faced with the opacity of art as an asset class, since it is bought and sold in an inefficient and unregulated marketplace about which there is asymmetry of information.

Often, the more sophisticated the investment strategy, the less likely that it will be achieved in practice, since the acquisition process is largely opportunistic and determined less by adherence to a plan than by the availability of appropriately priced investment-quality works. Many funds' acquisitions policies refer to the ready availability of art to "cash buyers," but such a policy is impractical unless there are only a limited number of funds (buyers) chasing the works. Competition among more than a small number of funds will ultimately prove to be self-defeating. The alternative is to seek out ever more niche-investment opportunities, such as in specific sectors, or in emerging markets—but the relatively modest size of many of these markets can lead to blockage, when too much money is seeking investment opportunities at the same time.

The Problems of Administrative Costs

Apart from basic administrative matters common to any fund, an art fund also has to deal with another dimension peculiar to its unique asset quality: such matters as transportation and storage of the acquired artworks, insurance, and ongoing portfolio management.

Since art is a commodity that yields no income stream, all these administrative functions have to be achieved within the constraints of the fees charged to investors. In order to be able to market itself successfully, an art fund, more often than not, feels constrained to offer broadly the same fee structure as is traditionally associated with hedge funds—a fee of about 2 percent and an incentive fee of 20 percent based on profits, all of this implying that for the exercise of running an art fund to be cost efficient, the investment funds under management must achieve a certain critical mass. All these factors present significant challenges to emerging art funds.

Existing Fund Structures

There are several different fund structures in operation:

❏ The *pooled-funds approach*, which is used by some private banks who buy art with an eye to investment potential on behalf of high-net-worth clients

❏ The *"art expert as adviser" approach*, which offer investors the guidance of an art expert in order for them to pool their money and acquire a selection of investment-quality art, with emphasis here on the nature and quality of advice offered by the expert

❏ The *fund of funds structure*, such as used in 2004 by ABN Amro, which sought to establish a fund of funds based on a spread of individual art funds; the initiative failed, because there were too few funds that met the bank's stringent financial criteria.

❏ The *art hedge fund*, which hedges against a potential market downturn using derivative securities.[11]

The number of art funds in existence even at this writing is difficult to assess because some funds have no obligation to register anywhere. Market experts estimate that there were, at the beginning of 2009, around fifty active art funds, with, interestingly, the majority based in India. Because such funds have not normally been open to outside investors, and the rules governing the share and disposition of their collections have tended to be rather basic, their structures lack the formal arrangements of true financial vehicles, and their operations are perhaps more like those of an investment club than a fund. Indeed, the number of operational funds would be at least halved if we were to limit the definition of an art fund to a formally structured investment vehicle that

❏ is open to outside investors,

❏ is subject to regulations governing such offerings regarding suitably qualified investors,

❏ has raised sufficient investment funds to embark on its trading strategy, and

❏ has a diversified allocation strategy based on categories of mainstream Western art.

Ultimately, the viability and attractiveness of art as an alternative asset class depends on the perceived relative prospects for the world's financial markets vis-à-vis the various sectors of the art market. Art appeals to certain investors because of its hard-asset–based backing and relatively favorable risk-adjusted return. In order to give these investors the necessary level of comfort and security, the emphasis will increasingly turn toward those art funds that have a sound approach to financial structure and management. When it comes to attracting serious investment money, what is needed to make art as attractive as other asset sectors is transparency, reliable market indicators, published track records, and the promise of sound portfolio management underlying the art investment strategy.

Art Funds: Current Strategies and Practices
Randall Willette

Earlier in this chapter, Jeremy Eckstein discussed the British Rail Pension Fund, which is the iconic reference point for all subsequent art funds. Since the BRPF, as interest in art as an alternative asset class has grown, a variety of different art-investment funds have sought to capitalize on the art market's inherent inefficiencies and provide the potential to identify, create, and execute art transactions at highly attractive terms. In 2008, there were estimated to be more than twenty-five established art funds globally at various stages of development—although, as mentioned earlier, since the funds are not always required to register, it is hard to determine exact numbers.[12] As the previous section pointed out, the greatest number of art funds seems to be in India, followed closely by Europe, the United States, Asia, and the Middle East.

Art fund managers seek to approach art investment in much the same way traditional fund managers would approach investments. Their investment strategy makes use of proven techniques and disciplines common to the management of every asset class:

❏ Modern portfolio theory
❏ Sophisticated risk-management tools
❏ Quantitative models
❏ Qualitative analysis

By employing the expertise and market intelligence of a fund manager, supported by robust financial and art market research, art investment funds seek to provide investors access to opportunities typically captured only by the world's top art collectors and dealers. Through an optimized exposure to art, these funds are designed for experienced and qualified investors seeking high levels of return in an inefficient market. With minimum subscriptions often as high as $250,000, art funds, like most alternative investments, are suited to the more sophisticated investor.

Depending on their objectives, art funds may be broadly diversified to spread the risk of the investment rather than to concentrate it in one sector, such as Contemporary art, which, though it might result in higher returns, also creates greater risk. Once the collection has been assembled and after the agreed-upon investment period, the acquired works are generally sold through an orderly disposal process over a set period of time, and the proceeds, after payment of management and administration fees, are distributed to investors. There are a number of ways in which art funds can help to mitigate some of the risks of investing in art. Some of the key benefits are:

❏ Art funds offer diversification of art market sectors across a diversified portfolio of works—e.g., Old Masters, Impressionist, Modern, or Contemporary works—that may have low correlation with one another.

❏ A fund structure can reduce costs associated with the purchase, sale, and holding of art by investing in art on a pooled basis, because, with their greater cash resources, funds are often able to negotiate advantageous fees and conditions with appraisers, auction houses, insurers, and other service providers that would not normally be available to an individual buyer or dealer.

❏ A fund's art acquisitions are based on expected investment returns, liquidity, diversification, and market conditions and are normally selected by leading experts in their field. Locating the right works of art to buy and then disposing of them at the right time requires more expert knowledge than most investors possess.

❏ Given the fund's significant available financial resources, it may also have unique access to works of art that are fresh, rarely seen on the market, and therefore more valuable. A fund's buyers and advisers might have the ability to source works of art directly from private estates and collectors, allowing them to bypass dealers and auction houses.

❏ For those investors who are passionate about art, a fund can sometimes even provide the opportunity to borrow the works of art for a limited and enjoy them personally in their own homes.

❏ Some funds have the connections to arrange lending of the fund's art to major museums or exhibitions, thereby raising its profile in the international art market and enhancing its investment value.

❏ Art funds are often structured to provide investors with a tax-efficient means of investing in art, including advantages regarding estate tax, sales tax, value-added tax, and capital gains tax.

❑ Art funds usually acquire works of art over a period of years and therefore can take advantage of potential price fluctuations and avoid art that they consider overpriced.

Of course, all the benefits described are only achievable if the art fund is well managed and the decisions to buy and sell are made by experienced, independent, and objective advisers. Unfortunately, some art advisers engage in such a broad spectrum of art market activities that their interests conflict with the interests of the investor, but well-structured art funds protect investors from such risks. Also, regardless of a fund's advisers' expertise, since art is not a liquid investment, the group might not be able to divest at the times or on the terms it desires. If the fund has a target maturity, the fund manager may have limited control over the timing of disposals, a circumstance that can result in divestiture under suboptimal market conditions.

Art Fund Models and Management

In their simplest form, many existing art funds are most comparable to private equity funds, in that the goal of both models is asset appreciation. Private-equity-style investment is based not on portfolio management but on the purchase of equity in private companies through leveraged buyouts and acquisitions in the hope of later selling the business at a higher valuation.

Similarly, art fund managers buy works of art in the hope that the value of the artworks will appreciate over time and, through active management, generate opportunities for returns that outperform other investments. Just as with any other asset class, if managers can use sector expertise, market intelligence, and creative investment strategies to recognize and capture the unique opportunities in the marketplace, they can generate highly attractive returns for their investors.

But there are also differences between private equity funds and art funds, in that art fund managers, unlike private-equity-fund managers, lack a track record of performance. Lacking any robust historical data on their funds, most art-fund-management companies try to assemble a management group consisting of art experts with a strong art-dealing background, thereby building capacity and developing some sort of proxy for a track record.

Critical Measures of an Art Fund's Success

There are a number of specialized skills art fund managers need in order to ensure the success of the fund. These include the following:

❏ *The ability to mine market intelligence.* Art fund managers must be able to use market research and intelligence to find attractive investment opportunities on favorable terms. Economic and behavioral research and market intelligence can help them spot regional and sector trends and be opportunistic when they find anomalies in pricing. Proprietary deal flow is an important consideration for investors selecting an art fund manager, and those strategic market positioning is a major competitive advantage.

❏ *The ability to enhance the value of a fund's assets.* Like private-equity-fund managers, art fund managers seek to enhance the value of the assets in the fund. They can do so through a variety of curatorial and marketing activities commonly practiced by successful collectors and dealers.

❏ *The ability to provide risk management.* Art fund managers must be able to manage their portfolio risk on several levels. They need constantly to monitor, review, and analyze economic developments and market trends that could affect future buying or selling, and they need to diversify their assets to mitigate risk of exposure to a single opportunity. Good art fund managers will be keenly familiar with the individual risks associated with the purchase of artworks—such as questions of authenticity, title, condition, and provenance—and be able to assess them wisely through the expertise, market intelligence, and depth of experience.

❏ *The ability to network within the art market.* The most successful art fund managers are those who have not only built an internal team but also formed exclusive partnerships with dealers, curators, economists, art sector experts and investment specialists, as well as quantitative and qualitative researchers to derive unique art-market insights.

Art fund managers must engage in the right transactions at the right time and at the right price. The type of business transactions in which successful art funds will engage include

❏ trades in the primary and secondary art market,

❏ transactions focused on a major art sector,

❏ regional and decorative niche opportunities, and

❏ art-related business and financing transactions.

Although existing funds vary in their exact market strategies, there are two basic approaches that have emerged as a basis for fund investment. They reflect the successful activity of two different groups of art-world professionals: the sector-allocation approach and the opportunistic approach.

THE SECTOR-ALLOCATION APPROACH

The sector-allocation approach to art-fund-management strategy is to acquire works of art, or interests in works of art, which, in the opinion of the manager, will be more highly valued in the marketplace either immediately or at some future time. The fund aims to attain its investment objective of significant capital appreciation through active management of a broadly diversified portfolio of art across multiple sectors of the art market, each having distinct performance attributes. Art funds that take the sector-allocation approach typically invest in works within the most-established or most-popular collecting categories, such as Old Masters, Impressionists, Modern, and Contemporary. Each sector chosen will usually have to also meet such key criteria as significant size and maturity of the collector base (i.e., its market size[13]); independent market behavior, including price performance and volatility; and long relative transaction history, allowing for greater trackability and predictability.

In practice, the fund manager makes top-down allocations among the sectors and periodically rebalances the portfolio, based on proprietary macroeconomic research and analysis of long-term art market trends. The fund assets will be actively managed through the strategic purchase, ongoing curatorial management, and sales of works of art.

THE OPPORTUNISTIC APPROACH

The second approach translates the activities of the world's leading art dealers and auction houses into identifying opportunistic financial transactions and direct investments that can result in superior shorter-term returns. Funds that pursue an opportunistic strategy replicate the activity of, and in some cases partner with, art market professionals to pursue investments across a range of regional and niche opportunities. Moreover, these funds make strategic investments in collections or portfolios of new works, which can be resold through traditional art-market channels. Works may be purchased for long-term capital appreciation or short-term arbitrage and, up until the beginning of 2009, focused predominantly on Contemporary art-works from such emerging art markets as China, India, the Middle East, and Latin America, along with niche sectors like photography and collectibles.[14] Types of transactions include opportunistic buying and selling of works to achieve an immediate return as well as financing opportunities and equity participations with significant upside potential. These opportunities are generated by the underlying dynamic of the art market, which includes inefficiencies, illiquidity, opacity, and extreme product differentiation or heterogeneity.

Whatever the approach, most art fund managers favor tax-efficient structures that achieve greater tax transparency for investors depending on their tax residence. Among some of the favorable tax jurisdictions that have been used for art investment vehicles are Jersey, Guernsey, British Virgin Islands, Luxembourg, Gibraltar, and the Cayman Islands.

Another differentiating feature of art funds is that they may be either open ended or closed ended. A closed-ended fund, in principle, does not allow its investors to redeem shares at will, but insists that they wait until the fund's target maturity date. Open-ended structures are difficult for art funds, as their investment strategy typically does not fit with providing investors with a regular right to redeem.

An art fund may also be structured as an "umbrella fund" that comprises several segregated subfunds, each displaying different characteristics or sectors of art investment. Whatever the legal form of the fund, its managing entity may delegate all or part of its functions to third-party service providers. Since extensive proprietary research and market-intelligence-gathering drives the selection of the art funds' market opportunities, they will often call upon both internal and external teams' expertise to assess such factors as economic conditions, financial and art market dynamics, and other such variables that could influence the prices, activity, and supply.

Chapter Notes

1. The Sharpe ratio is used to measure risk-adjusted performance, or the excess return of a portfolio per unit of risk it takes on. It is calculated by subtracting the risk-free rate (e.g., a 10-year U.S. Treasury bond) from the rate of return for a portfolio and dividing the result by the standard deviation of the portfolio returns.

2. High-net-worth individuals are those with investable assets of over $1 million, whereas ultra-high-net-worth individuals have investable assets exceeding $30 million (excluding their primary residences).

3. During the last quarter of 1974, this premium was equivalent to approximately 58 percent.

4. This further expenditure still did not take the total beyond the previously agreed-upon total limit of £40 million.

5. The principal beneficiaries in the United Kingdom were the Victoria and Albert Museum and the British Museum in London and the Doncaster Museum and Leeds Castle in Kent. Beneficiaries in the United States included the Detroit Institute of Arts, Minneapolis Institute of Arts, Dallas Museum of Art, San Antonio Museum of Art, Archer M. Huntington Art Gallery in Texas, National Gallery of Art in Washington, Yale Center for British Art, J. Paul Getty Museum in California, and Frick Collection and Brooklyn Museum in New York.

6. There was also some small-scale rationalization, involving trading up and buying works to replace certain items of lesser quality that had been acquired at a time when nothing better was available.

7. The first significant disposal following the reactivation of the selling program was the fund's collection of Old Master pictures. The collection was dispersed in four separate sales: (i) in December 1994, yielding a cash IRR of 12.8 percent per annum (5.6 percent after inflation); (ii) in July 1995, yielding a cash IRR of 6.9 percent per annum (1.3 percent after inflation); (iii) in July 1996, yielding a cash IRR of 5.4 percent per annum (a loss after inflation); (iv) in January 1997 in New York, yielding a cash IRR of 6.8 percent per annum (0.5 percent after inflation). Other significant collections sold after 1994 included Persian and Indian miniatures in April 1996, yielding a return of 0.5 percent per annum after inflation; European works of art in July 1996, yielding a return of 2.3 percent per annum after inflation; and ancient glass in November 1997, yielding a return of 1.5 percent per annum after inflation.

8. The only significant exceptions were their small collections of tribal and oceanic art, both of which sold for little more than their book cost, from a combination of the works being overpriced on purchase, and generally thin market-trading conditions throughout the period.

9. For example, eight individual works from the collection of twenty-five Impressionist pictures sold by the fund in April 1989 yielded returns greater than would have been achieved on the U.K. equity market over the same period. The collection as a whole yielded a return of 21.3 percent per year, just 1 percent per year less than an equivalent equity-market investment.

10. For example, when the fund sold its Impressionist and Modern art collection in April 1989, just 4 of the 25 works accounted for over 60 percent of the total realized sale proceeds, and 11 accounted for over 90 percent. The remaining 14 works (56 percent) accounted for less than 10 percent of the sale proceeds. In the sale of its Chinese ceramics in London in December 1989, just 3 out of 75 lots sold accounted for over 50 percent of the total sale proceeds, and 20 lots accounted for 90 percent of the sale proceeds. The remaining 55 lots (73 percent) accounted for only 10 percent of the proceeds. Over the four sales of its Old Master pictures, 5 out of a total of 78 works together accounted for 50 percent of the total proceeds, 33 lots accounted for 90 percent of the value, and the remaining 45 lots (58 percent) accounted for just 10 percent of the value.

11. The Art Trading Fund (ATF) was the first-ever regulated art fund with an art market hedge. When the fund observed a quarter-on-quarter drop in equities or the front end of the yield curve, it bought puts on equities in related industries that have a high correlation to the art market such as shares in Sotheby's (ticker BID) or in the luxury goods market such as LVMH or Richemont. The fund therefore created a synthetic hedge consisting primarily of exchange-traded options on liquid stocks, which offered some downside protection in case of a decline in the art market.

12. Some funds in the U.K. for example may not be required to register with the Financial Services Authority (FSA), but are required to register with the authority in the offshore tax jurisdiction in which they have set up operations such as Caymans, Guernsey, or Luxembourg.

13. As measured by number of players and volume of transactions.

14. The fallout from the economic crisis in 2008 and 2009 hit the Contemporary art market the hardest, with many art funds delaying their launch.

7

The Government and the Art Trade

Dr. Clare McAndrew
Rena Neville, Sotheby's NY
Anthony Browne, BAMF

EDITOR'S NOTE: The role of government in the art market has always been something of a double-edged sword. The state, on the one hand, can be an important support to the market, for example, through helping to fund the careers of Contemporary artists and support to the art trade. Through regulating the market, it also plays a role in protecting works of art, particularly those that form part of the national heritage or patrimony, and can also help to stimulate art investment through a variety of fiscal incentives. On the other hand, regulations, taxes, and levies imposed by the state can have a negative impact on the market, adding layers of costs and red tape and causing disincentives to trade, investment, and production of works of art. Differences in regulatory regimes between governments can also have distributional consequences for the international art market, with regulatory arbitrage leading to trade diversions and distortions, often resulting in concentrations of art trade in global centers with the most conducive and liberal regimes, such as the United States.

The first section, written by Clare McAndrew, looks at the rationale for government in the art market and analyzes in detail the arguments related to trade restrictions and the national patrimony. It also details the various forms of trade regulations that governments can impose on art and their effects. The second section, by Rena Neville, looks at the relationship between the government and the art market in the United States and discusses the issues related to the lack of a federal department for the arts as well as outlines some of the key federal laws that affect the market. The final section, by Anthony Browne, discusses the interaction between the state and the market from a British perspective and analyzes some of the main legislation affecting the market on a national and European Union level.

Trade and the Market for Works of Art

Clare McAndrew

There are a number of ways in which the government directly affects the art trade through subsidies and other direct funding of artists, as well as acting as an important consumer and investor in the market. The function of government that has the most impact on investors in the art market, however, is as a regulator, and some of the most relevant areas of current regulation include tax and fiscal incentives to hold, buy, and sell art (discussed in Chapter 9 and Chapter 10) and trade regulations. These interventions can affect the potential value of an art investment at a given place and point in time, and they are important considerations in deciding what, when, and where to invest in the art market in order to maximize returns and minimize risk.

Most economists would argue that when markets are functioning efficiently, they should be left as free as possible from government interference. A fully functioning competitive economy can result in consumer preferences being satisfied optimally without the need for intervention and regulation. The burden of proof in justifying any government interference in the market, therefore, should always lie in showing where the market, left to its own devices, fails to produce an optimal outcome or where there are "market failures." There are generally two principal grounds in economics to justify government intervention:

❏ *Market failures* occur when some market imperfection leads to an inefficient allocation of resources, which it is the task of government to correct. Examples of these failures are failures of competition (such as monopolies), public goods,[1] and positive and negative externalities.[2] The external benefits that works of important national art produce for society, for example, are often used as a justification for restricting exports.

❏ *Equity concerns* center on the belief that the market, left to its own devices, can lead to an unsatisfactory distribution of income.

In other words, while a free market may produce an efficient outcome, it may be inequitable to participants, which is used as a justification for redistributive taxation. This train of thought relates to egalitarian arguments, which would suggest, for example, that all citizens should have access to art and culture, and therefore subsidies could be used to overcome barriers such as high prices, low incomes, or geographical inaccessibility.

Although the rationale for government intervention to correct market failures in the art market is valid in many cases, regulation and taxation bring their own costs (including monitoring and enforcement) and can also often have detrimental side effects that run contrary to their objectives. Investors need to therefore be aware of the nature of government intervention and its impact (intended and otherwise), as well as ways to structure their investments to minimize its negative consequences and maximize any opportunities it offers.

Restricting Trade in National Patrimony Art

An awareness of any trade restrictions that apply to a work of art is crucial prior to investing, as they can directly affect the ability to sell and sometimes even transport works between locations. One of the most common reasons given for restricting trade in art and offering it a special position outside of many international free trade agreements is to protect the "national patrimony." It is important, therefore, to understand what this term means and what art belongs in this category. It is also interesting to examine the case for the state either purchasing or preventing the sale of objects that belong to the national patrimony.[3]

Trying to come up with a global definition of what makes up the national patrimony is impossible, as the concept is subjective and definitions vary considerably from country to country. Artworks belonging to the national patrimony are generally unique fine and decorative art and artifacts; however, not all unique art belongs to the national patrimony, and in most countries there is an age requirement, for example, objects of fifty or one hundred years or more. Not all "old" art belongs to the national patrimony, either, and it is generally only art that fulfills some important function that is categorized as belonging to it. Central to the definition, though, is that objects belonging to the national patrimony are of long standing and contribute in an integral way to the cultural identity and traditions of a country or region.

The national patrimony can also be categorized into two types: movable works of art (such as paintings and sculpture) and immovable art (collective sites, buildings, monuments and their attachments). While this discussion concentrates on movable art, there is a certain degree of overlap often caused by looting, pillaging, and even legal trade that involves breaking up sites and monuments and leads to a considerable blurring of the boundaries.

Another important question concerns where the national patrimony is physically located. Much of it is in public ownership in museums, public institutions, or publicly owned sites. Some is in private hands, such as galleries or homes, some is in churches, and finally some may be in sites where legal ownership is unclear. A critical issue in relation to this type of art that arises in the art market is stealing and looting, especially where access is "open" and protection is difficult to enforce. Many international agreements address this issue, but it is a problem that has existed for thousands of years with a long history of looting of works of art by invading armies and colonizers. The issue remains topical today, especially in relation to the large number of claims arising from activities during the period around the Second World War. It is estimated that the Nazis stole an estimated 220,000 pieces of art from both museums and private collections throughout Europe, worth $2.5 billion in 1945 prices, or over $30 billion today.[4] (Some of the issues that collectors face in relation to these claims are discussed in Chapter 12.) An even larger number of works also have dubious provenance in relation to the war and have come under investigation regarding ownership and rightful claims. Artistic treasures in Iraq are now also suffering the perils of war, with many works being looted from national museums and showing up on international black markets for art and others simply being destroyed amidst bombing and other violence throughout the region.

Much of the national patrimony worldwide tends already to be in state ownership or public museums. This ownership is apt to derive more from historical accident than from any economic rationale. A large number of the national treasures in Europe, for example, came from what were once the private collections of wealthy royal families, and many of these works of art had de facto been paid for by public money. Also in the United States, much of what is in state collections came from donations by private individuals, aided by tax expenditures by the state. As it is extremely rare for any of these museum works to come on to the open market for sale, they are not directly relevant to investors in the art market.[5]

Art and National Identity

The exact nature and extent of the external benefits derived from the national patrimony is a question open to some interpretation, and a wide variety have been identified, with more substance to some claims than to others. One of the arguments used most frequently in relation to the protection of the national art heritage relates to national identity and the extent to which artistic heritage can define the elements of national life which characterize a country and distinguish its attitudes, institutions, behavior, and way of life from those of other countries. This argument goes that just as the physical well-being of people and lands needs to be cherished and protected, so does their cultural identity, and the protection of the cultural well-being or "cultural capital" of a country creates benefits for all of its citizens, which need to be paid for collectively and usually owned by the state.

Some analysts have questioned the link between art and national identity. One argument is that art is, by nature, international in character and it in fact helps to eliminate parochialism if it is allowed to circulate freely and internationally.[6] Others have argued that in an increasingly multicultural society such as the United States, freely trading art can act as a means by which immigrant populations and ethnic groups can maintain contact with culture of their mother country, or even that an emphasis on national identity and a common cultural heritage could lead to the exclusion of these "foreigners" from the national cultural debate, as well as to a resistance to change over time. Another pro-trade case is that foreign buyers may appreciate a work of art long before it is given any recognition at home, which often acts as an external stimulus in the revaluation of a nation's own art and culture.[7]

Finally, there is a more general question of whether the very notion of national identity is still valid in the twenty-first century, with immigration resulting in an increasingly multicultural society. The United States is one of the biggest melting pots in the world, so much so that the notion of finding a universal American identity is both impossible and divisive (with the result that there is also much less emphasis on this argument for cultural support in the United States than would be the case in most European countries).

Despite these views, the national identity argument is used pervasively, particularly in relation to restricting the export of art, and holds tremendous appeal for most people, even in the United States. There are, of course, a large number of other activities besides art that generate national identity, and directing funds toward ownership and retention of national art treasures has an opportunity cost in taking away funds from other potentially worthwhile causes. However, it is generally accepted that art has an important function in the social cohesion, continuity, and identity of a nation, and hence is worth devoting public funds to its support, the extent of which is the outcome of political choice.

While the notion of national identity as a valid argument for restricting the art trade in major art markets such as the United States is open to debate, there is more universal agreement of its validity in certain less-well-off nations. Removing art and antiquities from a culture in which it is embedded may deprive these smaller communities of enjoying its benefits and threaten their sense of identity, alienate them from traditional sources of authority, and even weaken their institutional frameworks. The loss of traditional art, such as happened to the Mayan community, often occurs insidiously and gradually over many years, or in extreme cases, such as during wartime or colonial exploitation, there may be sudden and excessive movement.[8] This type of movement of art in the market has the potential to destroy important records of history or even civilizations, as seen in excessive depletion of the Mayan sites. This can be through actual physical damage or simply the lack of context for interpretation of the history and culture recorded in these works of art.

Besides national identity, there are a number of other nonprivate benefits from the national patrimony.

❑ *International recognition and national prestige.* Art can act as a means for a nation to gain international status and recognition. Although it could be argued that, for example, the national football team may provide more recognition to a wider international audience, in many cases art holds a special place in defining the origin, identity, or spirit of a nation, plus it could possibly not sustain itself commercially without some form of subsidy (at levels that generate national prestige).

❏ *Economic spillover benefits.* Related to international prestige is the fact that a country's historical artistic patrimony may act as an important magnet for tourists, for example, the Louvre in Paris. Tourists spend money and help create employment, so protecting the national patrimony produces additional benefits in the ancillary business it generates in the economy.[9]

❏ *Option demand for future and present generations.* This argument is that there is a benefit for present generations involved in knowing that, regardless of whether they are interested in art or not, future generations will be able to enjoy and consume historic cultural assets. In other words, they are prepared to pay in taxes for preserving these assets even though they may derive no benefit themselves from their existence.

Another option-demand argument is that people derive benefit from knowing that the cultural facility exists, thereby allowing them the option at some future date of attending it themselves, either on their own or with visitors. However, people may want an art treasure to exist, even though they never wish to see it, for several reasons, therefore option-demand value is simply a small subset of the existence-value argument, with national identity again forming a much more important part.

Because of these arguments, particularly the strongest case of national identity, most national treasures will be in public museums and the issue of their sale or the restrictions of it will not even be up for discussion. If these works do leave the country, it is often only via a lending scheme or other exchange with another country on the basis of reciprocity. The Dutch economist Arjo Klamer (1996) summarizes the arguments in relation to the national patrimony in considering the hypothetical case of the Chinese wishing to buy Rembrandt's *Night Watch* from the Rijksmuseum in Amsterdam:

> Because of the identification of the Dutch with the painting, it cannot be sold. Time is involved as well as bonding. Some "products" need time; people have invested in them, and once they begin to bear fruit—in the form of feelings of love, pride, awe even—giving them up is inconceivable; selling our friendship would be a betrayal of all we stand for. Another factor is uncertainty. We can never be sure of the value of those special products. How much is

your child worth to you? How much do you want for your wedding ring? Is a *Night Watch* worth $100 million or $1 billion? If we have to exchange what is precious to us, we may prefer to do so in a deal involving some form of reciprocity. So we might lend out the *Night Watch*—but only if the Chinese were to return the favor somehow, royally, at a later date. That way we may discover value in the deal itself, that is, in the quality of the reciprocal exchange.[10]

This quotation captures a number of things pertinent to the discussion. First, there is the point that all goods are not the same, and certain things quite literally do not have a price for most people. The example of one's child is a good case in point, and certain works of art also belonging to this group for some people. Second, it is clear that many of the important things to a person in their daily life are not bought in the marketplace but are received through reciprocal exchange between family, work colleagues, and friends. And third, the point about ascertaining the value, or price, at which one would be willing to sell, takes considerable time for some objects, especially, say, family heirlooms or national historical artifacts. It also raises the concept that over time the utility derived from some objects can change, because of "bonding." This relates back to the idea of national identity, with a feeling of identity generated by art objects resulting from such a bonding process.[11]

With these points established, what is relevant then in considering restrictions on trade or investment in works of art is the case where the work may start off in private or public hands but the question of selling it to pay for other worthy projects such as hospitals arises. If the work is in private hands, then whether or not it is sold and at what price is basically up to the individual. It may be that a nation has identified with this work, but it does not belong to the nation, and the only way it can be obtained is by the government or an individual investor paying the full market price (and it would run contrary to the principle of private property and individual freedom to suggest otherwise). The issue here, then, is how the nation is to obtain the object in question, with finance being the major factor. However, other devices are used that can facilitate sales to the state or make it undesirable or impossible for private investors to purchase or ultimately resell the work, especially overseas, should they buy it. The bulk of the policies that do exist in relation to the national patrimony relate to how objects held in private hands can be prevented from export, and this is a critical dimension of the potential return on an investment in particular works of art. The main devices used by governments to keep objects within national boundaries include export restrictions and preemptive rights, import regulations, and certain tax breaks.

Export Restrictions and Preemptive Rights

The most common form of regulation in art markets, in place in over 150 countries with the notable exception of the United States, is restrictions on exports of art objects belonging to the national patrimony. Legislation in this area concerns limiting, controlling, or prohibiting the export of works of art through subjecting them to approval or notification systems prior to export. Most countries try to limit the number of items subject to restrictions by criteria of age or value (or both) to ensure they are practical to enforce, but there is a wide variation in the degree of controls between nations, with regulations applied in very different intensities.[12] There are five main methods of export regulation.

1. *Embargo or prohibition.* The prohibition on export may refer either to an entire class of items, such as all antiquities, or some precisely defined list of works. The effect of embargo is to eliminate all legal trade in listed items and, as such, is often applied only to a limited number of works of art, and often with some exceptions.[13] Prohibition can only be useful for countries with strict border controls and low international trade, as export bans raise the value of art on illegal markets, encouraging smuggling and illicit export.

2. *Export quotas.* This system sets export quotas by reference to the volume of imports but is not used in any of the larger global art markets.

3. *Export licensing.* This is the most flexible and widely used instrument for export control, with a variety of systems in place ranging from genuine screening devices to effective embargo in that licenses are rarely granted (in other words, an "administratively enforced embargo"). Liberal systems are in place in countries such as the United Kingdom, which maintains high age and value criteria. Strict systems are found in countries such as Italy and Greece, in which any item deemed of a rather subjective interest by the state requires license authorization.[14]

4. *Preemptive rights.* These are rights associated with export licensing and give public museums or other institutions the first right to purchase the work of art to be exported at either a competitive market price or one set or agreed on through negotiation. License application is initially needed to defer export and allows time for potential domestic purchasers to mobilize the necessary funds.[15]

5. *Export taxes.* Some states also impose taxes once an export license is granted to act as a further disincentive to export. There are no export taxes in the United States and they are not permitted internally in the European Union, although some countries apply them to sales to extra-EU countries. Taxes are based on the value of the object to be exported and vary in size and application—for example, a flat rate of 5 percent in France and a sliding scale in Spain from 5 percent to 30 percent, depending on the value.

The United States has one of the most liberal systems, with no legislation barring or limiting the export of art, except very specific laws protecting Native American sacred sites. This lack of restrictions could be due both to the predominance of a free market ideology in the U.S. economic system, plus the fact that those involved are and always have been predominantly buyers rather than sellers of art. The United Kingdom, the second largest international art market, also has one of the most liberal national export systems in Europe, particularly in comparison to Italy and some of the other Mediterranean countries. All EU countries, including the United Kingdom, are however subject to European law governing trade between the member states, which may in some cases be more restrictive than national legislation. Whatever the system in place, the more restrictive the export control and the more conditions attached to it, the harder a work of art will be to sell overseas, and this places a limit on the potential buyers and ultimately on the value of the investment.

Import Regulations

For a system of control on the loss of national patrimony to function properly, import regulations are a necessary corollary to export restrictions, which implies that states have to rely on the cooperation of other nations—the ultimate consumers of exported art. Import regulations in other cultural goods often relate to protective measures, but in the case of fine and decorative art, they are in place to try to reduce illicit trade by making those who provide a potential market agree not to purchase works they believe are stolen or in breach of some export regulation. Generally this implies that all imports must be accompanied by some form of pedigree such as proof of origin, ownership, or legal export.

The United States is the most significant importing state as well as one of the largest markets for stolen and illegally exported art. Its policy on imports is as liberal as that on exports, with no restrictions on imports, apart from some pre-Colombian sculptures and murals. In January 2009, in their last week in office, the Bush administration signed an initial agreement to embargo a wide range of Chinese art and antiquities from the Paleolithic period through the Tang period ending in A.D. 907 plus all monumental sculpture and wall art that is at least 250 years old. The aim of the agreement was to deter looting of ancient sites and the illicit trade in stolen artifacts. Many in the art trade however (including Chinese art dealers and museum professional in the U.S.) believe that it will not achieve this because of its broad and inclusive nature, and will end up harming legitimate collectors. (The legality of the embargo is in question and is expected to be challenged in the high courts once it is applied.)

The United Kingdom, another important collecting and exporting nation, imposes relatively liberal controls on imports[16] and in some cases does not recognize and enforce the export controls of other states, claiming it would work against their status as a major international market. These and other wealthy art markets such as Japan are all major importers and, to maximize the range of acquisitions available, generally are against import controls. While they can be forced to deal legally with issues of stolen property, illegal export (and subsequent import) does not often in itself constitute an offense.

Other states have a variety of measures in place which range from "blank check controls," which effectively bar the import of all art whose export has not been legally authorized,[17] to more selective controls or import limitations, such as restraining imports in stolen works of art (stolen from their state of origin and therefore not declared as part of their exports), illegally exported objects (exported in violation of the state-of-origin laws), or objects from clandestinely excavated sites.

In the case of stolen art, most states, including the United States, provide remedies in the form of judicial action, giving the owner rights to sue for recovery in the courts of the importing nation, provided they can furnish sufficient proof of ownership and theft. For illegally exported objects, it is not as clear-cut, as the complaining party for this case is the state whose export laws have been violated, rather than the original owner seeking return. As a general rule, exporting states will have no standing in the importing state to recover the stolen object or sue for its value and must seek remedy directly against those who violated its laws. Illegal export in itself does not constitute theft in the United States, therefore it is not a violation to import an item of art or anything else into the United States just because it has been illegally exported from another state.[18]

To prevent the trade in stolen or illegally exported artworks, many museums and other institutional purchasers will also voluntarily decline purchases, with many having some form of "ethical acquisition" policy. Most large museums have explicit policy statements regarding acquisitions, which generally include that works will not be accepted into collections if illegal export is suspected or until some valid title can be proven.[19]

Although not all museums enforce such policies (and there is no way to control the acquisitions of private and individual collectors), media attention concerning acquisition controversies and substantial public interest especially from potential donors has exerted considerable pressure on large institutions to refrain from dealing in unlawfully traded material. There is also now substantial international agreement in imposing import controls if the art is stolen or looted or if its illicit export is damaging an important category of art or a nation's legitimate national patrimony. However, without a multilateral system operating, illegal flows of art will tend to continue in the direction of the countries with the least controls.

For most states there are works of art that form a special part of a nation's cultural and historical legacy. Many in even the most pro-trade markets such as the United States would argue that such objects should remain within the geographic boundaries of the state or region concerned, and many would go further to argue that they should be purchased and maintained by the state. The effect on the value of the works and the fact that they may be maintained and conserved somewhere abroad appears often to be neglected in this debate, which tends to focus on which objects to include and how much governments (that is, indirectly a nation's population) should pay to obtain them.

Any restrictions on works of art such as export licenses can significantly affect the value of an investment by reducing the possibility of selling the work or being constrained to do so on the domestic market at a potentially lower price. It is a moot point whether this is an acceptable constraint on private ownership or sales. Some people see works of historical art as belonging outside the normal range of trade and investment, no matter who owns them. Another debatable argument that is put forward is that many works of art at that level are probably owned by wealthy people, who may have made their wealth in that country, and therefore "should" make an appropriate return to the nation by either retaining historical art objects within the country or by donating them to the state, with or without state assistance.

However perhaps the most rational case is that such philanthropic gestures should be voluntary and not enforced through some state regulation or action. A very easy next step, if you followed the previous argument, could be enforced "appropriation" of all art objects held by wealthy individuals without any compensation whatsoever. For those who believe that the existence of private property and its protection under the law is a *sine qua non* of an economically strong and civilized society, this would be unacceptable.

The U.S. Government and the Art Market

Rena Neville

The U.S. government has great power to affect the world's largest art market. However, in this center of the art trade, there is no single point of contact on the myriad of issues affecting this broad and complicated market, which ranges from Contemporary art to early twentieth-century decorative art to antiquities and ethnographic art. There is a similarly broad array of members of this market, from individual collectors (many of whom prefer confidentiality for security and privacy reasons) to major public institutions, such as museums and auction houses. Recognizing the economic and public importance of the U.S. art trade, the formation of a united national trade association bears consideration, given that there is currently no centralized trade association or government agency in the United States to address the complex, unique issues facing the art market.

The United States is exceptional in that it is among the minority of countries that do not have a Ministry or Department of Culture that establishes and monitors cultural property policy. This issue has been debated in the past. In the absence of a federal agency establishing policy in this area, the Pew Charitable Trusts announced in 1999 that it would devote close to $50 million dollars over the next five years to the study of cultural policy in the United States.[20]

The idea of establishing a Cabinet-level post or secretary of the arts also gained momentum with the election of President Barack Obama in 2008.[21] However, the discussion around the scope of responsibility of such a post focused primarily around coordinating arts education and support for the arts, as opposed to any discussion of creating a legal basis for government interference with privately owned works of art.

The United States also differs from European nations in that there is dramatically less legislation articulating the government's right to "national patrimony" or "national heritage." The rare, well-established concept of "national trust" and "national heritage" in the United States relates to preserving America's heritage in historic properties and buildings but not to cultural property or works of art.[22]

Historically, the U.S. government has been reluctant to regulate the private ownership, sale, or transfer domestically or internationally of cultural property. Thus, the federal legislation that does exist in the United States affecting the art market tends to be narrowly drafted and focused on isolated issues and often in relation to some form of federal government involvement. For example, there is legislation regulating antiquities and archaeological property discovered on federal or Native American lands or property owned or controlled by museums or institutions receiving federal funding.

Further, examples include the Antiquities Act of 1906, which authorizes the imposition of penalties and possibly imprisonment for any person destroying or damaging historic ruins on public lands or excavating or destroying ruins, monuments, or antiquities on lands owned or controlled by the federal government. The National Environmental Policy Act of 1969 states that in assessing federal projects, the government must consider cultural and environmental values, and the government must use "all practicable means and measures ... [to] preserve important historic, cultural, and natural aspects of the national heritage." Others include the Archaeological Resources and

Protection Act of 1979 (which supplements the Antiquities Act of 1906 and protects archaeological resources on public or Indian land from sale, purchase, transport, exchange, or receipt, absent permission); the Abandoned Shipwreck Act of 1987 (which essentially vests title to abandoned shipwrecks found in state-owned waters to the federal government, which subsequently transfers such title to the states); the Native American Graves Protection and Repatriation Act of 1991 (which requires museums receiving federal funds and federal agencies to prepare inventories of Native American human remains and associated funerary objects to be provided to the tribal governments and traditional religious leaders if an affiliation is established with a Native American tribe). However, these laws do not generally extend to interference with objects legally purchased with private funds found on privately owned property. Moreover, there is no standardized definition in federal law for works of art or cultural property.[23]

There are much stricter and broader areas of regulation in other major, historic art-market nations such as the United Kingdom and France. These areas include the regulation of ownership, import, and export of national treasures. This regulation often takes the form of prohibitions against the sale or export of works of art even if privately owned or found on one's own land. There are also special taxes imposed at the time of sale, import, or export. In contrast, the United States has historically had no or very little taxation on the import and export of works of art, and there is no separate sales tax scheme uniquely for works of art.[24]

A notable difference from the United Kingdom in particular, is that the U.S. art market does not have a dominant national trade or lobbying association that represents the various participants in the commercial art market. The participants range in size and purpose from individual collectors, art advisers, and artists to much larger dealers, museums, and auction houses. The trade associations that exist tend to interact with individual government agencies or representatives. There are numerous art-related associations in the United States, which represent the specialized interests of their members but which have no regular or formalized national method of communication. Prominent examples include the National Antique & Art Dealers Association of America (NAADAA), whose members are antique dealers, and the Art Dealers Association of America (ADAA), whose members sell fine arts.[25]

There are also issue-specific artists groups, such as the Artists Rights Society, which focuses on licensing and copyright monitoring for visual artists. Museums have their own separate organizations, such as the Association of Art Museum Directors, which acts as a representative and advocate for the member institutions. There is no national art auctioneers trade association, nor is there a well-established national collectors trade association.

It is striking that in the world's largest and most diverse international art market nation, there is no single point of government contact and no national association representing the diverse interests of the commercial sector. It may be that these differences account in part for the flexibility and strength of the market. However, these omissions also result in uncoordinated and sporadic communications between the government and the trade without the benefit of holistically considering the impact of the individual interactions on the overall market. The discussion that follows examines some examples of the possible combined effects of the lack of a Department of the Arts and a national art market trade association exchanging ideas with respect to cultural property policy.

Key Federal Laws Affecting the Art Market

Endangered Species

The United States is a signatory to the Convention on International Trade in Endangered Species of Wild Fauna and Flora (CITES), which has also been implemented in the European Union.[26] The United States is also subject to the stricter restrictions enacted under its Endangered Species Act of 1973 (ESA).[27] The ESA restricts or prohibits the movement of endangered or otherwise protected plants or animals and related items such as feathers, corals, ivories, tortoiseshell, walrus, seal, and certain types of woods.

The ESA unnecessarily adversely affects U.S. collectors and the domestic art market in restricting trade in certain items. Although there is an exception in the ESA for "antiques" which are defined as articles that are at least one hundred years old, it is inconsistent with other nations' application of CITES. For example, the European Union has a similar exception, but it is for worked specimens taken from the wild and significantly altered prior to June 1947. Many items from the first half of the last century contain currently rare or endangered items such as tortoiseshell, ivory, or rosewood in such items as Art Deco watches, furniture, and jewelry. The inability of the U.S. art market to import or sell such items places it at a disadvantage to the European market.

Precluding the sale, import, or export of these items also seems to offer no benefit to animals and plants currently in need of protection from extinction, as such animals and plants were killed over fifty years ago. Rather, the strict regulations of ESA deter and inhibit the trade in many important and valuable items created more than twenty years before the act's implementation. The wildlife lobby in the United States is sophisticated, well funded, and well organized and makes any efforts to alter the existing legislation, however reasonable, extremely difficult to achieve. Moreover, as the ESA does not affect all aspects of the art market and there is no perceived benefit to the unaffected aspects of the commercial market to lobby to change such a discrepancy, the imbalance will likely continue. Arguably, it is the combination of the lack of a federal department of the arts and the lack of a national trade association that results in harming unnecessarily one aspect of an important national market without truly benefiting or protecting endangered plants and animals.

Import Regulations

Excluding specialized import restrictions regarding endangered species, there are few federal laws specifically regulating the import into the United States of cultural property. One other exception is in relation to restrictions on trade connected to political embargoes: certain types of works of art may not be imported (or sold or owned by U.S. citizens or by foreign subsidiaries or affiliates of U.S. companies, depending on which country is at issue) as a consequence of various trade embargoes with countries such as Iraq, Iran, and Cuba. The laws restricting trade with these countries are all dealt with in their own specific legislation and are exceptions to the broad historic U.S. policy in favor of free imports into the United States of cultural property and of the legitimate goal of furthering the exchange of cultural property.[28]

However, U.S. Customs and Border Protection (Customs) has broad criminal authority to seize and forfeit property, including cultural property, that illegally enters the United States. A general statement of the relevant applicable laws is set forth in a 2006 Customs statement that provides guidance to the trade regarding cultural property.[29]

When Customs was drafting its statement, there was a clear lack of ongoing formal dialogue between Customs and any national trade association, which arguably weakened the trade's ability to inform Customs of the full potential impact of the interpretation and application of its statutory powers.

Specifically, the forfeiture provision of the U.S. Code title 19, section 1595 (Custom Duties) grants to Customs a broad authority to obtain warrants to search for and seize property *otherwise* subject to forfeiture. Section 1595 requires the application of another provision of law, whether criminal or civil. Although there are numerous possibilities for Customs to exercise its forfeiture powers under section 1595,[30] the two most frequently used sections applied in instances of seizure of cultural property are sections 542 and 545 of title 18, the Crimes and Criminal Procedure Act. Section 542 is directed primarily at errors or omissions in declarations made in the entry process. Section 545 includes imports made generally "contrary to law," which often includes an allegation of a violation of the National Stolen Property Act.

National Stolen Property Act

One of the more frequent claims made by foreign governments is that an item of cultural property is stolen and should therefore be seized by Customs after importation into the United States. This results in an application of the National Stolen Property Act (NSPA) to imported cultural property. The act provides that

> Whosoever transports, transmits, or transfers in interstate or foreign commerce any goods, wares, merchandise ... of the value of $5,000 or more, knowing the same to have been stolen, converted or taken by fraud ... shall be fined under this title or imprisoned not more than ten years or both.[31]

There is no debate that the NSPA applies to domestically stolen cultural property (in the traditional meaning in the United States of the word "stolen" meaning to take without right or permission). Nor is there any debate that the NSPA applies to property stolen (in the traditional sense of the word) within the borders of a foreign nation and subsequently imported into the United States.[32] However, there is a question about the appropriate scope of the NSPA when dealing with stolen cultural property.[33] American courts have interpreted the NSPA to apply to cases in which property was never physically possessed by a foreign institution, museum, or nation. Rather, property has been deemed by a foreign nation to be owned by it simply by operation of foreign local law, such as a finder's law or export control law. There is a question as to whether it is appropriate to use the NSPA in the context of cultural property claims based in essence on foreign export-control laws.[34]

Customs acknowledges that there is an open question of whether the NSPA should be extended to apply to all foreign government cultural property claims. In its previous 1991 Directive on Cultural Property, Customs explains that as of 1991, U.S. courts have "only determined that [one country's] laws claiming ownership of cultural artifacts are sufficient for a successful criminal prosecution." The directive notes that U.S. courts have accepted claims by Mexico, while the cultural property claims of ownership by "Peru, Guatemala and Ecuador [are] more open to challenge."[35] Courts have refused to enforce the cultural property laws of Peru, Croatia, and Hungary for a variety of reasons in connection with cultural property claims.[36] In its more recent 2006 statement, Customs again acknowledges that "A violation of a foreign export control law is not in and of itself grounds for [Customs] action."[37] Customs further explains that "To qualify for protection as cultural property, an imported item *must* generally fall under one of the Acts listed below." The two federal laws then discussed are the Pre-Columbian Monumental and Architectural Sculpture and Murals Statute and the Cultural Property Implementation Act.[38]

The lack of a national art market association that can address the federal government in a consistent, coordinated, and organized fashion on issues of the proper application of the NSPA to cultural property means that U.S. judges are by default creating national policy in this problematic and important area of the law. The United States has an unusual history and framework within which to consider these issues. Historically, private citizens own objects found on privately owned land and are free to transfer or export such items regardless of their national importance.

Recently, for example, a version of the Magna Carta was offered at public auction and in the 1990s, a Declaration of Independence and the skeleton of a *Tyrannosaurus rex* were freely offered for sale. The T. rex is of particular interest in that it is an example of an important item, found in the ground on private property, for which the government had no power to restrict the sale or export. There was no legal means to interfere with the private property rights of the owners. All three items have remained in the United States. The Magna Carta and the T. rex are both on public view, at the National Archives in Washington, D.C., and Chicago's Field Museum of Natural History, respectively. Similarly, the Declaration of Independence was purchased by an American private collector and remained in the United States. Had these items been purchased and exported, it might have served the United States well. The documents have huge importance to democracy and history, and the T. rex to North American prehistory. A foreign country would make a perfectly good home, and the existence of these important items abroad might engender greater understanding of U.S. history and encourage tourism.

Thus, although there is an interest in promoting international diplomacy by accommodating foreign government requests, these interests must be balanced with domestic history and concerns. As the art market has not united on these issues across all categories, it is de facto allowing U.S. judges to create domestic cultural property policy in a patchwork of decisions. This is happening in isolated circumstances, without the courts or the market perhaps completely appreciating the cumulative impact of each decision. Fully respecting that other nations sometimes preempt citizen's private property rights, such decisions fly in the face of U.S. legal traditions and inch the nation toward a system in which it is compelled to ignore private ownership of cultural property.

The slippery slope here leads to some peculiar and extreme implications. Consider an individual who is denied rights of ownership based on his or her sexual preference, gender, religious beliefs, or ethnic background. Assume that title to such property has by operation of foreign law transferred to the foreign nation. What if that individual then properly declares the property when entering the United States and the country of origin requests assistance in recovering the property as stolen? It would be an odd situation for the United States to seize previously privately owned property that by operation of foreign law wholly inconsistent with its own had transferred to a foreign government.

Convention on Cultural Property Implementation Act (CCPIA)

One of the principle notable exceptions to the lack of import controls for cultural property in the United States is the Convention on Cultural Property Implementation Act (CCPIA.) The CCPIA implements the UNESCO Convention of 1970 on the Means of Prohibiting and Preventing the Illicit Import, Export and Ownership of Cultural Property.[39] One of the most noticeable features of the 1970 UNESCO convention is that it creates an international legal scheme that grants recovery rights for both smuggled and stolen property.

Although the United States ratified the convention in 1972, it was not self-executing. For over ten years, there was debate about how to strike an appropriate balance between the legitimate interest in preventing the import into the United States of stolen and recently smuggled works of art while endeavoring to protect the import into the United States of cultural property that is legitimately owned. The implementing legislation is narrower than the convention and did not take effect until 1983.

The CCPIA makes it illegal to import property stolen from a museum or religious or secular public monument. In addition, provided specifically identified cultural material is in "jeopardy of pillage" and that either "less drastic remedies are not available" or the pillage is of "crisis proportions," the United States may restrict imports by (a) entering into bilateral or multilateral agreements with other state parties or (b) imposing emergency import restrictions. Currently twelve countries have some form of import restriction in place, namely, Bolivia, Cambodia, the People's Republic of China, Colombia, Cyprus, El Salvador, Guatemala, Honduras, Italy, Mali, Nicaragua, and Peru.

Before making a determination either to enter an international agreement or to impose emergency restrictions, there must be a request for such relief from a signatory to the UNESCO treaty, a "state party." To lawfully import property from any of the countries for which special import restrictions are in place, one must establish either that (a) the property at issue is accompanied by a valid export certificate from the country of origin or (b) the property existed outside of the country of origin as of the effective date of the U.S. import restrictions. Pursuant to section 2604 of the CCPIA, the secretary of the treasury (or delegate) must produce a list of the protected archaeological or ethnological property that is "sufficiently specific and precise to insure: (1) the import restrictions under section 2606 are applied only to the archaeological and ethnological material covered by the agreement or emergency actions; and (2) fair notice is given to importers and other persons as to what material is subject to such restrictions."

To assist in determining whether to grant requested import restrictions, the president may consider the views of the Cultural Property Advisory Committee, established pursuant to the CCPIA.[40] The committee consists of eleven members appointed by the president, representing museums; the fields of archaeology, anthropology, ethnology, or related areas; specialists in the international sale of archaeological, ethnological, and other cultural property; and the interests of the general public. The committee reviews requests made by the state party and submits its recommendations to the president's delegate. According to the CCPIA, the committee must make recommendations to the president or his delegate within 150 days of receipt of information regarding a bilateral agreement or within ninety days of receipt of information regarding a request for emergency restrictions. In reality, the president's delegate has yet to make any decisions or determinations absent receiving a recommendation of the committee, even if such recommendations were well outside of the statutory deadline. The president's delegate has consistently followed the committee's recommendations. Although the committee has no statutory decision-making authority, it appears that it has de facto authority to implement the CCPIA.

Although individually affected members of the U.S. art market are free to submit comment and information to the committee, its deliberations and decision-making criteria are not made public. The committee in effect holds quite broad authority, which is troublesome given the lack of transparency and accountability. If there were a department of the arts to facilitate consideration of these requests, there would be no need to convene a special committee of appointees who have varying degrees of experience with what appears in reality to be full power to implement these requests. Moreover, there would be an ongoing dialogue about the appropriate scope and impact of the restrictions on the domestic market, rather than sporadic and isolated communications about each individual request.

The United States is the largest art market in the world. Yet, the relationship between the U.S. government and the art market is sporadic, poorly defined, and uncoordinated. The lack of a national art and antiques trade association to represent its interests to the various government agencies touching the art market no doubt weakens the trade's position. Moreover, it is one of the few countries in the world that does not have a central policy-making body of government whose primary function is to consider and address issues of cultural property. Both factors contribute to instances of imbalance with the international art market as well as a degree of needless uncertainty for the trade.

Government and Art Market Relations: A British Perspective
Anthony Browne

The diversity of the art and antiques market makes it subject to a wide range of legislation and international conventions, from measures specifically related to the art trade to those that appear on first examination not to have any connection with it. The corpus of legislation that applies in some form to art sales increases each year. It is therefore now more necessary than ever for the market to engage with governments in a formal and consistent way than may have been the case in the past.

In recognition of this, the British Art Market Federation (BAMF) was brought into being in 1996, marking the beginning of a new concerted approach toward relations between the art market and government at both British and European levels. Until then, contact between the British art market and successive governments had been sporadic, depending on the legislation that was under discussion at the time. There was no single organization communicating a coherent message on behalf of the market as a whole, leading to confusion and misunderstanding on both sides. For this reason, the British government suggested that channels of communication would be improved by having a single body to represent the entire art trade, both dealers and auction houses.

The proposal acknowledged the importance that the British government attached to fostering its art market and of the need to ensure that the market was not unintentionally damaged by new legislation both from within the United Kingdom and from the European Union.

BAMF therefore became the body through which the government could consult the views of the art market as a whole and could communicate its own policy.

Britain's membership in the European Union makes it subject to legislation designed to harmonize taxation and other matters within Europe as a whole. EU "directives" can, and do, have a profound impact on the British art market, particularly as the United Kingdom accounts for over half of the European Union's art market.

By emphasizing the economic and employment benefits generated by a successful art market, as well as the cultural contribution that it makes, BAMF has been successful in building political support. Research commissioned shortly after BAMF's founding revealed the extent of those benefits: in addition to providing employment for 40,000 people, it contributed invisible earnings from overseas visitors of over £2.8 billion ($4.6 billion) and tax revenues of £469 million (around $770 million). Since then the British art market has grown further, and more recent research has underlined the continuing contribution it makes to the British economy.[41] Successive British governments have recognized that this active sector deserves support, and they have been careful to avoid unnecessary legislation that might undermine its position in the highly competitive global art market.

European Union Directives

When governments are addressing new legislative initiatives, vigilance is necessary, particularly when the formulation of policy is in its early stages. Often a measure that appears to have no relationship with the art market can have unexpected consequences for a specialized sector. A recent example of this was an EU directive aimed at reducing the polluting effect of mercury on the environment. In its original form, this directive would have prevented the import of early barometers and scientific instruments containing mercury. Few would disagree with the public health benefits of reducing the amounts of mercury in circulation, but equally, most would recognize the historical and cultural benefits of preserving these old instruments. By arguing that they represent a special case, BAMF, with the support of the British government, successfully secured an amendment to the directive, exempting barometers and measuring instruments that are more than fifty years old.

Environmental and conservation considerations also have impact on works of art that incorporate materials such as ivory and tortoise-shell, protected under the CITES,[42] and here similar exemptions have been negotiated to protect the market for culturally important artifacts. Even the European Union's initiative to reduce energy consumption by encouraging the use of low-energy light bulbs has had unexpected consequences for dealers who sell early lamps and chandeliers, which may be unsuited to the shape and size of low-energy bulbs—another example of the surprising range of issues that have to be considered.

Even legislation intended to address street crime can affect the art and antiques market. The British government's initiative to restrict the sale of knives could have outlawed the market in historic and culturally important weapons, such as Japanese swords. After legislators were alerted to the significance of these artifacts, they introduced exemptions to protect this small but important sector of the market.

Taxation

A more clear-cut subject for concern has been fiscal legislation. Taxation can have a major influence on the location of art markets, either through sales taxes or indirectly through the way in which buyers and sellers of art are themselves taxed. Art is mobile and the fiscal environment in one country compared with another can easily lead to a migration of the market. A striking example of this was provided by the French art market, which had been Europe's dominant market in the early part of the twentieth century but which ceded this position to the United Kingdom as a result of tax increases introduced in the 1950s.

Sales taxes have a direct impact on the market, and as a result, value-added tax (VAT) has long been a concern to the U.K. art trade, since it not only applies to art sales themselves but also to imports of art for sale on the British market on behalf of vendors from outside the European Union. VAT is a tax on sales that is levied on the value added by each transaction. To avoid double taxation on final consumption, exports (consumed abroad) are usually not subject to VAT, or there is a system whereby VAT can be refunded at export.

Works of art pose a special problem compared with other goods to which VAT applies in that they are mainly sold in secondary markets and they are usually traded between former and future consumers (e.g., private collectors, investors, dealers, or museums) rather than between producers and final consumers. To take this into account, in the Seventh VAT Directive, the European Union introduced special rules concerning the taxation of secondhand goods, objects of art and antiquity, and collections. It established the system of taxing the profit margin made by taxable dealers (rather than the full price), or the difference between the selling price charged by the dealer for the good and the purchase price. This avoids double taxation and ensures that VAT is levied only on the real value added. The scheme is only available to taxable dealers, and the rate of VAT charged is generally the standard rate applicable in the European Union (currently between 15 percent and 25 percent).

A controversial provision incorporated in the Seventh VAT Directive was the introduction of common rules on the import of works of art from third countries. With the aim of harmonizing the conditions of trade within the European art market, the directive imposed a minimum effective rate of 5 percent VAT on the import of works of art from outside the European Union.

This was a particularly detrimental move for the United Kingdom, which, prior to the directive, did not apply any import VAT for artworks entering the United Kingdom from outside the European Union.[43] It was feared that the introduction of import VAT would threaten the U.K. trading position, particularly vis-à-vis the competing extra-EU markets of Switzerland and the United States. In recognition of this, a special case was made for the United Kingdom, which was given a derogation (an exemption from the full terms of the directive) until June 1999 to apply a super-reduced rate to imports of works of art of 2.5 percent. However, the directive did not interfere with the tax-exempt status of temporary imports to the European Union, but increased the period in which they become due for reexport from six months to two years.

The gestation of the Europe-wide legislation on import VAT was long and complex, but it resulted in a regime that recognizes the difference between art and other consumer goods, and although bureaucratic, it has so far enabled the British art market to continue to attract business from non-European collectors. This outcome did not come about by accident: it resulted from many years of discussion between the British government, the European Commission, and the art market.

Intellectual Property

Intellectual property legislation is another area of regulation that affects the market in a number of ways. Copyright protection interacts with the need to reproduce a work of art in a catalogue for the purposes of selling it. As a result of representations by the art market, an exemption from copyright was secured in both British domestic legislation and in the EU Directive on Copyright to permit the reproduction of a work of art for the purposes of sale. Without this, the art market would have faced added complications and costs when selling works subject to copyright.

But the longest-running dispute concerning intellectual property has revolved around the EU directive, agreed in 2000, to introduce the artist's resale right (or *droit de suite*)—a levy on art resales aimed at benefiting artists and their heirs—throughout Europe.[44]

The European Commission had first published its draft directive in 1996, proposing new legislation in order to remove what was a perceived as being a trade distortion within the internal EU art market, caused by the absence of the levy in some member states together with the varying ways in which it was administered in others. This situation was considered to have prejudiced the proper functioning of the EU art market and therefore needed to be remedied.

It was therefore argued that *droit de suite* had either to be applied uniformly throughout the European Union or abolished in all member states. The commission decided to pursue the former option, since eleven of the fifteen member states at the time either applied the levy or had the legislation in place to do so. Since *droit de suite* existed in few countries outside the European Union, the directive was also seen as a means of encouraging other countries also to introduce it. This could be achieved by means of an amendment to the Berne Convention on Copyright.

Agreement was reached in 2001 (although the British government voted against the final text), and on January 1, 2006, EU Directive 2001/84EC on resale rights for the benefit of the author of an original work was introduced throughout the European Union. The directive imposed a uniform system of resale royalties in all EU member states. It introduced the right for the first time in some EU countries (the United Kingdom, Ireland, Austria, and the Netherlands) and obliged others to change their existing arrangements in order to conform with the terms of the harmonized arrangements that the directive imposed.

The directive allows for the introduction of a levy for the benefit of living artists and their heirs for up to seventy years following their death, based on a sliding scale starting at 4 percent for works of art over 3,000 euros to 0.25 percent on works worth over 500,000 euros or up to a maximum limit of royalties payable of 12,500 euros. The ceiling on the royalty means that there is no additional levy when the sale price exceeds around 2 million euros. It is applicable to all professional resales but does not apply to resales between individuals acting in their private capacity, without the participation of an art market professional, or to private resales to museums that are not for profit and are open to the public. The deadline for the implementation of the directive throughout member states was January 1, 2006, but those member states that had not applied *droit de suite* before were allowed a derogation limiting the levy to the work of living artists only. This derogation ends January 1, 2012.

The directive committed the European Commission to negotiate an international agreement on the resale right. But no progress has been made so far; therefore, the directive has merely replaced an internal trade distortion within the EU art market with a distortion between the European Union and its international competitors.

The British government, which opposed the directive from the outset, argued that a levy on sales in the United Kingdom that did not apply in the United States or other competing markets outside the European Union would endanger the competitiveness of the British art market in the valuable global market for Contemporary and twentieth-century art. BAMF has been at the forefront in arguing that only a global agreement, or the repeal of the directive, can ensure that European art markets are not at a disadvantage to their competitors elsewhere. Emotions run high on both sides of the debate and there is a sharp disagreement between the organizations set up to collect and distribute the levy, on the one hand, and the art market, on the other. However, it remains clear that if other countries adopt the resale right, then the existing differential in transaction charges would be eliminated. If not, the European art market as a whole will continue to suffer from administrative costs and additional charges that are absent elsewhere.

Cultural Heritage Protection

Although taxation has tended to dominate discussions between the art market and governments, another enduring theme has been the debate concerning the relationship between the art market and cultural heritage protection. This involves balancing the needs of a free market art with the state's perceived responsibility to protect what it considers to be its national cultural patrimony. This affects both British and EU legislation.

The creation in 1992 of a Europe-wide system of export licensing with a parallel provision for the return of objects that had been illegally exported from one member state to another revealed a gulf between the free market traditions of many northern European countries and the more protectionist traditions of those bordering the Mediterranean. It was a tribute to the negotiators that they found a way to make the export licensing system feasible by applying value thresholds to different categories of works of art. The objectives of the art market were to have a system that is clearly understood, workable in practice, and fairly administered and that recognized a fair balance between the property rights of the individual and the interests of the state. It is the last consideration that can create the sharpest division of opinion.

Recently, a matter generating considerable controversy has been the market for antiquities. Some archaeologists have blamed the looting of sites on the high prices paid for antiquities in the open market. This has led to demands in some quarters that the licit market for these objects should cease altogether, even though the works of art of the ancient world have been bought and sold throughout their history.

The extent of the black market for the works of art of the ancient world and its effect on the legitimate market became the main focus of this debate. In order to address this, the British government brought together a group of archaeologists, academics, museum directors, and representatives of the art market to examine evidence of the size and extent of the illicit market and to suggest ways of countering it. In spite of the variety of views and interests represented, the Illicit Trade Advisory Panel was able to produce a unanimous report, proposing a number of actions designed to eliminate the illicit trade in antiquities in the United Kingdom. The British government accepted the panel's recommendations and has since acted on most of them, including accession to the UNESCO Convention and the enactment of a new law designed to target those dealing in illicitly removed artifacts.

Only by explaining the practical problems confronted by those operating in the legitimate market is it possible to arrive at solutions that work in practice. The United Kingdom's Dealing in Cultural Objects (Offences) Act (2003), which grew out of one of the panel's recommendations, was supported by BAMF because it successfully reconciled the need to introduce a law that targeted criminal activity without, at the same time, enveloping the legitimate market in unnecessary red tape.

Other issues that have concerned BAMF since its formation have included money-laundering legislation, consumer protection law, the hallmarking of silver, the protection of cultural property at times of military occupation, and other regulatory matters relating to the art and antiques market. Underlying all of these topics is the need for a proper dialogue between legislators and the art market, so that each has a clear understanding of the other's concerns. In this, BAMF has been guided by the principle that it is always better to be at the table than on the menu.

Chapter Notes

1. In economics, public goods are goods within the economy that are nonrival and nonexclusive in consumption. What this means is that, once produced, one person's consumption of the good does not interfere or detract from anyone else's, and it is generally not possible to exclude anyone from consumption.

2. In economics, an externality is a cost or benefit from an economic transaction that third parties who are external to the transaction are forced to bear. It can be either positive (external benefit) or negative (when an extra cost is imposed, e.g., pollution). The externality occurs when the direct participants do not bear all the costs or reap all the gains from a decision or action, and it causes extra costs or benefits to third parties. In a competitive market, the result can be that too much or too little of the good may be produced and consumed from the point of view of society.

3. This is dealt with in more detail in C. McAndrew, *The Art Economy* (Dublin: Liffey Press, 2007); and C. McAndrew and J. O'Hagan, "Restricting Trade in the National Artistic Patrimony: Economic Rationale and Policy Instruments," *International Journal of Cultural Property* vol. 10, no1 (2001): 32–54, on which much of the discussion in this section is based.

4. From M. Bazyler, "Litigating the Holocaust," *University of Richmond Law Review* vol. 33 (May 1999).

5. One question of interest is why the state should purchase works that come on to the open market or restrict their sale outside a particular country. The main economic rationale for state ownership of works of art is that they have positive

externalities: national-patrimony works create not just a benefit for those who view the objects (for which they can be charged) but also a benefit that accrues to those who do not. This nonprivate benefit cannot be charged individually to people but has to be paid for and, for objects owned by the state, funded out of general taxation. These works can also have public-good characteristics, another form of market failure. Both of these features are, in principle, strong arguments for public ownership and are based on economic reasoning rather than on some rhetorical special pleading in the case of art. They purport that there are objects the very existence of which creates a benefit—be it psychic, material, or whatever else—for most of the population. Despite benefiting from it, it would be virtually impossible to charge people according to their individual gains, and therefore they have to be paid for by the state using a device such as compulsory taxation.

6. The internationally renowned legal academic and expert on art and cultural property law John H. Merryman once noted, "If parochialism is a sickness, a free trade in artistic and cultural treasures is part of the cure."

7. See L. Prott and P. O'Keefe, *Law and the Cultural Heritage*, vol. 3, *Movement* (London: Butterworths, 1989).

8. Prott and O'Keefe (1989) also point out the problem, especially with tribal and traditional communities, that through buying and reselling certain artworks, Western collectors transform objects that may have been intended for religious worship or even some functional use into materialistic consumer goods.

9. There are dangers in this argument. For example, it could be claimed that good golfing facilities are a key factor in attracting entrepreneurs to an area, with consequential benefits for museums. As such, it could be argued that government should subsidize the golf clubs rather than museums. However, most would probably agree that the Louvre, for example, creates benefits for ancillary businesses in Paris and that the direction of causation is not the other way, so there are in fact economic spillover effects that, while not the key rationale, are important to an overall assessment of public ownership of, and increased expenditure on, specific national cultural works of art.

10. From A. Klamer, "Economic Aspects of Cultural Exchange" in *Trading Culture: GATT, European Cultural Policies, and the Transatlantic Market*, ed. V. Hemel et al. (Amsterdam: Boekman Foundation, 1996), 46.

11. The concept of bonding is related to the wider so-called "endowment effect" and relates to the phenomenon that people often demand much more to give up an object than they would be willing to pay to acquire it. The reason is that in the case of artworks, the nature of the service derived from the good changes with possession: there is not only the pleasure of looking at the painting but the psychic benefits associated with past consumption of the painting. These psychic benefits do not exist at the point of purchase but build up over time, implying that what you would therefore be prepared to sell the painting for would be considerably higher than what you originally paid for it (even adjusting fully for inflation and other factors).

12. A useful source of information on export (and other) regulations relating to cultural heritage in a number of countries worldwide is provided via the UNESCO Cultural Heritage Law Database. This database was launched by UNESCO in 2003 to offer all stakeholders involved (collectors, governments, customs officials, art dealers, organizations, lawyers, buyers, and so forth) a complete and easily accessible source of information on national legislation available online in the event of a legal question about the origin of an object (which may have been stolen, pillaged, or illegally exported, imported, or acquired). The database is accessible at www.unesco.org/culture/natlaws.

13. For example, China until recently prohibited the export of all works of art except for the purpose of exhibition subject to the issuance of a special license. Because of the boom in demand for its works of art, the law evolved and now states that only antiques or any items over one hundred years old require a license (and are generally banned from export if they are considered to be of national importance). For a full discussion on trade laws in emerging markets see C. McAndrew, *Globalization and the Art Market* (Helvoirt: TEFAF, 2009).

14. The Italian system is in one of the strictest in the European Union. Any piece of art within Italy can be served with a listing notice by the Ministry for Cultural Heritage and Activities, which means that it cannot be exported without the permission of the state, which is never granted, and owners must inform the authorities every time they wish to move the object within Italy or if they are about to undertake any form of restoration or maintenance. If the state feels that it is in the public interest, it may also expropriate or assume guardianship of endangered objects of significant interest.

15. National systems vary as to whether the price offered by the exporter has to be matched or a new price be negotiated or settled by the courts. Some states, such as Italy and Greece, retain the right to withhold the license even when the delay period is due and no offer is forthcoming (which is simply equivalent to export prohibition). Others, such as France, retain this right but offer compensation to the owner. In states such as the United Kingdom and Canada, however, export licenses must be granted if the state or domestic institution does not exercise its rights of acquisition within the legislated time frame.

16. The United Kingdom does adhere to import controls under the Convention on International Trade in Endangered Species of Wild Fauna and Flora (CITES), which means that when importing certain objects, (particularly antiques) into the United Kingdom, you need to have both a CITES export permit to cover the departure from the source country and a separate CITES import permit for the arrival in the United Kingdom. This convention is discussed in the next sections.

17. This system was proposed in the original draft of the UNESCO Convention. The United States rejected and defeated this draft stating that it could not adopt a rule banning imports simply because their export was in violation of another state's law. The UNESCO Convention refers to the 1970 United Nations Educational, Scientific and Cultural Organization (UNESCO) Convention on the Means of Prohibiting and Preventing the Illicit Import, Export and Transfer of Ownership of Cultural Property. The purpose of the convention is the prevention of illicit import, export, and transfer of ownership of cultural property. It enables members to recover stolen art and

antiquities that surface in the countries of the nearly one hundred fellow signatories. The United States and the United Kingdom have accepted the Convention but have not fully ratified it.

18. A problem that arises in legal cases is the difficulty in distinguishing between stolen and illegally exported goods. For example, in the case of *United States v. McClain (1977)*, in which Mexican artifacts were being looted from sites and illegally exported to the United States, emphasized the necessity of establishing ownership. Many of the pieces involved were not known or registered with the Mexican government, and so the court ruled that while it was illegal to deal in stolen goods, theft could not be established unless there was a bona fide declaration of ownership.

19. International organizations such as the International Council of Museums (ICOM, with 26,000 members in 151 countries) have been instrumental in developing ethical acquisition codes and policies that they expect their members to comply with.

20. See, J. Dobrzynski, "Heavyweight Foundation Throws Itself Behind Idea of a Cultural Policy," *New York Times*, August 2, 1999, noting that the United States unlike most other countries, does not have a formal government body establishing a national cultural property policy.

21. See http://www.petitiononline.com/esnyc/petition.html and as of January 24th, there were 193,718 signatories to the petition. See also J. Trescott, "Quincy Jones Leads Chorus Urging a Cabinet-Level Arts Czar," *Washington Post*, January 14, 2009.

22. For information regarding the history and purpose of the National Trust for Historic Preservation, see http://www.preservationnation.org/about-us/history.html. See also Executive Order 13287, Preserve America, March 3, 2003 (establishing federal policy and leadership in part to preserve historic properties owned by the federal government).

23. See, e.g., P. Bator, "An Essay on the International Trade in Art," *Stanford Law Review* vol. 34 (1982): 275–284. Bator notes that "art historians, archaeologists and anthropologists differ on what should be called a 'work of art' and what should be called an 'artifact.'" See also J. H. Merryman, "Two Ways of Thinking About Cultural Property," *American Journal of International Law* vol. 80 (October 1986): 831–833.

24. See, e.g., *Underwood Tariff Act of 1913*, §§ 652–655, Public Law 63-16, *U.S. Statutes at Large* 38 (1913): 114, exempting works of art from import duties.

25. However, both the NAADAA and the ADAA are members of an international dealers' association, the Confédération Internationale du Négociants en Oeuvres d'Art (CINOA).

26. CITES was signed in Washington, D.C., on March 3, 1973, and amended in Bonn on June 22, 1979. See European Council Regulation 338/97 and Commission Regulation 939/97, which set out the rules for the import, export, sale, and movement of CITES species; see also the commission's environment Web site, http://ec.europa.eu/environment/cites/home_en.htm.

27. In addition to the ESA, the United States has additional laws affecting the movement and sale of endangered species such as the Migratory Bird Treaty Act (protecting most birds and bird parts, including feathers, from sale, ownership, or transfer within the United States); Bald Eagle Protection Act; Marine Mammal Protection Act; and Lacey Act (restricting imports of certain mammals, birds, fish, amphibians, and reptiles).

28. See J. Merryman, "Two Ways of Thinking About Cultural Property," *American Journal of International Law* vol. 80, no. 4 (1986): 851–852. Merryman notes the historic U.S. policy of free movement of works of art in terms of the lack of import duties on most works of art and limited export restrictions and points out that there have been few import control restrictions implemented since 1970 in the form of the treaties or laws. The U.S. import restrictions that have been imposed over the last thirty years are limited in scope and generally address specific regional concerns or temporary assistance in response to current situations of pillage or looting.

29. "What Every Member of the Trade Community Should Know About: Works of Art, Collector's Pieces, Antiques, and Other Cultural Property, U.S. Customs and Border Protection, U.S. Department of Homeland Security, May 2006, see http://www.cbp.gov.

30. The fact that most works of art may enter the United States duty free is not in any way a defense to underdeclaring or misclassifying an imported item. Although not a loss of revenue to the government, nonrevenue loss violations may nevertheless be prosecuted because the incorrect data skews the trade statistics on which the government relies in international trade negotiations. An example is discussed in Jack Licensing, "Customs Takes Importer to Court for Allegedly Overvaluing Goods," *Journal of Commerce*, http://www.joc.com (reporting on a trial in which an importer was prosecuted for overvaluing goods and the government argued that the overvaluation "skewed trade statistics which the government uses to establish foreign policy").

31. See U.S. Code 18, § 2314.

32. See, e.g., the case of *United States v. Hollinshead* (1974), in which it was stated that there was "overwhelming evidence that the defendants knew that it was contrary to Guatemalan law to remove the stele, and that the stele was stolen."

33. The courts have in other contexts refused to extend the concept of "stolen" in the NSPA beyond its common understanding. See *United States v. Carman* (1978) where in the context of an NSPA prosecution in the area of interstate transfer of money knowing such funds were taken by fraud, the Court followed *McClain*, quoting that section 2314 "should not be expanded at the government's will beyond the connotation depriving an owner of its rights in property conventionally called to mind"; and *United States v. Rogers* (1986), where the Court refused to expand the definition of "stolen" to include the defendant's taking his own property which had not yet been declared forfeited.

34. See, e.g., *United States v. McClain* (1979) and *United States v. An Antique Platter of Gold, known as a Gold Phiale Mesomphalos* (1999).

35. See 1991 U.S. Customs Directive titled "Detention and Seizure of Cultural Property," p. 11.

36. See *Republic of Croatia v. Trustee of the Marquess of Northampton 1987 Settlement* (1994). Croatia and Hungary failed to satisfy their burden of proof supporting their respective claims of title to a collection of ancient Roman silver. The original plaintiff, the Republic of Lebanon, withdrew its claim shortly before the trial. Also *Government of Peru v. Johnson* (1989). The Government of Peru was unable to establish its claim for recovery of eighty-nine artifacts it alleged had originated in Peru.

37. "What Every Member of the Trade Community Should Know About: Works of Art, Collector's Pieces, Antiques, and Other Cultural Property, U.S. Customs and Border Protection, U.S. Department of Homeland Security, May 2006; see http:// www.cbp.gov.

38. Ibid.

39. There were also several treaties entered in the early 1970s between the United States and individual Central American countries regarding recovery of stolen, as opposed to illegally exported, archaeological and historical cultural properties. Examples include the Agreement between the U.S. of America and the Republic of Peru for the Recovery and Return of Stolen Archaeological, Historical and Cultural Properties, 1981; Agreement for Recovery and Return of Stolen Archaeological, Historical and Cultural Properties, United States–Guatemala, 1984; and Agreement for Recovery and Return of Stolen and Archaeological, Historical and Cultural Properties, United States–Ecuador, 1983; and Treaty of Co-operation between the United States of America and the United Mexican States Providing for the Recovery and Return of Stolen Archaeological, Historical and Cultural Properties, 1970 (or the "U. S. / Mexican Co-operation Treaty"). Although available as remedies, in some cases for more than twenty-five years, these treaties are rarely invoked to recover property. The American Society of International Law on International Movement of National Art Treasures (also involved in recommending an international response to the problem of the illicit art market in the form of the UNESCO Treaty) recommended to the State Department that there was a need for legislation to restrict the import of illegally exported pre-Columbian monumental and architectural sculpture and murals.

40. From 1986 to 1999, the president delegated his authority to enter into such agreements to the director of the U.S. Information Agency. In 1999, the U.S. Information Agency was merged into the Department of State, and such authority was assumed by the latter

41. A recent survey carried out for The European Fine Art Foundation (TEFAF), found that in 2006, the British art market had accounted for total sales of 11,595 million euros, through 8,900 businesses employing 48,500. See C. McAndrew, *The International Art Market, A Survey of Europe in a Global Context* (Helvoirt: TEFAF 2008).

42. CITES is an international agreement between governments that aims to ensure that international trade in specimens of wild animals and plants does not threaten their survival. It was drafted as a result of a resolution adopted in 1963 at a meeting of members of the International Union for Conservation of Nature (IUCN), and it entered into force on July 1, 1975. Countries adhere to CITES

voluntarily, and current signatories number 175. Although it is legally binding on those that sign, it does not take the place of national laws, and each country must adopt its own domestic legislation to ensure that CITES is implemented at the national level.

43. The British art market was, and is, heavily dependent on cross-border trade. The United Kingdom has a high level of imports, particularly from outside the European Union, underpinning its status as an entrepôt market for the international art trade. In 2006, art to the value of £2.4 billion (around $4.4 billion) was imported into the United Kingdom from outside the European Union.

44. France was the first to introduce droit de suite in 1920. It was intended to enable the heirs of artists killed in the First World War to benefit from a percentage of the value of the deceased artist's work when it was resold. Although droit de suite was taken up by some other European countries, it was not introduced widely elsewhere. The Berne Convention for the Protection of Literary and Artistic Works (Paris revision 1971), Article 14 leaves it to the decision of individual signatories as to whether or not they implement the right.

8

Insurance and the Art Market

*Christiane Fischer and Jill Arnold,
AXA Art Insurance Corporation*

EDITOR'S NOTE: There are a number of risks associated with ownership and investment in art, some of which do not exist for other financial asset classes. Because art is a tangible, material asset, there are risks related to the actual physicality of the asset, such as breakage and accidental damage. Some of the risks related to wear and tear over time can be reduced through proper care of a collection; however, others are sometimes beyond the direct control of a collector. A work of art that is lost through damage or theft, for example, can arguably never be replaced because of the unique nature of this asset class. However, the financial value of the investment can at least be protected to some degree with adequate insurance.

Insurance is a critical part of any art investment, and an industry has developed to specifically address the needs of collectors, investors, and the art trade. It is now possible to insure against many of the risks associated with art investment and purchases (and to pay for maintenance, repairs, and restoration). All of these activities accrue extra costs that are not relevant to investment in most financial assets, therefore an understanding of their impact and the financial indemnity available is critical for art owners.

This chapter chronicles the development of the market for art insurance and its current practices and discusses issues related to regulation and reinsurance in the art market.

The Origins of Art Insurance

In 1990, two men broke into the Isabella Stewart Gardner Museum in Boston and stole a dozen uninsured valuable paintings by artists such as

Johannes Vermeer, Rembrandt Harmenszoon van Rijn, Édouard Manet, and Edgar Degas. The FBI estimated that while in the museum from the hours of 1:24 a.m. to 2:45 a.m. on March 18, the thieves (dressed as policemen) seized the works with a value of over $300 million. This famous heist stands as one of the world's largest unsolved art thefts. To this day, the small museum has not been able to collect insurance, since it carried no insurance policy at the time of the heist. While replacement of the stolen masterpieces is impossible without recovery, the proceeds from the insurance settlement could have facilitated the purchase of pieces of a similar time and period.[1]

Insurance in its simplest form is a transfer system, formalized by a legal contract addressing the duties and responsibilities of two parties. It exists as a transfer system by which one party (the insured) transfers the financial risk or uncertainty of loss to another party (the insurance company). By transferring the risk to an insurance company, the insured is exchanging a policy premium for the promise of payment, formalized through an insurance contract, or policy, at the time of loss. Insurance as a business is designed to take in more premiums through the payment of policies than it pays out through claims. The insurance industry in the United States provides over 2.3 million jobs and, in 2007, had a combined worldwide market share of $4.1 trillion that included property, casualty, and life insurance premiums.[2]

Measuring and controlling risk is a relatively modern concept, but since the beginning of recorded history, gambling, which is the very essence of risk taking, has been a popular pastime.[3] The concept of insurance is now an integral part of the modern financial economy. The Great Fire of London, which destroyed over 13,000 homes in 1666, was the trigger for the insurance industry as we know it today. In the aftermath of this disaster, Nicholas Barbon, an English economist and financial speculator, started a business that offered insurance for buildings, and in 1680, he established England's first fire insurance company, the Fire Office, offering insurance for brick and frame homes.

Towards the end of the seventeenth century, London's growing importance as a center for shipping trade increased the demand for marine insurance. In the late 1680s, Edward Lloyd opened a coffee house that became a popular haunt for ship owners, merchants, and ships' captains, and thereby a reliable source for the latest shipping news.

It also became the meeting place for parties wishing to insure cargoes and ships, and those willing to underwrite such ventures. Insurance as a business is credited as originating at Lloyd's coffee shop, where captains of industry recognized that by joining forces they could pool risks and be safeguarded from financial catastrophes. Today, Lloyd's of London remains the leading market for marine and other specialist types of insurance. It is not a company, but a market with multiple financial backers, which can be individuals or corporations, that come together to pool and spread risk.

Although art was sometimes covered under early contents insurance, it was not until the 1960s that specialist art insurance companies began to develop. The roots of what is today known as AXA Art Insurance Corporation trace back to the mid-nineteenth century, when the company was founded in Berlin as a fire insurance company called Nordstern Versicherungs AG (Nordstern Insurance Company). In the early 1960s, some of the high-level executives of Nordstern, all of them collectors in their own right, decided that wealthy private individuals needed a specialty product for their art, antiques, antiquities, and other valuable collectibles. The key issue is that art needs to be insured separately from ordinary contents, as only those things that can be replaced with reasonable ease can be insured with ordinary replacement-value insurance. Given its unique and original nature, art presented a new challenge in that it could not be easily replaced. These executives took what was originally designed as an "inland marine floater" (a policy that was designed to insure exposures that include property and merchandise while in transit or "floating," including valuable papers and documents as well as mobile equipment and other supplies), and expanded the product to cover objects of art.

Nordstern started its fine art insurance business (which is historically the aggregate term for insuring all categories of collective activity, from painting, drawing, sculpture, ceramics, photography, jewelry, and silver to any perceivable category of collecting, including wine, Civil War swords, dolls, and baseball cards) in Germany and France, later expanding to Western Europe, Eastern Europe, the United States, Canada, and most recently Asia and the Middle East. Since the mid-nineties, the company has been part of the global AXA Group and has subsequently changed its name to AXA Art Insurance Corporation. It is the only insurance company solely dedicated to providing products and services to the art world and provides fine art and collectibles coverage for individual and corporate collectors plus professional services to the art trade, including coverage for exhibitions, dealers, and museums.

Besides the major global providers, there are now hundreds of smaller specialist insurance companies and agents that offer specialized fine art insurance, and many other larger general insurance companies that have added fine art to their portfolio of services. Insurance products are generally sold through three different venues: direct contact with clients (mostly through the Internet), agents (which are part of a company-owned distribution network), or third-party independent brokers (who represent the buyer of the insurance product and are compensated by a commission paid by the insurance company). The majority of the high-end personal insurance market that is most relevant to art collectors and the art trade, however, is serviced by independent insurance brokers. A qualified broker will have access to many important insurance markets and thus be able to provide the client with a variety of competitive quotes. The art and valuable objects insurance market has developed into an industry of many players and consequently is a very competitive arena.

Financial Monitoring of Insurance Companies

From a valuation perspective, insurance companies are evaluated and monitored based on the size of assets under management and financial strength. This monitoring correlates to the insurance companies' ability to pay obligations to their policyholders. Founded in 1899, A.M. Best Company evaluates insurance companies from A++, the most preferred rating of superior, to S, where the rating has been suspended. *Table 8.1* below illustrates the rating modifiers and affiliation codes.

The company also assigns a letter rating (A++ through D) to assess the financial size category (FSC) of an insurance company. The FSC is designed to provide an assessment based on the size of a company in terms of its policyholders' surplus and related accounts. These range from 1, for adjusted policyholders' surplus, to 15 to surplus of 2,000 or greater. Since the credit crunch and global financial crisis of 2007–2008, many art insurance buyers have become increasingly cognizant of the financial strength of insurance carriers and its correlation to their ability to pay a claim. Wary buyers only want to consider

TABLE 8.1 Insurance Company Ratings

Secure	Vulnerable
A++, A+ (Superior)—Assigned to companies that have a superior ability to meet their ongoing insurance obligations.	B, B– (Fair)—Assigned to companies that have a fair ability to meet their ongoing insurance obligations. Financial strength is vulnerable to adverse changes in underwriting and economic conditions.
A, A– (Excellent)—Assigned to companies that have an excellent ability to meet their ongoing insurance obligations.	C++, C+ (Marginal)—Assigned to companies that have a marginal ability to meet their ongoing insurance obligations. Financial strength is vulnerable to adverse changes in underwriting and economic conditions.
B++, B+ (Good)—Assigned to companies that have a fair ability to meet their ongoing insurance obligations.	C, C– (Weak)—Assigned to companies that have a weak ability to meet their ongoing insurance obligations. Financial strength is vulnerable to adverse changes in underwriting and economic conditions.
	D (Poor)—Assigned to companies that have a weak ability to meet their ongoing insurance obligations. Financial strength is extremely vulnerable to adverse changes in underwriting and economic conditions.
	E (Under regulatory supervision)—Assigned to companies (and possibly their subsidiaries/affiliates) placed under a significant form of regulatory supervision, control, or restraint—including cease and desist orders, conservatorship, or rehabilitation but not liquidation—that prevents conduct of normal, ongoing insurance operations.
	F (In liquidation)—Assigned to companies placed in liquidation by a court of law or under a voluntary agreement. Note: Companies voluntarily liquidated/dissolved generally are not insolvent.
	S (Rating suspended)—Assigned to rated companies when sudden and significant events affect their balance-sheet strength or operating performance and rating implications cannot be evaluated due to lack of timely or adequate information
	NR (Not Rated)— Not assigned a Best's rating due to a number of reasons, such as insufficient data, size, or operating experience, or due to a request from the company

Source: http://www.ambest.com/ratings/guide.asp

buying insurance coverage from a company that they believe have sufficient financial strength to provide the necessary policy limits to insure their risks.

Reinsurance

Besides building sufficient capital surplus, insurance companies buy insurance policies to protect their capital base against losses, especially losses of a catastrophic nature. This insurance is called reinsurance and is a critical element of an insurance company's risk-management activities, as it helps make the company's underwriting results more predictable by absorbing larger losses and reducing the amount of capital needed to provide coverage. Reinsurance allows the company to offer higher limits of insurance to a policyholder than its size would otherwise allow, as well as secure catastrophe protection against shock losses. It can also act as a substitute for capital as per the capital requirements of the regulator.

For example, an insurance company with a surplus of $50 million is able to write an insurance policy for $100 million by retaining a small portion, say $1 million, of the risk and transferring (ceding) the remaining $99 million to one or several reinsurers. Since insurance companies are obliged to fully indemnify the policyholder for a loss under the insurance policy, independent from the company's ability to collect from their reinsurer, companies select their reinsurers with great care and consistently monitor their financial ratings.

Art Insurance

The underlying contract for fine art insurance is an inland marine policy. Inland marine insurance was originally developed as an extension to ocean marine insurance to cover the goods for the nonocean portion of a sea journey. Inland marine insurance policies are also known as "floaters" because they indemnify against the physical loss or damage to moving or movable property. Therefore, the basic coverage of the "fine art floater" is for property at all named locations, in transit, and at any other location (AOL, which is for fixed locations that are an element of transportation, such as a warehouse).

Most fine art insurance policies are so-called all-risks policies, which means that they cover loss that is not specifically excluded, in contrast to named-peril policies, which protect against certain causes of loss that are explicitly named in the policy, such as fire or theft. In the case of the iconic painting *The Scream*, by Edvard Munch, which was stolen from the Munch Museum in Oslo in August 2004 (along with another work by the artist titled *Madonna*), the insurance policy for the collection, a named-peril policy, was designed to cover water and fire damage but not theft. Fortunately for the museum, this story ended happily enough, as the painting was later recovered, but this case highlighted gaps in the insurance of major works around the world, with a large number not covered against theft, particularly in public collections.

All risk policies exclude coverage for wear and tear, any quality in the product that causes it to damage or destroy itself, gradual deterioration, mold, or damage from insects, vermin, or rodents. Often these policies will also exclude damage sustained due to or resulting from any repair, restoration, or retouching, although some include coverage up to a certain amount (typically $10,000), provided prior approval is obtained from the insurance carrier.

From a natural-catastrophe perspective, most risk policies will exclude coverage for any earth movement, including earthquake, sinkhole collapse, mine subsidence, landslide, or earth sinking, rising or shifting, expansion or contraction, or any other shifting of earth. In addition, they will exclude coverage for volcanic eruption, explosion, lava flow, or particulate matter. There are a few carriers will provide coverage for loss due to earthquake, and the policies they provide will reflect an additional charge for this coverage.

Fine art policies exclude war, governmental action, and nuclear hazard. With regard to war, this includes undeclared war, civil war, insurrection, rebellion, revolution, warlike act by a military force or military personnel, destruction or seizure or use for a military purpose, and including any consequence of any of these. Governmental action includes the seizure or destruction of property by order of governmental authority. However, some carriers will pay for acts of destruction ordered by governmental authority and taken at the time of a fire to prevent its spread if the fire would be covered. Nuclear hazard means any nuclear reaction, radiation or radioactive contamination, all whether controlled or uncontrolled or however caused, or any consequence of any of these.

The typical fine art insurance policy is an annual contract and can incept at any given date. Exhibition policies usually cover the time period of the actual exhibition as well as the transport to and from the venue (called "nail-to-nail" or "wall-to-wall" insurance). In addition there are short-term policies that are designed to provide coverage for a single shipment of property, including temporary storage mid transit, which is called "trip-transit insurance."

Risk Management

A recent example of the kinds of physical risks art is subject to can be seen in the case of collector and casino mogul Steve Wynn, who had agreed to a reported $139 million deal in September 2006 for the sale of Pablo Picasso's painting *Le Rêve* to hedge fund manager Steve Cohen. While showing the work to friends, Wynn's elbow punctured the painting causing a two-inch tear and the cancellation of the deal. With insurance, the painting was able to be repaired and has been exhibited publicly at the Acquavella Gallery in New York in 2008, and in the *Cézanne and Beyond* show at the Philadelphia Museum of Art in 2009. Wynn sued insurer Lloyd's of London in 2007 for the $54 million he claimed to have lost as a result of the damage. However, he was reported to have commented: "This has nothing to do with money. The money means nothing to me. It's that I had this painting in my care and I've damaged it."[4]

For Wynn, and for many fine art collectors, the primary goal is to preserve the objects in their care for the good of their own enjoyment and the collective cultural legacy. However, given accidents such as this do happen, insurance exists to financially restore the value of the policyholder's collection.

Overall, there are three important steps in protecting a collection:

❏ Create a risk-management program to avoid exposure to fire, theft, and water damage in the first place.

❏ Select a qualified fine art insurance broker who can work with an insurance company that specializes in fine art coverage.

❏ Have a firm understanding of the value of the collection as well as a complete inventory by location.

Most fine art insurance policies are designed to safeguard against three basic risks: fire, theft, and water damage. In an effort to protect the items in a collection, a risk-management program will therefore include recommendations to minimize or avoid exposure to these dangers. Baseline risk-management techniques could include a centrally monitored fire and burglar alarm system to reduce the exposure to fire and theft, as well as low-temperature sensors to detect frozen pipes to reduce exposure to water damage.

Fine art insurance policies are generally not designed to cover the gradual deterioration of works of art subjected to the elements, such as light and heat, resulting in fading, chipping, or melting. There are several techniques that can be used to minimize these effects. For example, ultraviolet protective Plexiglas and window blinds are recommended to protect against sunlight damage. These and other methods for preserving works of art are discussed in more detail in Chapter 11. Insurance policies rarely cover these forms of gradual deterioration as the impact from them cannot be correlated to a distinct moment in time. In contrast, the perils of fire, theft, and water damage on an object, sudden or accidental, are fixed to a moment in time and specific event and, hence, can be insured against.

Underwriting and Loss Prevention

Underwriting fine art insurance has been historically profitable, so many carriers now compete through broad policy language and competitive rates. Fortunately, there are a variety of carriers specializing in this area, including AXA Art Insurance Corporation, AIG Private Client Group, Chubb Group of Insurance, Fireman's Fund, and St. Paul Travelers. A reputable fine art broker should provide access to these carriers and negotiate policy terms and premium.

Depending on the collection's total value, rates range from 7 cents to 20 cents per hundred dollars. In the United States, Hurricane Katrina reminded underwriters of nature's awesome power, which is why many promptly revisited the pricing of their programs in flood-, windstorm-, and earthquake-prone areas. Collectors living in these zones are therefore likely to have already encountered higher rates and more limited insurance availability.

The experience of Hurricane Katrina also provided many collectors with an appreciation for a proactive approach to collection management in emergency situations. Planning, discovery, and loss mitigation are critical aspects to protecting any collection of art, and it is crucial to have a list of resources that can be secured quickly as they rapidly become scarce in disaster situations.

The New Orleans Museum of Art was significantly threatened by the impact of Hurricane Katrina. No one was prepared to deal with the kind of catastrophe that ensued. E. John Bullard, the museum's director, commented that having endured the turmoil of a natural disaster and recovery, he could not emphasize enough the importance of a preemptive plan that allows museum professionals to take an immediate proactive approach to keeping a collection safe in the event of an emergency. In the days following Katrina when Bullard was unable to return to New Orleans, he was in constant communication with his insurance company (AXA Art Insurance Corporation), who provided an international security team to respond to reports of looting. Large generators were arranged to restore electricity to the building in an attempt to maintain and preserve the museum's collection.

For many museums, galleries, and private collectors, an essential aspect of collection management is maintaining a loss prevention plan for natural disasters such as tropical storms and hurricanes. In areas vulnerable to hurricanes or windstorms, an evacuation plan should be established that takes into consideration the movement and storage of valuable items when advance warning of a storm is available. Another alternative is to establish a watertight "safe room" in the interior of the building that can sustain wind velocity of 120 miles per hour. Storm shutters are also recommended and may be required by carriers to minimize loss. Unfortunately, there is no forecasting system for earthquakes, but most insurance carriers now require special hanging hardware that prevents objects from slipping off the wall. Bookshelves should be attached to the wall, and fragile items secured with bases or museum wax.

Given that most collectors have spent considerable time cultivating their collections, it is important for them to rely on experts to help develop an insurance program. At an initial meeting with a broker, it is important to address the specific questions about what types of fine art programs they design, what carriers they work with, how they are paid, the process for adding items to an insurance schedule, and details of what happens in the event of a claim. Fine art insurance is a relatively sophisticated sector of the insurance market that demands an understanding of the marketplace, access to specialists in the fields of appraisal and conservation, and an understanding of art storage facilities and shipping companies.

Policy and Valuation

Fine art insurance policies for collectors, dealers, and museums are written on an annual basis with renewable pricing and terms offered each year before the policy expires. Exhibition policies for museums are an exception in that they are generally designed to cover the length of the loan and pricing is reflective of the items insured and locations where the items will be exhibited.

For personal collections, it is important to remember that there is a significant difference between the protection that collectors will purchase for their home and the one used for their art. Homeowner's insurance is designed to repair or replace a damaged residence with like kind and quality material. Fine art insurance is designed to reimburse the insured for a financial loss to objects that are damaged and often difficult or impossible to replace. A client-focused art insurer will make every effort to work with the collector regarding his or her preferences when a claim occurs. Some collectors wish for claims to be resolved financially by paying for the loss or loss in value to a piece, while other collectors prefer assistance in locating and acquiring a similar piece to replace the object that was lost from the collection.

The valuation clause in a fine arts policy defines what the policy-holder will receive in the event of loss or damage. It also specifies how the company will make the payment. A broker can help identify which valuation clause is most appropriate. Depending on the nature of the collection and the extent of the supporting documentation, the collector may opt for an agreed-value policy, which offers faster claims settlement as the insurer has "agreed" to the value prior to the loss. In contrast to an agreed-value policy, blanket coverage at current market value should be reserved for a large quantity of small objects such as collectibles, multiples, silver, and figurines. Many insurance contracts contain both agreed-value and blanket-value amounts. Insurance companies typically will accept invoices or bills of sale and appraisals from reputable appraisers to establish the value of a work of art or collection. Some insurance companies also employ their own in-house art experts to monitor changes in the art market and subsequent changes to values for fine art schedules.

Another valuation option is current market value, which insurance carriers traditionally cap at 150 percent of the stated value of the policy for individual items. However, there is generally a stipulation that if there is a total loss to all objects in the collection, the policyholder will only receive an amount equal to the total value of the collection and not 150 percent of that total value. By illustration, the policyholder and the insurance carrier may agree that, in the event of a loss, an estimated current market value will be agreed on by both parties whether the value is higher or lower than the schedule value of the piece of the insurance policy. Obviously, for both parties it is necessary for this type of valuation to be monitored as the various art markets move up or down. In the current economic climate, it is recommended that values should be reevaluated every two to four years, depending on the object and collecting class.

A reputable fine art broker should also guide collectors to evaluate the exclusions section of the insurance policy. For example, some fine art policies do not offer coverage for mysterious disappearance or theft by employees. Both of these potential events are important coverages that would make a significant impact in the monetary payment of a claim or the dismissal of a claim by the insurance carrier.

In addition, the policy should also cover any appreciation in the value of the items in the collection over time. Insurance appraisals are necessary to maintain an accurate valuation and ensure an accurate settlement with the insurance carrier in the event of a claim. A collector or curator should also maintain precise inventory records, photographs, and invoices in addition to the appraisal so that the provenance and ownership of the object can easily be explained.

Policies should also cover what happens if the collector suffers a loss, such as the theft of a vase, and the insurance company pays the insured value as listed on the policy, but the item is then recovered. If the vase is recovered years later, for example, when it has greatly appreciated in value, what happens? In the event that the collector is able to reclaim title and is not barred by a statute of limitations, a problem still exists because technically the insurance company owns the vase. When the claim was submitted and paid to the collector after the theft of the vase, the collector lost his or her rights to the object. In some insurance policies, there is an option for the client to reacquire title to the vase from the insurance company for the amount paid to the collector at the time of the loss. An insurance company will sometimes require that an interest factor be added before agreeing to such a provision. This provision is essential, because the current fair market value of the vase may be many times the amount of the insurance payment that was received by the collector.

Art Fund Insurance

As discussed in Chapter 6, there are now a number of art funds functioning within the art market such as the Fine Art Fund (FAF), Art Trading Fund (ATF), and The Collectors Fund (TCF). In addition to market volatility, art funds must factor in the risk of physical damage to their artworks and also the fact that they might be sued for mismanagement, misrepresentation, or failure to adequately disclose the various risks associated with their investment offering. Most therefore select an insurance broker that understands this specialized market, as well as all aspects of their holdings such as value, location, and inventory.

For insurance companies, art funds are challenging to underwrite and insure because they constitute a very young industry, with scant benchmarking data about past claims. Also, unlike other commodities such as oil or grain, the art market lacks a centralized clearinghouse for reporting private sales data, making it especially inscrutable. Therefore, both investors and underwriters pay particular attention to an art fund's track record, relationships with experts, and abilities to raise capital and educate investors. No matter how impressive a fund's investment returns may be, its bottom line may never add up if it does not first minimize and transfer all possible risks.

Lending and Consigning Works of Art

A work of art is particularly vulnerable to damage and theft when it is being moved. Therefore, before items are placed on loan to a museum or consigned to a gallery, the collector should take the opportunity to review and minimize all possible risks. Initial considerations include the following:

❏ Is the work too fragile to be moved?

❏ Who is responsible for the packing and shipping, and are the people involved qualified and specialized enough to handle works of art?

❏ Who will be responsible for the insurance?

For example, when selling a painting on consignment through a dealer, the owner should require that the dealer insures this work from the time it leaves the owner's home until the sale is complete. To avoid miscommunication, the dealer should furnish a copy of the policy to confirm that all losses will be paid in full by its insurance policy, regardless of the size or type of loss that may occur, as well as a certificate of insurance providing such coverage to the owner.

Like a collector, an artist exhibiting and consigning works to a dealer should also make certain that the works are fully covered by the dealer's policy. The artist should also have insurance covering works of art when they are on the artist's premises.

Whether the collector's relationship with art is in pursuit of a passion or for a financial return, a significant responsibility is to care for and safeguard the items in the collection against damage and theft. Therefore any collection management program should include a risk-management and loss-prevention component to minimize the potential risks. Accidents do happen, and that is when collectors start to appreciate the value of their fine art insurance policy.

Chapter Notes

1. This most noteworthy unsolved art heist is featured in Ulrich Boser's *The Gardner Heist: The True Story of the World's Largest Unsolved Art Theft* (New York: Harper-Collins, 2009), in which he estimates the current value of the stolen works at over $600 million.

2. See http://www.iii.org/media/facts/statsbyissue/industry/.

3. An interesting history of risk taking and insurance is detailed in P. Bernstein, *Against the Gods: The Remarkable Story of Risk* (New York: Wiley, 1996).

4. Nora Ephron, "My Weekend in Vegas," *Huffington Post*, October 16, 2006, http://www.huffingtonpost.com.

9

Art and Taxation in the United States

Ralph E. Lerner, Withers

EDITOR'S NOTE: National governments have a vested interest in enhancing their cultural heritage and their international reputations by encouraging the creation, preservation, and acquisition of art. Financial policies that affect the art market can be in the form of direct funding through subsidies and grants or indirect funding through fiscal or tax incentives. Although very different in their use and application, both methods have a similar impact on the art trade, since they both result in directing funds domestic art institutions or toward individual artists.

When direct government funding takes the form of subsidies to art institutions, it helps them to continue in business or to increase acquisitions. Often, because these institutions rarely go on to sell any of the works that become part of their collections, encouraging museums to own art is virtually equivalent to discouraging exports. In Europe, for example, many museums not only are financed by the state but also are prevented by the state from "deaccessioning," or selling artworks from the museum's permanent collection. In the United States, however, deaccessioning is not illegal, so long as any terms accompanying the original donation of artwork are respected. That said, even in the United States, deaccessioning is used as a means to expand, protect, or care for collection, rather than simply to raise money in times of financial hardship.[1]

Direct subsidies to individual artists allow them to increase or at least maintain their production of art and to enhance their professional careers.

Indirect funding for art takes the form of tax incentives and is likely to encourage investment and retention of art in three ways: (1) to encourage people and organizations to make donations to museums, which, like subsidies, enable museums to buy more art and retain it domestically; (2) to encourage people or organizations to hold their own wealth in the form of art and therefore encourage investment in art; or (3) to offer tax relief in return for public access and ownership by domestic museums and art institutions (which again discourages exports).

Although nearly all countries use some form of incentives, there are marked differences in the preferred level and balance between this and more direct aid such as subsidies. This chapter focuses on tax incentives and other tax issues related to art collecting in the United States.

Art collectors and investors face a number of important tax issues related to the collection of art, the valuation of a collection for tax purposes, and the transfer of works of art from one person to another or across generations.

This chapter and Chapter 10 offer some insight into the relationships between taxation and art in the two largest global art markets, the United States and the United Kingdom. Regardless of their fiscal home, most tax incentives are generally applied to the receipt of income or transfer of works of art by sale, gift, or death. Although systems may vary regionally, most incentives are designed with similar goals and to have equivalent effects, and they have played an important part in shaping the art trade over time.

Art, by its nature, follows money. Not surprisingly, donations—of both art and money—follow tax incentives, and those cities with the most attractive tax incentives (or the fewest tax burdens) have therefore become the biggest art centers, with New York, London, Hong Kong and the emerging market of Dubai, offering good examples. Any investor in the art market must be aware of national fiscal incentives and disincentives that can affect the return on either holding or divesting art.

Maintaining an art collection in good condition is expensive. Costs include such items as framing, lighting, air and humidity controls, cleaning, restoration, security, publications, and insurance. As a collector, you may also incur travel and other buying expenses and fees whenever you add to a collection, and all these costs have increased substantially in recent years.

What determines the tax that you pay, therefore, is whether all—or, at least, some—of the expenses and losses incurred in holding art as an investment *are* tax deductible, because they are business or investment expenses, or *are not* deductible, because they are personal expenses that are simply incurred in the pursuit of a hobby for your own enjoyment. If, for example, you were to purchase ten prints as a private collector, intending to keep one and sell the others, are you an investor or a dealer? Or might you perhaps still be a collector?

Defining Your Role for Taxation Purposes

The availability of deductions will differ according to how you are classified:

❏ A *dealer* is taxed on the gain from the sale of his or her artworks at ordinary income tax rates up to a maximum of 35 percent.

❏ An *investor or collector* is taxed at long-term capital gains rates from the sale of works held for more than one year at the rate of 28 percent; *but*

❏ An *owner selling a piece of art he has held for one year or less* has his gain treated as ordinary income, up to a maximum of 35 percent.

In addition, whereas the long-term capital gains tax on the sale of securities and real estate is currently 15 percent, the Tax Relief Act of 2003 imposed a 28 percent rate on the long-term gain from the sale of "collectibles." It is this seemingly unfair high tax rate of 28 percent on long-term capital gains from the sale of collectibles that has stimulated interest in tax planning.

For tax purposes, here are the distinctions among these three roles:

1. A *dealer* is someone engaged in the trade or business of selling works of art, primarily to customers. Although the terms "trade" and "business" are not specifically defined in the Internal Revenue Code, court cases indicate that it means the pursuit or occupation to which one contributes a major or substantial part of one's time for the purpose of livelihood or profit. The courts have also stated that in order to be engaged in a trade or business, the taxpayer must be involved in the activity with "continuity and

regularity," and his primary purpose for engaging in the activity must be for income or profit. Collecting and selling art as a sporadic activity, a hobby, or a diversion does not make you a dealer, and a collector's art-investment activities do not constitute a trade or business.

2. An *investor* is someone who buys and sells works of art primarily for investment, rather than either for personal use and enjoyment or as a trade or business. The cases in the securities markets that distinguish a dealer from an investor are equally applicable to the art world. The word "primarily" means "of first importance," and the key to this is whether or not you are engaged in the investment activity with the primary objective of making a profit. This is determined by a range of factors, and objective factors carry more weight than subjective statements of intent.

3. A *collector* is someone who buys and sells works of art primarily for personal pleasure and is neither a dealer nor an investor. Ordinarily, a collector cannot deduct expenses and losses.

Establishing Your Motive for Buying Art

The statutory framework covering expense deductions is given in the Internal Revenue Code (IRC) of 1986. It says that all ordinary and necessary expenses incurred in a trade or business, as well as those incurred in the production or collection of income, may be deducted from gross income. Section 165 of the IRC also permits deduction of losses sustained in a trade or business or in a transaction entered into for profit.[2] In other words, you have to show your activities had a profit motive in order to claim expenses on them as deductions.

Deductions and losses from activities not engaged in for profit are disallowed, but certain investment-related expenses are allowed.[3] Deductions of expenses can be problematic, because the Internal Revenue Service (IRS) places an onerous burden of proof on the taxpayer, who must prove that he incurred the expenses in connection with works of art held primarily for investment and with a primary motivation of earning profit.[4] The question of a collector's intent is obviously subjective inquiry, but it generally needs to be shown with a number of objective facts and circumstances.

Under the law, no single factor determines intent, but some of the factors considered include the following:

1. *The manner in which you carry on the activity.* A "businesslike manner," with complete and accurate books and records, is probably the most important factor in indicating a profit motive.
2. *Your expertise or the expertise of your advisers.* For example, preparation for the activity by extensive study of accepted business, economic, and scientific practices, or by consultations with experts, may help you to indicate a profit motive.
3. *The time and effort you expend in carrying on the activity.* The more you spend, the more a profit motive is indicated.
4. *The expectation that artworks used in the activity may appreciate in value.*
5. *Your success in carrying on other similar or dissimilar activities for a profit.* The fact that you have engaged in similar activities in the past, and converted them from unprofitable to profitable, may indicate that you are engaged in the present activity for profit, even if the activity is presently unprofitable.
6. *Your history of income or losses with respect to the activity.*
7. *The amount of occasional profits, if any, that you have earned.*
8. *Your financial status.* The fact that you do not have substantial income or capital from other sources may indicate your need to engage in the activity for profit.
9. *Elements of personal pleasure or recreation.* According to the regulations, the greater the pleasure, the less likely your profit motive.

Insurance and Taxation

Insurance is a significant consideration for collectors, investors, artists, and dealers. As discussed in the previous chapter, an insurance policy covers the risk of losses that may result from any number of natural and unnatural causes. As with any other contract, an insurance policy needs to be examined in detail to make sure that all risks that the collector wants covered are included and that any tax implications planned for.

Given the often-high cost of insuring an art collection, one option that may be worth considering is becoming a "self-insurer." The idea behind self-insuring is that the allowable deduction for a loss from fire, theft, or other casualty may save a high-bracket taxpayer more in taxes than he would pay for insurance.

Self-insuring, however, is not always the best decision, since the allowable "casualty-loss deduction" is limited to the lower of cost or the fair market value of the damaged art, and then only to the amount in excess of 10 percent of the taxpayer's adjusted gross income.

In an insurance case, before applying the limitation, the collector must first determine the amount of the loss. Only the amount of loss that exceeds the above limitations can be claimed as a casualty loss.[5] The amount of the loss from the casualty is the lower of either

1. the fair market value of the artwork immediately before the casualty, reduced by the fair market value of the property immediately after the casualty (which is zero, in the case of a theft), or
2. the artwork's adjusted basis (or original cost). From that lower amount, the collector must first subtract $100 for each casualty, then subtract 10 percent of his adjusted gross income.

Let's suppose that, in 1995, a collector purchased a painting for $10,000. Ten years later, in 2005, when it had a market value of $50,000, it was stolen. Let's further suppose there was no insurance, and the taxpayer's adjusted gross income in the year of the theft was $100,000. The calculation for his casualty-loss deduction would be $10,000 (the lower of fair value or cost) minus $100 (required deduction per casualty) minus $10,000 (10 percent of his adjusted gross income).[6]

When making an insurance claim on art works, it is important to be aware that your recovered costs will have tax implications.

❏ *You will be considered to have made a taxable gain* if the amount of insurance proceeds you receive is greater than the original cost of the artwork stolen, unless you fall within the exceptions laid out in the regulations.

❏ *You will not be considered to have made a taxable gain from the insurance payout*[7] if the insurance proceeds were used to purchase a similar work within two years after the gain was realized.

In the above example, if the collector received a $50,000 insurance recovery on the painting, he would have realized a taxable gain of $40,000, unless he reinvested the insurance proceeds in a similar painting within the applicable time period.[8]

Sales Taxes and Use Taxes

There are a number of sales and use taxes that can apply to both art collectors and art dealers. All art dealers in the United States must register with their state sales tax department and obtain a resale certificate and number from the state in which they are doing business. With a resale number, the dealer is not required to pay a sales tax on works of art purchased in any state, since the works are being bought for resale. When a dealer sells the works, he collects the sales tax from the customer, and the sales tax is paid by the ultimate consumer, usually the investor or the collector. The sales tax is a transaction tax, liability for which occurs when the transaction takes place.

A use tax is designed to complement the sales tax, and imposes a tax on the use, within a state, of works of art that would have been subject to the sales tax if they had been purchased within the state. This means that an investor or collector who resides in one state and buys an artwork in another state for delivery in the state where he resides, will not owe a sales tax in the state in which he bought the art, but will owe use tax to the state in which he is a resident.

Some collectors attempt to avoid paying the sales or use tax by registering for a resale certificate and number, either in their own names or in the name of a corporation set up for that purpose. Doing so, however, is usually a big mistake. Consider the scenarios that could result:

❏ The art, if sold, will be considered ordinary income property that will produce income and not capital gains and, if donated to charity, will allow a tax deduction only for the cost of the artwork, not the appreciated value.

❏ The collector could face criminal charges.[9]

Although an analysis of sales tax law in every U.S. state is beyond the scope of this chapter, a review of the law as it applies in New York State can serve as a guide for dealers, investors, and collectors in all states.

The New York State sales tax on the sale of art in the state must be paid by the buyer, and collected by the seller, unless

1. the property is sold to a buyer for delivery out of the state of New York, or
2. the property is purchased by a dealer exclusively for resale.

Since the sales tax is a "destination tax," the location to which the work is delivered, or to which possession is transferred, controls both the tax rate and, ultimately, the tax burden. Because of this, the sales tax applies only to sales for which delivery takes place within New York State.

In order to avoid liability for collecting the sales tax, however, an art gallery in New York State is required to deliver the work of art physically to the purchaser out of New York State. The clearest way this can be done is for the art gallery to organize and pay for the delivery (even if the gallery seeks reimbursement from the purchaser). Another way this can be handled, and in which the gallery will not be liable for the tax, is for the purchaser to select the carrier and be invoiced directly for the costs (as long as it is the art gallery that delivers the work to the carrier).[10]

In addition, if a purchaser has an item shipped to an out-of-state location, even if he does not have a New York State tax liability, he might have a use tax liability in the state of delivery, and, under certain circumstances, if that individual later brings the item back into New York State, New York State could also impose a use tax. That said, those situations affect the purchaser, not the art gallery, unless it can be shown that the art gallery conspired in some way to assist the purchaser in avoiding the New York State sales tax.

Art Advisory Services' Tax Liability

It is worth noting that interior decorating and design services are also subject to the New York State sales tax, but an art adviser's service, of consulting with a client for the sole purpose of making a recommendation on the client's purchase of certain works of art from the perspective of investment potential, is not classified as a taxable interior decorating and design service. It is not always clear, however, where the line is drawn between art advisory services that are and are not subject to the sales tax.

When an adviser advises a private collector within New York State regarding the quality and investment potential of art acquisitions with respect to specific artists and works, the adviser is considered to be performing a consulting service and is not subject to the tax. Neither is the adviser subject to the tax when advising on the proper framing or restoration procedure of an artwork—so long as he or she does not perform or arrange for the actual framing or restoration service. If, however, the adviser supervises the installation of a piece of art in a client's home, the art adviser is considered to be performing interior decorating and design services; in that case, total charges to the client, including any charges for the above-noted consulting services, are subject to the New York sales tax.

When a work of art is purchased at Sotheby's, Christie's, or most other auction houses, the buyer pays a buyer's premium over and above the hammer price. This premium is considered part of the purchase price and is subject to sales tax.

Determining Valuation for Tax Purposes

Perhaps the most difficult problem collectors face in planning their estate is knowing what they really want. Most collectors have some degree of emotional involvement with their artworks, especially if, for example, a painting has been in the family for generations. Collectors may own items that they consider very valuable when in fact they are worthless— but the reverse may also be true. Some collectors may be secretive about what artworks they have and about the true worth of their collection. One moment, they might want their children to have the collection, and, the next moment, they might prefer to donate it to their favorite museum.

The care and maintenance of the collection may be the most important part of the collector's life, taking up a great amount of time and energy, and any encroachment on that activity, or even suggestion of less involvement with it, may appear threatening. For that reason, making a decision with respect to the transfer or eventual relinquishing of a collection may also be something that the collector would rather avoid, and is a factor that needs to be considered.

Regardless of your testamentary decisions, however, valuation of your estate is of the utmost importance—for many reasons:

❏ *For income tax purposes,* if the collection is transferred during life to a charitable donee[11]

❏ *For gift tax purposes*, if the property is transferred during life to a noncharitable donee

❏ *For estate tax purposes*, if the artwork or collection is owned at the time of the owner's death

❏ *For insurance purposes,* if the collection is maintained during life (since insurance companies require an appraisal in order to determine the premiums for coverage)

As important as the concept of valuation is, there is no simple rule or answer regarding how best to approach it, especially in respect to art. The IRS has attempted to create rules of valuation, but these are not workable in all situations and are particularly difficult to apply to unique items such as works of art.

In his treatise on federal estate and gift taxation, Randolph Paul, one of the architects of the U.S. federal income tax, wrote that value is "essentially and peculiarly a difficult question of fact, with the burden of proof falling on the taxpayer."[12] The treatise pointed out, however, that valuation is more than a question of fact; it is also a prophecy, a matter of opinion, and a judgment. In the valuation process, it is not safe to neglect any apparent factor. It is the composite of all the factors involved in a single case that should lead to a conclusion. He further pointed out that the courts have observed that market value is dependent on times, places, conditions, and people, to such an extent that what is a good rule in one case may be no rule at all under other circumstances.

The Concept of "Fair Market Value"

The IRS regulations for estate tax, gift tax, and income tax, although they are not consistent in every respect, do contain certain parallel provisions. The estate tax regulation defines "fair market value" as "the price which a willing buyer would pay to a willing seller, neither being under any compulsion to buy or to sell and both having reasonable knowledge of relevant facts." (The gift tax and income tax regulations contain identical language.) When trying to place a value on a unique collection, however, those guidelines do not offer much practical help. The hypothetical sale must be in the market in which the artwork is most commonly sold to the public, but such regulations contemplate a retail market that, in the case of art and collectibles, may not exist.

To illustrate an example of a retail market, the regulations offer the example of a used car, and state that "market value" is the market price for which the general public can buy the car, not the wholesale price for which a dealer can buy the car. When dealing with an average automobile, there is no problem, since the automobile market is fairly standardized in price and is liquid. If the automobile is a rare antique, however, such a market may not exist. Thus, the retail-market rule is an attempt by the IRS to formulate a simple rule that does not fit a complex situation.

Neither the rule that "value is the price at which an item can be sold at retail to the public" nor the rule that "value is the price that a member of the public can obtain on the sale of the item" is appropriate in every estate, gift, and income tax situation. The IRS's inappropriate and rather mechanical rules cause unfair valuations, and, in practice, there *is* no simple rule. Value cannot always be made to depend on a retail market. If a rule exists, it should be that fair market value depends on all the facts and circumstances in each case.

IRS Valuation Procedures

An appraisal of a collection for tax purposes should include the following:

1. A complete description of the object, including the size, subject matter, medium, name or names of the artist or artists, approximate date created, and interest transferred
2. The cost, date, and manner of acquisition
3. A history of the item, including proof of its authenticity
4. A photograph of a size and quality sufficient to identify the subject matter fully, preferably a 10-inch-by-12-inch–or–larger print
5. A statement of the factors on which the appraisal was based, including information about the sales of other works by the same artist or artists (particularly on or around the valuation date), quoted prices in dealers' catalogues of the works by the artist or of other comparable artists, the economic state of the art market at or around the time of valuation, a record of any exhibitions at which the particular art object was displayed, and a statement as to the standing of the artist in the profession and in the particular school, time, or period.

IRS Publication 561, *Determining the Value of Donated Property*, gives additional information on preparing appraisals and choosing an appraiser. It states that material available to assist individuals in valuing collections includes catalogues, dealers' price lists, bibliographies, textbooks, specialized hobby periodicals, and other materials that help in determining fair market value, but it also notes that "these sources are not always reliable indicators of fair market value and should be supported by other evidence."

In a discussion of "fair market value," consider a dealer who may, after a particular item has remained unsold for a long period of time, sell it for considerably less than the price shown on a price list. That example is consistent with IRS policy, which indicates that the best measure of value is an arm's-length sale in the market. Certainly, if a dealer puts an extremely high price on an object and is unable to sell it at that price, the list price of the item should not be the measure of its fair market value; the price the item is actually sold for is the fair market value the IRS will accept.

The weight given by the IRS to the appraisal depends largely on the appraiser's competence and knowledge about the work of art and the market for it. Choosing the proper appraiser is the most important consideration, and it is critical to find one who specializes in the particular genre or category of art in question. To be considered qualified, an appraiser must present himself to the public as an expert appraiser of a particular type of art or property and must be completely independent of the donor. To present a "qualified appraisal," he must prepare the appraisal document not more than sixty days before the date appraised property is to be contributed.

If a person acquires a painting from an art dealer and later donates the painting to a museum, then neither the donor, the dealer who sold the painting, the museum, any person employed by the donor or dealer or museum, nor any person related to any of the foregoing is a qualified appraiser. The regulations are so broad that they appear to disqualify an auction house from being a qualified appraiser if the donor has previously purchased the property at auction from that auction house. The regulations also retain a provision that disqualifies someone who performs appraisals exclusively for that donor, as well as anyone who might falsely overstate the value of the donated artwork. It is crucial to find someone who meets these criteria, because if the appraiser is not deemed qualified, the entire charitable deduction may be lost.

The Pension Protection Act of 2006 defines a "qualified appraiser" as an individual who has earned an appraisal designation from a recognized professional appraiser organization or has otherwise met minimum education and experience requirements set forth in regulations, who regularly performs appraisals for pay, and who meets other requirements that the IRS may prescribe in regulations or other guidance. It is now also imperative that the appraiser's credentials show that he or she is an expert for the particular item being appraised. In other words, an expert appraiser for seventeenth-century Flemish drawings will not be the correct appraiser for a work of Contemporary art.

Requirements for a Qualified Appraisal

An appraisal must be signed and dated by a qualified appraiser, and the fee charged cannot be based on a percentage of value of the object. It should contain these elements:

❏ A detailed description of the work of art and its physical condition

❏ A detailed description of the appraiser's background and qualifications

❏ The appraised fair market value and the method of valuation used to determine that value, including the specific basis for the valuation (such as any specific comparable sales transactions)

❏ A description of the fee arrangement between the donor and the appraiser[13]

The cost to the taxpayer of obtaining a qualified appraisal can be high, because of the detailed information required, and separate qualified appraisals are generally required for each artwork[14] that is not included in a group of similar works.

A twenty-two-person art-advisory panel of art experts has been appointed to help the IRS determine whether realistic appraisals of fair market value have been placed on works of art (generally for any works over $20,000). The panel, which was set up in 1968, classifies the valuation submitted by a taxpayer as either "clearly justified," "questionable," or "clearly unjustified." The panel also recommends appraisers to the IRS and reviews appraisals.[15] Following the successful format of the IRS

Art Panel and because of the recent popularity and increase in value of art prints, the IRS also established an Art Print Panel in 1980.

Determining a "Comparable Market": Rulings on Four Cases

The question of the fair market value of a collection is difficult, and the answer must rest on expert appraisals. As demonstrated by the actual cases litigated, resolving valuation disputes with the IRS can be time consuming and expensive.[16] A number of interesting cases have arisen that highlight some of the problems in valuing works of art, particularly in finding appropriate comparable markets.

1. *Anselmo v. Commissioner*: When "Fair Market Value" Is the Wholesale Price

Evidence of IRS willingness to litigate charitable-contribution schemes that have no economic reality is found in *Anselmo v. Commissioner*, which involved the valuation of gems donated to the Smithsonian Institution. In this case, the taxpayer purchased colored gemstones and donated them nine months after purchase, after the long-term capital gains holding period had been satisfied. In determining fair market value, the tax court found that it was not members of the public who generally purchased unset gems, but rather manufacturing and retail jewelers, who used them to create jewelry. The court looked to the definition of "retail market," and found that the comparable-value market for the donated gems was the wholesale market, in which the jewelry stores made their purchases, and not the public retail market (via a retail jewelry store). In effect, the tax court said there can be more than one retail market, and the market that is closest to the taxpayer's activities is the market the court looks to for comparable values.

2. *Heriberto A. Ferrari*: When the Fair Market Is the Art Gallery, Not the Auction House

The *Heriberto A. Ferrari* case involved the valuation of twenty-one pieces of pre-Columbian art donated to the Duke University Museum of Art and the Mint Museum of Art.[17] The court correctly pointed out that the comparable market was the retail sales at art galleries, not the sales at auction houses. In purchasing pre-Columbian art or antiquities, most buyers want to rely on the connoisseurship and the guarantee of authenticity of an art dealer. Unless the buyers themselves are dealers or experts, they often do not want to buy at auction, because some auction houses may not cover the purchased antiquity with a warranty of authenticity. In noting that gallery prices were the correct comparable marketplace, the court also found that different galleries price even the same or similar objects at different levels. Therefore, the court found that fair market value in this case was not a single price but a range of prices, and then not necessarily the highest price at which an object changed hands between a willing buyer and a willing seller.

3. *The Quedlinburg Treasures*: When Stolen Art Is Included in the Value of an Estate and When the "Fair Market" Is the "Discreet Retail Market"

An interesting twist to the identification of the proper market in which to value works of art was discussed in Private Letter Ruling 91-52-005. The ruling closely follows the facts in what became known in the press as the story of the Quedlinburg Treasures. In 1945, the decedent's[18] U.S. Army unit had been placed in charge of guarding some rare medieval art objects in Quedlinburg, Germany. The decedent had stolen and shipped the art objects to his home in Texas, and, when he died, in 1980, his inheritance tax return did not list any of them. No federal estate tax return had ever been filed, even though the art objects had a value of many millions of dollars, and the decedent had successfully sold a number of the stolen items during his lifetime and retained possession and enjoyment of the remaining objects until his death. The IRS ruled that, under section 2033, the stolen art property was includable in the decedent's gross estate, because the nature of ownership required for inclusion was based on his possession of the "economic equivalent of ownership," rather than upon a technical legal title.

In deciding how the property should be valued, the decedent's attorney argued that, in this case, the comparable market for valuation purposes would have to be the illicit market in which stolen art objects were regularly sold, and since there was no market for stolen medieval art objects, the value of the items must be zero. The IRS rejected that argument, referencing, in part, income tax cases in which they had placed a value on cocaine and marijuana by referring to its street-market price. The IRS further noted that the objects were of great historical, artistic, cultural, and religious significance and that there were individuals in the "discreet retail market" who were eager to purchase such otherwise unobtainable objects at premium prices. They concluded that the fair market value of the objects was "the highest price that would have been paid, at the time of the decedent's death, whether in the discreet retail market or in the legitimate art market."[19]

4. The *George O. Doherty* Case: When Experts Disagree

The *George O. Doherty* case pitted against each other the two foremost authorities on the paintings of Charles M. Russell. The taxpayer had donated a painting to the Charles M. Russell Museum, and valued the donation at $200,000. The IRS, however, claimed the painting was a forgery. Both experts were beyond question, and yet they had reached different conclusions, and so the court itself declined to rule on the authenticity of the painting. In reaching its conclusion that the painting therefore had a value of $30,000, the court recognized that a dispute over the authenticity of a painting, in and of itself, acts as a depressant on its value.

Blockage Discounts: When Excess Supply Depresses Value

A blockage discount is appropriate when an estate contains a substantial block of the same general type of property. The blockage-discount concept had its genesis in stock-valuation cases but can also be applied in valuing works of art. The concept was originally applied when the size of a block of stocks to be sold off would overtax the market, thereby depressing the selling price. In these circumstances, the courts routinely discounted the value of the securities to take that effect into account.

The concept of blockage discount is essentially one of timing. A discount may be allowed when such a large quantity of any one type of art is offered on the market at one time that it would substantially depress market valuations. The amount of discount is determined, in part, by a reasonable estimate of the time it would take to sell the entire quantity in smaller lots.

Some of the factors used to determine the availability of a blockage discount are

❏ the opportunity cost of holding the inventory,

❏ the carrying costs of the inventory, and

❏ the expected period of time it will take to dispose of the inventory.

The courts and the IRS concede a blockage discount, but no specific percentage is applicable in all cases. The amount of discount will be based on

❏ an art appraiser's opinion of the effect on the market of offering a large number of works by the same artist, at the same time,

❏ the number of such works on hand,

❏ the number of such works previously sold,

❏ the size of the potential market, and

❏ the necessity of price reductions and concessions to make sales.

Relative price also enters into the determination; the market for oil paintings selling for more than $1 million, for example, is probably smaller than the market for those selling for $10,000.

The *David Smith* Case: Sculptures from the Artist's Own Estate

Estate of David Smith is a landmark decision involving the application of a blockage discount to works of art in an artist's estate. Smith was a sculptor who died owning 425 pieces of his own work. He had sold fewer than 100 pieces during the twenty-five years before his death, and, although he had great artistic success, he had financial success only in the last few years before his death. The pieces were unusual in that most were very large: half were more than seven feet tall, and many weighed several tons and were located at his studio in New York. The executors valued the works at their highest hypothetical retail sale price (that is, the price each would bring if it were the only item offered for sale), subtracted 75 percent for a blockage discount, and subtracted 33 percent of the remainder for selling commissions that were contracted for, thus reaching a value of $714,000. The IRS proposed a final figure of $4,284,000, which was the executors' figure for the highest value at which the pieces would have sold in the retail art market on a one-at-a-time basis. The court decided that the appropriate value was $2,700,000, which was not far from the midway point between the IRS value and the executors' value, and ruled for a blockage discount in valuing the works, recognizing the impact of "simultaneous availability of an extremely large number of items of the same general category."

In the *David Smith* case, it seems logical that when each buyer in the retail art market was figuring out what he would be willing to pay, he would, at the very least, take into account the fact that 425 other items by the same artist were being offered for sale at the same time. This is particularly important in the art market, which is a supply-driven marketplace, and scarcity and rarity often drive high prices for works sold. The *Smith* case is an indication of some important considerations for valuing an artist's estate:

❑ The state of the artist's reputation at death (based on whether or not his or her reputation as an artist had fully blossomed)

❑ The market's acceptance of works of the size and character at issue

❑ The relationship of the works to all the artist's other works, including relative size and quality and the period in the artist's life when they were created

❑ Whether or not the works are part of a complete series created by the artist

❑ The number and the prices of sales during the artist's life and the prices at which sales were made during the period immediately before and after death[20]

❑ The accessibility of the works of art (such as high transportation costs or other expenses involved in getting the works of art to market)

Although the courts in the Smith case considered the above factors, the case is inconclusive, since it never discussed the weight and importance of each factor. It also stated that not every consideration had been taken in the case.

A court needs to consider the nature of the art market and how it functions—including such factors as the influence of art critics, museum shows, and gallery shows—and the possibility that the reason that the works on hand are unsold is that they are the artist's less-desirable works and, therefore, not worth as much as those sold before the artist's death. It is also important to consider the effect of the artist's death on the market value of his works. Obviously, once an artist dies, he can produce no more works, which might be considered to increase the value, but that is not necessarily the case. Often, after an artist dies, the executors must sell many of the works to raise cash for the administration of the estate, and such a sell-off can have an adverse effect on prices.

The other major issue in *Smith* dealt with the deductibility of the selling commissions from the value of the works of art. Generally, commission expenses are not a factor that affects value, but what *is* a factor is the number of years it takes to sell the property and an estimate of the net amount realized after the sales expenses have been subtracted.

Auction House Premium

At most auction houses, when art is purchased, a buyer's premium is added to the final auction bid price and paid by the buyer.[21] This premium is an additional factor that an appraiser needs to consider in the valuation process. The IRS's position is that, when an estate sells collectibles at auction, it must add the buyer's premium to the hammer price (the final auction-bid price) in order to calculate the federal estate tax value—even though the estate has no access to the buyer's premium, can never obtain it, and has no right to it.

The trend in valuation cases indicates that settlement is clearly the best course of action. Settlement is best achieved by being initially careful and thorough in selecting an appraiser and in making sure that the appraisal complies with all the requirements of the IRS regulations. What is most important is that the appraisal show comparable prices and identify the proper marketplace for valuing the donated property. Being thorough and complete at the time of a donation is most often the best course of action, because it enables the taxpayer to sustain the value of the donated property and avoid expensive litigation.

Charitable Transfers

The lifetime transfer of an art collection to a charitable organization can offer the donor income tax relief and save the expense and worry of maintaining a valuable collection. A painting that cost $1,000 some years ago may have a fair market value of $10,000 today. If you contribute the painting to a charity that meets all the requirements (discussed below), you receive an allowable charitable deduction of $10,000. For someone in the 35 percent tax bracket, that saves $3,500 in federal income taxes. Since your out-of-pocket cost was only $1,000, you have essentially made a $2,500 tax-free economic profit as well as had had the opportunity to enjoy the painting through the years of ownership.

A testamentary transfer (a transfer at death by will) of a collection to a charitable organization can also save your estate a great amount in estate taxes because of the allowable estate tax deduction. At the same time, it relieves the estate of the problem of trying to sell a potentially nonliquid asset to raise the cash necessary to pay the estate tax.

Inter Vivos (During Your Lifetime) Charitable Transfers

To claim a charitable deduction for the full fair market value of a donated collection, you must, before donating a collection to a charitable organization, have complied with specific requirements related to four areas.

1. The definition of the charity as public or private. The charitable organization must be considered a public charity. To receive a full deduction, the artworks must be contributed to a public charity, not a private foundation.

Public charities generally receive part of their support from the general public, and include churches, schools, hospitals, museums, and other publicly supported organizations, as well as private operating foundations and certain organizations operated in connection with another public organization. They also include those private foundations that distribute all their receipts each year.

Private charities, on the other hand, include all other exempt organizations and private foundations. Generally, you will receive a deduction only for the cost for a donation of works of art made to a private charity, whereas you will receive the full fair market value for a donation made to a public charity.

2. The definition of the property as capital gains or ordinary income property. The property must be long-term capital gains property, not ordinary income property. Most art collections are "capital gains property," a category that includes any property whose sale at its fair market value at the time of the contribution would result in long-term capital gains. Any appreciation in value, no matter how small, makes the work of art a capital gains property and allows it to receive the favorable tax treatment. For tax purposes, the distinction between ordinary income (including short-term capital gains) and long-term capital gains is that ordinary income is taxed as high at 35 percent, and long-term capital gains on collectibles is taxed at a maximum of 28 percent. The Jobs and Growth Tax Relief Reconciliation Act of 2003 reduced the long-term capital gains rate to 15 percent for sales of securities and other capital assets held for more than twelve months but maintained the 28 percent rate on gains from the sale of art and collectibles held for more than one year.

The characterization of donated property as either capital gains property or ordinary income property is particularly important with regard to charitable contributions. Generally, if the four requirements for making a charitable donation are satisfied, a taxpayer will receive a deduction for the full fair market value for a donation of long-term capital gains property but will be limited to his or her costs if the donation is classified as ordinary income property. Since the maximum ordinary income tax rate is currently 35 percent, there is now a smaller difference between ordinary income treatment and capital gains treatment on the sale of collectibles. This may serve as increased incentive for individuals to donate collectibles rather than to sell them. Another feature of this legislation is that losses from the sale of art and collectibles can now be used to offset gains from the sale of collectibles.

A work of art will be considered as ordinary income property under the following conditions:

❑ It was created by the donor (works created by the artist do not receive the favored capital gains property deduction treatment).

❑ It was received as a gift from the artist (a collector who receives artwork as a gift from an artist has the same basis in the property as the artist, and, since artwork is ordinary income property in the artist's hands, it cannot be a capital asset in the donee/collector's hands).

❏ It is held in inventory by a dealer.

❏ It would produce short-term capital gain if sold (that is, it is owned for one year or less before being donated).

❏ It would produce a capital loss if sold.

3. Related-use compliance. The use of works of art by the charity to which the work is donated must be related to the tax-exempt purpose of the charity. For example, if you were to donate a collection of works to a museum, the donation should be used for exhibition purposes and not sold off at auction. (The rule is met, however, if, in the case of a collection, the charity sells off only an "insubstantial" portion of the works.)

Formally, under section 501, the related-use rule requires that the use of the works by the charity be related to the purpose or function constituting the basis for their exemption. If the use of the works is unrelated to the exemption, the amount of the charitable deduction must be reduced by 100 percent of the collection's appreciation in value. In this case, after the 100 percent appreciation reduction, the remainder may be deducted up to 50 percent of the taxpayer's contribution base.

A donation of art will meet the related-use rule if you can establish that the charity will not put it to an unrelated use—or at least that you do not anticipate that they will. For example, if a collector donates a collection to a museum, and the works within it are of a general type normally retained by museums for exhibition, it is reasonable for the donor to anticipate that the collection will not be put to an unrelated use, even if it happens that the collection is later sold or exchanged by the museum. If an item is donated for the purpose of sale at a charitable art auction, however, that would be considered an unrelated use, and 100 percent of the appreciation in value is lost as a charitable deduction.

4. A qualified appraisal. A qualified appraisal prepared by a qualified appraiser must be obtained (based on requirements that appear elsewhere in this chapter).

Charitable-Deduction Limitations

A charitable-contribution deduction of collection is allowable to the extent of its full fair market value on the contribution date, but not to exceed

30 percent of the taxpayer's contribution base,[22] if it meets all of these conditions:

- ❑ It is long-term capital gain–type property.
- ❑ It is contributed to a public charity.
- ❑ It meets the related-use rule.
- ❑ There is a qualified appraisal prepared by a qualified appraiser.

If the collection satisfies the related-use rule, the taxpayer may increase the 30 percent limitation to 50 percent of his contribution base. However, in that case, the amount of the deduction must be reduced by 100 percent of the collection's appreciation in value; in other words, the deduction is limited to the donor's cost. It is easiest to see how these rules work by running through some examples, which are shown below.

Example 1: Gift from the artist diminishes potential deduction. Let's say you received a painting as a gift from a little-known artist. At the time of the gift, the painting has a basis of $100, representing the artist's cost for paint, canvas, and brushes. Some twenty years later, however, after the artist has become famous, the painting has a fair market value of $10,000. If you now donate the painting to an art museum, your maximum charitable deduction will be $100, because the property you have contributed is ordinary income property. The entire $9,900 of appreciation in value is lost as a charitable deduction. If you had paid $500 for the painting, the character of the property would be capital gain–type property and your deduction would be $10,000.

Example 2: Related-use rule raises the allowable deduction. Again, let's assume your salary is $100,000, and you donate to a public charity a painting you purchased for $10,000, which now has a fair market value of $50,000. If the donation satisfies the related-use rule and there is a qualified appraisal by a qualified appraiser, you will be allowed a deduction of $30,000 (30 percent of $100,000) and a carryover of $20,000. If the contribution does not satisfy the related-use rule, you will be allowed a deduction of $10,000 ($50,000 minus $40,000 appreciation), and there is no carryover.

Example 3: Higher purchase price allows higher deduction. Finally, again assume your salary is $100,000, and this time you donate to a public charity a painting that you bought for $40,000, which now has a fair market value of $60,000. If the donation satisfies the related-use rule and there is a qualified appraisal by a qualified appraiser, you will be allowed a deduction of $30,000 (30 percent of $100,000) and a carryover of $30,000. If it does not satisfy the related-use rule or you elect to increase the deduction, you will be allowed a slightly higher deduction of $40,000 ($60,000 minus $20,000 appreciation equals $40,000), and there is no carryover.

To summarize, in order to maximize the charitable deduction, you should do the following:

❏ Make the contribution of appreciated tangible personal property to a public charity (rather than private).[23]

❏ Be sure that the contribution satisfies the related-use rule. (Before making the gift, you should discuss this with the charity to ensure they will be willing and able to furnish proof that the rule will be met.)

❏ Make the contribution only with long-term capital gains property rather than ordinary income property.

❏ Be sure that there is a qualified appraisal by a qualified appraiser.

❏ Make the contribution when the alternative minimum tax (AMT) does not apply.[24]

Partial Lifetime Charitable Transfers

Although a complete transfer of a collection to a charitable organization has many tax- and estate-planning advantages, a collector must still give up possession of the works of art in order to receive the benefits from its transfer. Under the Pension Protection Act of 2006, the current formula is:

Initial contribution of fractional interest in work of art =
Full fair market value × Fractional interest donated

In determining the deductible amount of each additional contribution for the same work of art, the fair market value of the donated item is now limited to the lesser of

❏ the value used for purposes of determining the charitable deduction for the initial fractional contribution, or

❏ the fair market value of the item at the time of the subsequent contribution.

A collector who gives away a 50 percent interest in a painting worth $1 million can still claim a $500,000 deduction. Ten years later, however, when the collector donates the remaining 50 percent interest and the painting is worth $2 million, the collector's donation would be limited to 50 percent of the initial fair market value of $1 million, which is $500,000 (not 50 percent of the $2 million current value). The collector must also complete the donation of his entire interest in the work of art before his death or ten years from the initial contribution, whichever comes first.[25] Under the new provisions, the benefiting charity must

❏ have substantial physical possession of the work of art during the donor-allowed possession period (a maximum of ten years), and

❏ must use the work of art for an exempt use during such period (that is, satisfy the related-use rule).

Substantial Physical Possession

The *Joint Committee on Taxation Report* offers an example of an art museum's satisfying the related-use requirement (by including a painting in an art exhibit sponsored by the museum), but it does not explain the meaning of "substantial physical possession." For example, if a collector donates a 10 percent fractional interest in a painting to a museum, and plans on donating the remaining 90 percent ten years later, the regulations are unclear about whether the collector is violating the substantial-physical-possession rule if the museum has physical possession during the ten-year period for only 10 percent of that period. If the museum has physical possession for a period of time equal to the donated percentage interest, however, that should be sufficient to satisfy this requirement.

If the collector violates either the ten-year timing or the use limitation (the substantial-possession or related-use requirement), then his or her income and gift tax deductions for all previous contributions of interests in the work of art are recaptured, with interest. The statute also imposes an additional tax of 10 percent of the amount recaptured for all these cases.

Contributions of Fractional Interest in a Work of Art

There are no deductions allowed for contributions of a fractional interest in a work of art, unless

❏ all interests are owned by the collector, or

❏ all interests are owned jointly by the collector and the donee organization.

The IRS is authorized to make some exceptions to this rule in cases in which all those who hold an interest in the work of art make proportional contributions of undivided interests in their respective shares of such work of art to the donee organization.

Example of IRS Exception re: the Fractional-Interest Rule

If collector A owns a 50 percent interest in a painting, and his brother, collector B, owns the other 50 percent, the IRS may allow A to take a deduction for a charitable contribution of less than the entire interest held by A, provided that both A and B make proportional contributions of fractional interests in the work to the same donee organization (for example, if A contributes 25 percent of A's interest and B contributes 25 percent of B's interest).

The Pension Protection Act contains similar limitations to those described above for gift and estate tax purposes. Like the income tax provision, the estate tax provision limits the estate tax deduction to

❏ the lesser of the fair market value at the time of the initial fractional contribution, or

❏ the fair market value at the time of the subsequent contribution.

In order to avoid the recapture of the income tax deduction, the transfer to the donee charity must be completed upon the earlier of

❏ ten years from the initial contribution, or

❏ the donor's death.

Estate of Robert C. Scull v. Commissioner: **When Fractional Ownership Diminishes Value**

In *Estate of Robert C. Scull v. Commissioner,* the value of the decedent's 65 percent undivided interest in an art collection was reduced by 5 percent to reflect the uncertainties involved in any acquisition of the interest, which was the result of a divorce proceeding still being appealed. In *Robert G. Stone v. United States,* the court allowed a 5 percent discount to an estate that owned an undivided 50 percent interest in nineteen paintings that were left to family members.[26] This concept is discussed later in this chapter.

Tax-Planning Tools

A bargain sale of an art collection to a charitable organization occurs when the collection is sold to a charity for an amount less than its fair market value and has elements of both a sale and a gift. It can be a useful tax-planning technique. In a bargain sale,

❏ the sale element is the sales price the collector charges, and

❏ the gift element is the difference between the sales price paid by the charity and the fair market value.

An elderly client who has most of his assets tied up in a valuable collection that he wants to go to his favorite museum, and who does not have enough income, can sell the collection to a charitable organization under the bargain-sale rules. This will give him a low-tax way of giving him enough investable cash to increase current income yet still allow him to have an estate to pass on to his heirs.

In terms of taxes, the sale portion of the transaction is subject to taxation (capital gain or ordinary income), whereas the gift portion is allowed as a charitable deduction to the extent of its fair market value. All the rules discussed above govern the amount of the deduction.[27]

Charitable Remainder Trusts

Another useful tax-planning vehicle is a charitable remainder trust. Generally, a charitable remainder trust must distribute a specific amount, at least annually, to beneficiaries, at least one of whom is a noncharitable beneficiary. The payment period must be for the lives of the individual beneficiaries or for a term not to exceed twenty years. At the termination of the noncharitable interest, the remainder must be paid to one or more appropriate exempt organizations. The charitable remainder trust is exempt from income tax, and so the trustee can sell assets without having to pay capital gains tax, and the grantor of the trust is entitled to an income tax deduction based on the present value of the remainder interest.

There are two types of charitable remainder trusts:

❑ An annuity trust is required to pay a fixed yearly sum to the noncharitable beneficiary equal to no less than 5 percent but no more than 50 percent of the fair market value of the trust assets (which are valued when the trust is first created).

❑ A unitrust is required to pay a fixed yearly sum to the noncharitable beneficiary equal to no less than 5 percent but no more than 50 percent of the fair market value of the trust assets, valued each year on the valuation date.

The *J. W. Kluge* Case: Art Sold to the Collector's Own Corporation

In *J. W. Kluge*, the taxpayer sold valuable works of art to a closely held corporation (wholly owned by himself) but retained the works of art in his home after the sale. The tax court upheld the IRS in its judgment that, since Kluge retained the beneficial use of the objects in his home, he had received a taxable dividend equivalent to the sales prices allocated to the works of art. Therefore, the payment by the corporation was for his personal benefit rather than for a valid business purpose.

Complete Testamentary Charitable Transfers

An individual may wish to bequeath a collection to a charitable organization upon his or her death but keep possession of it during his lifetime. Doing so results in an estate tax charitable deduction equal to 100 percent of the fair market value of the property at the date of death. In the case of a bequest at death, there is no longer a distinction between a public charity and a private foundation; generally, the full estate tax charitable deduction is allowable for a bequest to either one. Neither, moreover, does the related-use rule generally apply.

When Art Appreciation Is Disproportionate to Other Assets' Appreciation

Whenever a valuable collection constitutes a substantial portion of the assets that an individual wants to bequeath to charity, consideration must be given to the extent of the charitable bequest. For example, an art collection left to charity at the time a will is drafted may constitute only 40 percent of the testator's estate, but the collection may have increased in value by the time of the testator's death, and other assets may have decreased in value. Such a change could result in the charitable bequest's constituting more than 50 percent of the estate. To avoid a problem under local state law, provision can be made by either drafting a clause with a percentage limitation or drafting the will in such a way as to allow for a change in relative value.

A bequest to a charitable organization of an undivided fractional interest in a collection does qualify for an estate tax charitable deduction. For example, if the testator gives an undivided three-quarters interest to the charitable organization during his or her life, the testator can give the remaining quarter under his or her will on death. The estate tax charitable deduction will be 100 percent of the fair market value of the remaining one-quarter interest as determined for estate tax purposes.

The Marital Tax Deduction

The Economic Recovery Tax Act (ERTA) of 1981 provides an unlimited estate tax marital deduction, regardless of charitable deduction. Even if the collector wants a charitable organization to receive the collection at his death, he should bequeath it not to the organization but to his surviving spouse and have the spouse make the donation either during her own life or at death (receiving an income tax charitable deduction for a lifetime transfer or a charitable deduction for a transfer at death). Because of the now-unlimited marital deduction, the surviving spouse would not then incur federal estate tax on the estate of the deceased spouse.

Outright testamentary charitable transfers are still important for unmarried partners. Such bequests allow the collection to be kept together as a unit and eliminate the need for a forced sale of the valuable collection to pay taxes on the gross estate.

Upon the death of the testator, the collection takes a new cost basis equal to the value at the date of death or within six months. Collectors should still maintain adequate records of their cost basis, since the law could change at some time in the future.[28]

Noncharitable Transfers

We have discussed bequests to charitable organizations, but sometimes there is a strong family tie to a particular item and the collector might prefer to keep it in the family, or possibly a young member of the family may have developed a particular interest in the collection. Sometimes the collection constitutes a substantial portion of the collector's estate. In such cases, noncharitable transfers must be considered.

Inter Vivos Transfers

Since the passage of the Tax Reform Act of 1976, only one tax-rate schedule covers both gift tax and estate tax.[29] To the extent that taxable gifts are made, they will push the donor's estate into a higher estate tax bracket. There are nevertheless still some advantages in making lifetime gifts of works of art, including the following:

❑ A married donor can take advantage of the unlimited gift tax marital deduction for gifts made to a spouse. Shifting assets to your spouse can be an effective estate-planning tool. For example, the gift can remove the value of the assets from your estate at no cost and can increase your spouse's estate to take maximum advantage of the unified credit. In that case, if you die first, there is no tax in your estate, thus leaving the donee's estate to the children or in trust for then without tax in the donee's estate.

❑ You can reduce any gift tax on gifts made to someone other than your spouse by having your spouse consent to those gifts and taking advantage of the gift-splitting provisions, which allow you to compute the gift tax as if one-half of the gifts had been made by your spouse.

❑ Property used to pay the gift tax is not included in your estate for estate tax purposes if you live at least three years after the date of the gift.

❑ A gift tax is paid only on the actual amount passing to the donee. An estate tax, on the other hand, is paid not only on the amount passing to the beneficiary but also on the money used to pay the estate tax. Any appreciation in value after the date of the gift is removed from the calculation of the donor's gross estate.

There are also other specific exclusions in the legislation—for example, the amount of the gift tax can also be reduced by taking advantage of the $13,000 annual exclusion or the $1 million exclusion (unified credit against gift tax)—and other disadvantages to inter vivos gifts, such as the loss of dominion and control of your collection. With a very valuable collection, the gift tax for a transfer to someone other than a spouse may also be so high as to make such a transfer impractical. Also, since the gift tax is payable in the year of the gift, the present loss of that money and the loss of future income on that money may be more painful than the prospect of a larger estate tax that is not due until nine months after death—and then only to the extent that the estate has not decreased in value or been consumed.

A married collector who is planning to take advantage of the unlimited estate tax marital deduction on death should also consider maintaining ownership of the collection up to death, so that the surviving spouse can receive a step-up in basis for the collection. This technique enables the surviving spouse to sell the collection and avoid the capital gains tax on any appreciation in value. If lifetime gifts are made, that advantage will be lost.

The lifetime gift can be outright or held in trust, or it can be a gift of a legal life estate. An intrafamily transfer, particularly if it is made to a family member living in the same household, can cause a difficult burden of proof on the question of completion of the gift. The transfer of a collection to a family member must be evidenced by

❏ a deed of gift with a signed acceptance,
❏ the filing of a gift tax return, and
❏ the transfer of any insurance policy to the new owner.

If possible, it is also advisable to arrange physical delivery of the collection or works being transferred, particularly to avoid the argument that the donor retained lifetime use of the collection, since that would make it includable in the donor's estate.

As noted above, the estate of a collector who owns a collection of works that has appreciated in value receives a step-up in the basis of the collection to its fair market value on the date of death or six months later. As a result of the unlimited gift tax marital deduction, transfers between spouses can be made at no gift tax cost. One spouse can transfer a collection to the other shortly before the donee spouse dies, for the purpose of receiving a step-up in basis for the transferred collection. If the donee spouse's will leaves the same collection to the surviving spouse, there will be no estate tax, because of the unlimited estate tax marital deduction. In that case, the surviving spouse will regain the collection at a stepped-up basis.[30]

For federal estate tax purposes, the value of a collection included in an individual's gross estate is generally the value as of the date of the person's death. However, the executor of the will may elect to value the collection on an alternative valuation date, generally within six months after the decedent's death. Since there is no estate tax on the estate of the first spouse to die, it is to the surviving spouse's advantage to have the collection valued on the date the value is the highest for federal estate tax purposes. An alternative valuation date may be used only when both the total value of all property in the gross estate and the federal estate tax liability of the estate are reduced. Therefore, in a zero-tax estate, the alternative valuation date cannot be used to obtain a larger stepped-up basis for a collection in a decedent's estate.

Finally, a lifetime sale of a collection generally results in a capital gain or a capital loss. A capital gain is taxable, and a capital loss is not, unless it can be shown that the collection was held as an investment property. If the collection is ordinary income property, the collector realizes ordinary income on its sale.

Testamentary Transfers

A collector who has not made a lifetime transfer of the collection must provide for its disposition on his death. If you intend to transfer works of art via your will, a specific bequest in the will should be used to bequeath the works or collection outright to a noncharitable beneficiary or beneficiaries. If you live in a different city from the beneficiary, you should consider that, unless specified, the cost of shipping will be borne by him or her. In addition to amounts that qualify for the marital deduction, the amount that can be bequeathed estate tax free is now $3.5 million (unified credit against estate tax). This means that there is no federal estate tax unless your assets are greater than $3.5 million. The increase in the amount of the available applicable exclusion was increased to $3.5 million effective January 1, 2009.[31]

Estate of Ludwig Neugass: A Marital Bequest

In *Estate of Ludwig Neugass,* the decedent had a valuable art collection, some of which he wished his wife to have outright. His will provided for his wife to have the right to take any items she chose within six months of his death. The IRS disallowed the marital deduction, alleging that such a right was a "terminable interest" (or one that would lapse over time), which did not qualify for the marital deduction, but the case was eventually reversed in her favor.

As discussed earlier in this chapter, when fractional donations are made to charity by testamentary bequests, the IRS accepts the undivided percentage of the fair market value given to the charitable organization, with no reduction for a minority interest as the allowable charitable deduction. The same is true for testamentary charitable and noncharitable bequests.

In *Estate of Robert C. Scull v. Commissioner* (cited earlier in this chapter), the value of the decedent's 65 percent undivided interest in an art collection was reduced by 5 percent to reflect the uncertainties involved in any acquisition of the interest that was the result of a divorce proceeding under appeal.

Robert G. Stone v. United States: Sale of Fractional Interest by Heirs

In the case of *Robert G. Stone v. United States,* in 2007, a 5 percent discount was allowed to an estate that owned an undivided 50 percent interest in nineteen paintings that were left to family members. In *Stone*, the estate claimed a 44 percent discount for the undivided 50 percent interest in the painting owned by the decedent on the date of death. "Art is simply not fungible," said the IRS, and the discount should be not more than 2 percent. The court concluded that a hypothetical seller of an undivided fractional interest in art would likely seek to sell the entire work of art and split the proceeds, rather than seeking to sell his or her fractional interest at a discount. In other words, the court thought that a hypothetical willing seller who was under no compulsion to sell would seek to gain consent from the other co-owners to sell the collection and divide the proceeds. The court decided that the taxpayer's appraisal methodology was flawed, because it failed to take into account that collectors of art are often drawn to the esthetics of a particular work of art, not only to viewing it as an investment vehicle, and the mathematical assumptions made by the appraiser as to the rate of return on investments in art and the appropriate net-present-value percentage were made without supporting evidence.[32]

Testamentary Transfers by Trust

Finally, a trust can be used to make testamentary transfers. A testator may wish to give the surviving spouse a life estate in a collection, with the remainder to go to their children on the spouse's death. The basic idea is to make one transfer cover two estates, with only one estate tax imposed. Although a legal life estate can be used, it is preferable to create a trust, because of its greater flexibility. The terms of the trust should specify who should pay for insurance, storage, and any other expenses. The trustee should be given the power to arrange a sale of any of the items, in which event the trust should provide how the proceeds are to be held and applied. This clause is necessary to allow for the event of a family misfortune, in which case the life tenant would not be left in the position of having a valuable collection but no money with which to pay bills. The trust can also be drafted so that it qualifies for the estate tax marital deduction if the surviving spouse can require the trustee to convert non-income-producing assets to income-producing assets.

Selling a Collection After Death

Since a collection may constitute the bulk of a decedent's estate, the executor may have to sell all or a part of the collection in order to pay estate taxes and other administrative expenses. The sale may also be necessary to make sure that the decedent's spouse or children are financially secure and will receive a yearly income. Since the commission expenses on the sale of a large collection can be significant, a will must be drafted to allow these commissions to be claimed as deductions on the federal estate tax return. (If the will contains a specific direction to sell, the expenses of the sale are deductible.)

The question of what qualifies as a deductible miscellaneous administration expense for federal estate tax purposes is not clear, and the allowability of an expense by a state probate court is no guarantee that the expense will be deductible for federal estate tax purposes. However, if it is anticipated that large or unusual administrative expenses will be incurred in administering an estate, the deductibility of those expenses should be planned for in advance.

One of the most important tax consequences of death is that property included in a decedent's gross estate for federal estate tax purposes acquires a step-up in cost basis for income tax purposes equal to its federal estate tax value. The regulations provide that the cost basis of property acquired from a decedent is the fair market value of the property at the date of the decedent's death or the alternate valuation date. In other words, if a collector purchases a painting for $10,000, but when he dies, the painting is valued at $100,000 for federal estate tax purposes, his heirs will acquire the painting with a step-up in cost basis equal to $100,000.

Chapter Notes

1. The American Association of Museums requires that its members use the proceeds from deaccessioning to expand its collection rather than to raise money to use toward capital needs or in times of general financial hardship.

2. There are, however, some specific sections that disallow deductions attributable to activities not engaged in for profit—with a few exceptions—and others that deny a deduction or loss for personal expenses.

3. There are also limitations based on gross income. Section 67, for example, limits miscellaneous deductions to those that exceed 2 percent of your adjusted gross income, while section 68 generally limits your ability to claim itemized deductions if your adjusted gross income exceeds a specified statutory amount.

4. The main objective of section 183 is to disallow most deductions for all collectors who are not dealers or investors. Section 183(b) does offer some help to collectors, however, by allowing them to claim deductions for expenses attributable to an activity not engaged in for profit up to the amount of the gross income derived from it, after first deducting allowable items, such as interest and taxes, that are without regard to whether an activity is engaged in for profit.

5. If an item in a collection is purchased and later discovered to be a forgery and, hence, almost worthless, it produces a deductible loss if the transaction amounted to a "theft," as defined by local law. For it to constitute a theft, the taxpayer must bear the burden of proving that the item was sold to him with an intent to defraud.

6. In other words, the limitations in this case are $100 plus $10,000, or $10,100. The loss in this case ($10,000) does not exceed the limitations ($10,100), and so there is no deductible amount.

7. According to section 1033 (a)(2).

8. The question of what is similar property for a collector was dealt with in Private Letter Ruling 81-27-089. A fire had caused extensive damage to a collector's lithographs and other art items. The collector had difficulty in replacing the lithographs and wanted to use part of the insurance proceeds to purchase artwork in other artistic media. The IRS ruled that artwork in one medium that is destroyed in whole or

in part and that is replaced with artwork in another medium will not be considered property similar or related in service or use. The ruling appears to be unduly narrow in its interpretation of the statute.

9. The Manhattan District Attorney's office has been conducting an intense investigation of art dealers and collectors who may be in violation of New York State sales and compensating use tax law. The continuing investigation has raised millions of dollars for New York State and has caught the attention of other states that are now focusing on the payment of the sales and use tax due in their states.

10. In the latter case, the art gallery is still required to have documented proof that it shipped the work by common carrier to the out-of-state purchaser. Therefore, if the purchaser wants to select the common carrier, it is always best if the art gallery is the entity that retains the common carrier at the request of the purchaser, even if the cost is to be paid by the purchaser.

11. A donee is the person or organization that receives the gift or inheritance of the works of art.

12. R. E. Paul, *Federal Estate and Gift Taxation* (Boston: Little Brown, 1942).

13. Treasury Regulations section 1.170 A-13(c)(4) sets out the paperwork that has to be supplied with the valuation. Completion of IRS Form 8283 (signed and dated by both the appraiser and the donee charitable organization) is required for all non-cash gifts of more than $500 to a charitable donee, along with a signed copy of the full appraisal. The IRS can also request a photograph for any individual art object valued at $20,000 or more. IRS Publication 561 provides a useful summary of what the IRS is looking for to support claimed values of works for donation or estate-tax purposes, and IRS Notice 2006-96 also offers some guidance as to the new appraisal rules introduced by the Pension Protection Act of 2006.

14. In excess of $500 in value.

15. Unfortunately, it often takes from six months to a year to have a request processed through the national office in Washington, D.C., since there is limited staff to process the huge volume of valuation cases referred. The art panel, which reviews the documentation prepared by the IRS, is also faced with an enormous volume of cases. Therefore, the taxpayer's documentation must be as complete as possible before the information is submitted to the national office.

16. The Tax Reform Act of 1976 recognized the plight of the taxpayer faced with a valuation issue and an IRS agent who supplies little or no information to support the IRS determination. To encourage early resolution, section 7517 provides that the IRS must, on written request, furnish a written statement explaining the basis on which the IRS has determined a valuation of property that is different from the valuation submitted by the donor. The IRS must comply within forty-five days and explain the basis of the valuation and any computations used.

17. This case includes an excellent discussion of what to look for in determining value. The court succinctly stated that value is determined by the item's condition, its uniqueness or rarity, its authenticity, its size, and the market value of comparable objects.

18. A decedent is the legal term referring to a deceased person.

19. The decedent's attorney then argued that if the objects were includable in the gross estate at their fair market value, the decedent should be entitled to claim a deduction for claims against the estate by the legitimate owners of the art objects. The IRS rejected the deduction, noting that in order to be enforceable under Texas law, a claim had to be submitted within a certain period of time, which had passed.

20. In *Smith*, the court noted that sales too far removed from the date of death should not be considered, and little weight was given to sales more than two years after the artist's death.

21. The current buyer's premium for art at auction at Christie's and Sotheby's in the United States is 25 percent on the first $50,000, 20 percent from $50,001 to $1 million, and 12 percent on the balance.

22. Any amount that exceeds the 30 percent limitation may be carried forward for five years.

23. It is worth noting that donors can also set up a private operating foundation that falls somewhere between a private foundation and a public charity and has the same tax advantages for donors as if contributions are made to a public charity, so long as the specific donation requirements are satisfied. Private operating foundations are organizations that devote their assets or income to the active conduct of a charitable purpose, rather than make grants to other organizations, and they have a number of qualifying features in the regulations. Since the donor is the creator of the foundation and can act as its president, he can keep a degree of control over the collection while also availing himself of the full deduction.

24. The IRS created the AMT to ensure that high-income individuals pay a minimum amount of tax, regardless of deductions, credits, or exemptions. It functions by adding certain tax-preference items back into adjusted gross income. If the AMT is higher than the regular tax liability for the year, the regular tax and the amount by which the AMT exceeds the regular tax must be paid.

25. If the charity is no longer in existence, the collector's remaining interest may be contributed to another section 170 (c) organization.

26. Generally, before a museum will accept a fractional gift, it wants assurances that it will receive the balance of the undivided interest when the collector dies, because it does not want to be left owning a fractional interest in a work of art with the donor's heirs' fighting over the remaining interest. The *Stone* case is discussed further later in this chapter.

27. Although this sounds straightforward, there can be significant problems of proof of fair market value on bargain sales, and it is often prudent to obtain two appraisals. In addition, the donor bears the burden of proof to show that he had the required "donative intent" that must be present for any gift to charity. When a donor makes an outright gift to a charity, the donative intent is clear, but in the case of a bargain sale, this is not always the case. For example, negotiations between the charity and the donor may suggest that the seller sought a high price but agreed to a lower price, simply because the charity would not pay. An attempt by the donor to characterize this sale as a bargain-sale donation after the fact is likely to fail, even

when a subsequent appraisal shows the fair market value to be greater than the sale price. Therefore, from the outset of negotiations, the donor must make the donative intent clear (perhaps expressed as a fraction of the value of the collection) and must outline the donative element in the final bargain-sale agreement.

28. The Economic Growth and Tax Relief Reconciliation Act of 2001 reinstates new carryover-basis rules for property included in a decedent's estate for anyone dying after December 31, 2009, which is when the federal estate tax is scheduled to be repealed. If the repeal goes into effect, a new modified carryover-basis system will apply, where the basis will equal the lower of the asset's fair market value at the decedent's death or the decedent's adjusted basis in the asset. In other words, for income-tax purposes, the basis may remain at the original cost of the property purchased.

29. Before 1977, a lifetime gift of a collection to a noncharitable beneficiary resulted in saving a large amount in estate taxes, because gift tax rates were only three-quarters as the amount of the corresponding estate tax rates.

30. To discourage the use of such pre-death transfers, there is no step-up in basis in the case of appreciated property acquired by a decedent by gift during the one-year period before the death if that property is then reacquired by the donor under the decedent's will.

31. The estate tax has been repealed beginning for decedents dying in 2010 but will be reinstated in 2011 if the 2001 Act provisions are not affirmed by Congress. If the 2001 Act provisions are not again passed, the estate tax applicable exclusion amount reverts to $1 million in 2011.

32. The taxpayer in this case could not meet his burden of persuading the court that a hypothetical buyer would demand a discount greater than 5 percent and be able to get a seller to agree to it. This case is an important warning sign that art is treated differently from real estate or closely held businesses when it comes to applying discounts. Accordingly, it should not be assumed that the discounts usually available for lack of 100 percent ownership interest will be available in the same manner for art as for real estate.

10

Art and Taxation in the United Kingdom and Beyond

Pierre Valentin, Philip Munro, and Samantha Morgan,
Withers

EDITOR'S NOTE: This chapter offers an alternative perspective on the art market and taxation from that of Chapter 9 and deals with fiscal regulations in the United Kingdom, the second-largest global art market next to the United States. The discussion focuses mostly on U.K. tax rules but extends beyond the United Kingdom in some areas regarding offshore trusts and provides some brief notes on tax principles in the European Union.

U.K. Tax Regime

The structure of the U.K. tax regime is in many respects broadly similar to that of the United States:

❑ *Income tax* must be paid by individuals, on income from employment, investments, and trading.

❑ *Capital gains tax* is separate and distinct from income tax.

❑ *Corporate tax* is imposed on companies, where it is structured as an amalgam of income tax and capital gains tax.

❑ *Value-added tax* (VAT) in the United Kingdom is an indirect tax comparable to sales tax in the United States, and its principles apply across the European Union.

❑ *Inheritance tax* is relevant upon death and to certain inter vivos gifts in much the same way as U.S. estate tax and gift tax.

For U.K. tax purposes, before considering these taxes and their application, it is important to consider the concepts of residency and domicile, since they determine an individual's tax profile. (The nationality of the taxpayer is normally irrelevant for U.K. purposes.) The residence of the taxpayer is fundamental in determining his liability to U.K. income tax and capital gains tax.

Residence

For purposes of taxation, an individual will be deemed to be a U.K. resident in any of the following circumstances:

❏ He has spent 183 days or more in the United Kingdom in any one tax year (the U.K. tax year runs from April 6 to April 5).

❏ He has spent less than 183 days in the United Kingdom, but his visits to the United Kingdom are, on average, ninety-one days or more per year over a period of four years.

❏ Upon arrival in the United Kingdom, he comes to the United Kingdom to live permanently or intends to stay two years or more.

Domicile

Domicile (which should not be confused with nationality) is relevant to most U.K. taxes. In English law, domicile has a more technical meaning than is the case in most other jurisdictions, particularly in continental Europe where the concept is closer to that of habitual residence. A person is domiciled in a jurisdiction rather than in a country, and therefore, in a federal system, a person is domiciled in a particular state or province. The U.K. rules are complicated and can yield some strange results:

❏ Every person acquires a domicile of origin at birth (generally the domicile of his father at that time). When that individual is an adult, however, he can change his domicile by acquiring a domicile of choice if he becomes resident in a country with the intention of residing there permanently or indefinitely.

❏ A person may also then lose his domicile by leaving the country of choice if he does not intend to return to live there, at which point, unless a new domicile of choice is acquired, his domicile of origin is reestablished (even if he has no substantive connection with that country).

❏ Any person who has been resident in the United Kingdom for all or part of seventeen out of the preceding twenty years will be deemed to be domiciled in the United Kingdom, and this concept of deemed domicile applies for purposes of the inheritance tax and the pre-owned–assets income tax charge but not for purposes of other income or capital gains tax.

Direct Taxes

In the U.K., direct taxes are those taxes levied directly on an individual or company, and include income, capital gains and corporate taxes. (These are contrasted with indirect taxes, such as sales taxes or VAT, which are collected by an intermediary such as a retailer.)

Income Tax

As of 2008, the top rate of income tax is 40 percent, but in 2010, this will rise to 50 percent. A *U.K.-domiciled U.K. resident* is liable for income tax on his worldwide income, both U.K. sourced and non-U.K. sourced. A *non-U.K.-domiciled U.K. resident* is also liable for income tax on his worldwide income, both U.K. sourced and non-U.K. sourced, but in the latter case, the individual can elect to be taxed on a so-called remittance basis. When he has elected the remittance basis, he is subject to U.K. income tax only on overseas income, and only to the extent that such income is remitted or brought into the United Kingdom. For employment income to qualify as overseas earnings, the employment must be with a foreign employer (unless the individual is not ordinarily resident in the United Kingdom), the duties must be performed wholly outside the United Kingdom, and the income must be received outside the United Kingdom. Accordingly, where art professionals are based in the United Kingdom but employed internationally, it may be possible to shield some of their overseas employment earnings from U.K. tax.

Capital Gains Taxes

Currently charged at the rate of 18 percent, capital gains tax applies to the profits of sales of property and certain assets, as well as to gains arising on gifts of property.

A *dealer or an individual considered to be carrying on a trade in the United Kingdom* (e.g., as an art dealer), however, will have the profits of his trade subject to U.K. income tax, not capital gains tax.

An *individual collector* seeking to dispose of a number of artworks in the United Kingdom (particularly when they were originally acquired with a view to later resale) within a relatively short period of time should seek counsel regarding whether he might be considered to be carrying on a trade.

A *non-U.K.-resident collector* cannot be liable for capital gains tax and can therefore dispose of art at auction in the United Kingdom for a profit without incurring U.K. capital gains tax liability.

A *U.K.-resident, U.K.-domiciled collector* will be liable for capital gains taxes on gains arising on his worldwide assets. Gains made on an auction sale in New York, for example, will be taxable in the United Kingdom.

A *non-U.K.-domiciled U.K. resident* is liable for capital gains taxes on all gains arising from the sale of his U.K. assets, but he will pay capital gains tax only on those gains for non-U.K. property to the extent that he remits the proceeds of sale into the United Kingdom (assuming he claims the remittance basis of tax).

It should be noted that individuals have an annual exemption of £10,000, below which gains are not subject to capital gains taxes. Also, for an asset (e.g., a painting) that is tangible, movable property and is disposed of, and for which the consideration does not exceed £6,000, there is no gain; whereas if movable assets are sold for more than £6,000, the gain is limited to five-thirds of the difference between the consideration and £6,000. Further, in computing capital gains tax liability, such costs as incurred for acquisition and disposal, enhancement of the value of an asset (such as painting-restoration costs), and any costs of defending title to the asset can, in some instances, be taken into account and reduce the chargeable gain.

Capital Gains Regulations for Art

A number of specific capital gains tax rules apply to art:

❑ Profits can be exempt from capital gains tax if a disposal is made either in satisfaction of an inheritance tax liability or given to a museum in a way other than by a sale.

❑ Gains may sometimes be held over, or deferred, when art is transferred to a fund established for the maintenance of a historic building.

❑ When a person owns a set of articles (say a series of paintings by the same artist) and makes a number of disposals of single items from the set to the same person or to connected persons, the transactions can be treated as a single transaction for capital gains tax purposes.[1]

As explained above, the remittance basis for tax means that a non-U.K. domiciled U.K. resident may not be liable for the income and gains arising from his overseas assets' being exposed to tax (until they are brought into the United Kingdom). This has led to the perception that the United Kingdom is a jurisdiction that is very tax advantageous for the wealthy, but that is no longer so true as it once was. Now, following the Finance Act of 2008, if an individual has been a U.K. resident for seven out of the previous nine years and he elects to be taxed on the remittance basis in a particular tax year, he must pay a U.K. charge of £30,000. In some instances, this charge might be creditable against foreign taxes paid, but it has nevertheless reduced the attractiveness of the United Kingdom as a tax jurisdiction for the wealthy "international crowd."

The current U.K. remittance rules are wide enough to capture indirect remittances of overseas income and gains. Accordingly, there will be a remittance when foreign income or gain is used to settle a U.K. liability (such as a U.K. credit card bill) incurred by a non-U.K.-domiciled person. There will also now be a remittance due when foreign income or gain is used to purchase personal items, such as works of art, which are brought into the United Kingdom. That said, the remittance rules offer a number of exemptions that can be helpful when U.K. residents have overseas art collections. Although the parameters of these exemptions need to be considered specifically in each case, there are some generalities that can help indicate tax implications for works of art. Certain imports of the following items may not lead to a U.K. tax liability in some circumstances:

❏ Art brought into the United Kingdom for public display in an approved establishment

❏ Art brought into the United Kingdom for repair or restoration

❏ Art brought into the United Kingdom for less than nine months (e.g., for display in a commercial gallery)

❏ Art acquired on or before March 11, 2008, with untaxed foreign income

Charitable Donations

For donations to U.K. charities, an income tax relief is available for a gift of cash, land, or shares in listed companies but not specifically for a gift of art. There are some circumstances, however, when a capital gains tax deduction might be available in the event of an art gift or sale at an undervalue price to a charity or to certain national institutions, including the National Gallery, the British Museum, and the National Trust.

To be considered "charitable" under English law, a body must have purposes that are considered exclusively charitable under the law's definition of charity and must exist for the purposes of the public good. If an entity has any purpose that would not be considered charitable, it will not then, for the purposes of English law, be considered a charity.[2]

In order to determine whether an entity has exclusively charitable purposes, English law has used a process of precedent and analogy. The basis from which most of the case law is derived, however, is the four cornerstones of charity known as the Pemsel classification:

❏ The relief of poverty
❏ The advancement of education
❏ The advancement of religion
❏ Other purposes beneficial to the community

The meaning of charity under English law was also codified by the Charities Act 2006, which introduced a statutory definition of charity in early 2008 that expanded on the Pemsel classification and set out a list of thirteen charitable purposes that also included the advancement of the arts, culture, and heritage.[3]

Corporate Taxes

A brief discussion of corporate tax law is necessary, since works of art have often been acquired or donated by private companies, and more recently certain hedge funds and other investment vehicles have also invested in art as an alternative investment strategy.

A corporate tax is levied at a rate of up to 28 percent on worldwide profits (comprising both income and capital gains) of U.K. resident companies, whether or not these profits are remitted to the United

Kingdom. Rates below 28 percent apply where company profits do not exceed £300,000 per annum. A company may obtain tax relief against corporate tax by making a donation to a charity, which allows the amount of the donation to be offset against the amount of its taxable profits.

In most cases, for corporate tax purposes, a company incorporated in the United Kingdom is considered a U.K. resident, but it may be treated as a resident of another country when a double-tax treaty between the United Kingdom and another country makes a determination in favor of the other country. A company not incorporated in the United Kingdom will, for tax purposes, nonetheless be treated as a U.K. resident if its central management and control is located in the United Kingdom. This form of residency-deeming provision is alien to the U.S. tax code but is not uncommon globally, with similar principles applying, for example, in Switzerland.

The central-management-and-control test is a common-law test that was developed by the U.K. courts. This test looks at where, as a matter of fact, the ultimate management of the company takes place. Her Majesty's Revenue and Customs (HMRC) will look at where an overseas company's directors are making the highest-level company-management decisions and will consider the location of any person who, in practice, exercises influence over a company's strategic management, whether or not that person holds any formal position within the company. Regarding any overseas company that, through its personnel, advisers, or directors, has a presence in the United Kingdom, it is critical that no management decisions whatsoever be made in the United Kingdom, because unless the company intends to become a U.K. resident for tax purposes, its worldwide income and gains will then be subject to U.K. corporate tax.

Even a non-U.K.-resident company can be exposed to U.K. tax if it is trading in the United Kingdom or receiving U.K. income from investment properties or other sources. However, since a non-U.K.-resident company that is neither trading in the United Kingdom nor receiving U.K.-source income is not subject to U.K. taxes, such a company can profit from the disposal of art held in the United Kingdom for investment purposes without its profits being subject to U.K. tax. These rules enable offshore art funds to dispose of art at U.K. auctions without the funds being exposed to U.K. tax on sale proceeds. Where an offshore art fund is trading, rather than investing, in art, however, and has a U.K. presence (in the form, perhaps, of a U.K.-based investment manager or art consultant), then a U.K. corporate tax exposure could arise to the extent that it makes trading profits through its U.K. presence (where no presence exists, an offshore company could in some circumstances be subject to U.K. income tax if trading in the United Kingdom).

Like its U.S. counterpart, U.K. inheritance tax is a tax based on the value at death of an individual's estate and the value transferred during his lifetime by certain lifetime gifts, such as those to trusts. Inheritance tax is charged at two rates:

❑ The first £325,000 of a person's estate (known as the "nil-rate band") is taxed at 0 percent.

❑ Amounts in excess of the nil-rate band are charged at a rate of 40 percent (or 20 percent in the case of lifetime chargeable transfers).

Exemptions

Gifts between spouses and civil partners are exempt from inheritance tax (unless the donor is U.K. domiciled and the donee is not, in which case the exemption is restricted to £55,000). Gifts to U.K.-registered charities are entirely exempt.

INHERITANCE TAX AND RESIDENCY

Inheritance tax applies to the worldwide assets of individuals domiciled in the United Kingdom, but only to the U.K. assets of non-U.K. domiciled individuals.

A non-U.K.-domiciled individual should be aware that a U.K. inheritance tax exposure could arise to the extent that he keeps works of art in the United Kingdom (unless they are left by exempt gift upon death). Residence is not relevant in determining a person's liability to inheritance tax, except to the extent that long residence may cause an individual to be deemed, for inheritance tax purposes, domiciled in the United Kingdom.

GIFTS TO INDIVIDUALS

Outright gifts to other individuals made during an individual's lifetime do not give rise to an immediate charge of inheritance tax, and the gift will fall outside the U.K. inheritance tax net if the donor survives the gift by seven years.

TRUSTS

Care must be taken in settling art into trust for U.K. purposes, because, as noted above, lifetime gifts into trust now trigger an immediate inheritance tax charge at the rate of 20 percent[4] if

❏ they are made by a person who is actually domiciled in the United Kingdom,

❏ they are made by a person who is deemed domiciled in the United Kingdom, or

❏ they are of U.K. property.

A special inheritance tax regime applies to most U.K. trusts, which subjects the value of the trust fund to inheritance tax charges at the rate of 6 percent on ten-year anniversaries of the trust, and at a proportionate rate on capital distributions between anniversaries. Although trusts settled by U.K. nondomiciliaries[5] may be outside this inheritance tax regulation, the regime will still apply, to the extent that U.K.-situated property is held at trust level. Therefore, if consideration is being given to holding art within a trust, and the art might be located in the United Kingdom at ten-year anniversaries or when appointed from trust between anniversaries, a non-U.K. holding entity, such as an offshore company, should instead be set up between the art and the trust, and if there is no intermediate entity, it may be necessary to move the art outside the United Kingdom before inheritance tax liability events occur. In this case, however, consideration needs to be given to export-license requirements and to the VAT implications of exporting the art from the United Kingdom.

It can be possible for U.K. nondomiciliaries to avoid U.K. inheritance tax on U.K.-situated assets by holding them through an offshore trust or company structure (although this may have other tax implications, particularly where the asset continues to be used) or by borrowing against the asset, thereby reducing its value for tax purposes.

INHERITANCE TAX AND DOMICILE

When an individual owns art, the appropriate form of any inheritance tax planning depends very much on his U.K.-domicile status.

Whatever his status, gifts are exempt from inheritance tax if they are made to

❑ a surviving spouse,
❑ a surviving civil partner of the same domicile status, or
❑ a U.K. charity.

It is also possible to reduce the impact of an inheritance tax charge by taking out a suitable life insurance policy. If a life policy is written "in trust," the proceeds will not then be subject to inheritance tax on the death of the insured.

As a general principle, while gifts to trusts may be subject to upfront inheritance tax charges, it is possible to give assets absolutely without inheritance tax exposure if the donor then survives the gift by seven years.

ANTI-AVOIDANCE RULES

The U.K. inheritance tax rules are also complemented by two sets of anti-avoidance rules.

1. Gifts with the reservation of benefits.   These rules provide that a donor's work of art remains in his estate if he has reserved a benefit from it, no matter how long ago the gift was made. A benefit is considered reserved if either possession and enjoyment of the work is not assumed by the donee or the work is not enjoyed to the entire exclusion of the donor. If, for example, a painting is given to a child, but remains on the donor parent's wall, then it has not been given for U.K. inheritance tax purposes.[6] A gift of art into trust, where the donor as settler remains a beneficiary, will also come under these rules, on the basis that the donor could benefit from the art at the discretion of the trustees.

2. Pre-owned-assets charge.   The pre-owned-asset rules were introduced because there were attempts to circumvent the gift-with-reservation-of-benefit rules. These rules impose an income tax charge on individuals who use, occupy, or enjoy certain assets they previously owned or on those who contribute to someone else's purchase of property or assets, which they then use, occupy or enjoy.

Exemptions from inheritance taxes include all gifts to spouses and charities as well as the United Kingdom's leading national collections, including universities and other listed institutions.

As a mechanism to keep heritage property within families, there is a conditional-exemption system from inheritance tax that can be claimed in respect both to lifetime chargeable transfers of heritage assets (including art) and to chargeable transfers on death. Provided the artworks are of sufficient quality that they can be considered "preeminent" (which has a tightly defined technical meaning for U.K. tax purposes), a transfer will, for inheritance tax purposes, be treated as a "conditionally exempt transfer" if it is agreed that the objects will be retained permanently in the United Kingdom, that steps will be taken to preserve them, and that the public will have reasonable public access to them.[7] Under this regulation, inheritance tax is not completely avoided but is deferred until some chargeable event takes place, at which time it is recaptured according to the proceeds of sale or to the market value at the date of the event.[8]

Paying Inheritance Taxes with Works of Art

HMRC has the power to accept certain items in lieu of inheritance tax, including pictures, prints, books, manuscripts, or works of art that can be shown to be preeminent.[9]

Trusts of maintenance funds for historic buildings also carry special inheritance tax rules that are designed to encourage their preservation. While the rules primarily relate only to land of outstanding scenic, historic, or scientific interest and to buildings of outstanding historic or architectural interest, they are broad enough to include any object that is historically associated with a qualifying building and so can extend to include some artworks. There is no inheritance tax when property is settled into such a trust, or when the settlement comes to an end, and there are no periodic charges during the life of the settlement. After six years, the property may be returned to the settler, in which case there will be an income tax charge to put the settler back into the position he would have been in, had he simply paid out of net income to maintain the property. Because of this, properties are often held in maintenance trusts for the very long term.

Indirect Tax: Value-Added Tax

Value-added tax (VAT) is a tax on the supply of goods and services. Although the same VAT principles apply in all EU countries, each country uses a different tax rate and applies the principles differently, with the result that VAT should be considered separately in each EU country.

The sale of art is subject to VAT in the United Kingdom. In principle, every time a work of art is sold, where the sale is part of a business, the seller charges VAT at the standard rate on the sales price. If a dealer buys art and resells it at a profit, he will pay an input VAT on his purchase price and an output VAT on his sales price, with the difference paid to HMRC. There are, however, special VAT rules dealing with secondhand goods, including works of art. The purpose of these special rules is to avoid applying VAT on the full value of secondhand goods every time they are resold, and VAT is instead applied on the margin of the sale. Where a sale is in the margin scheme, no VAT is shown on the buyer's invoice.

Importing Art into the United Kingdom

Importing art into the United Kingdom from a non-EU country, such as the United States, will normally give rise to a liability to pay import VAT. The rate of import VAT on works of art is a reduced rate of currently 5 percent. The rate of import VAT on antiques is also 5 percent if the antique is more than one hundred years old. If the antique is less than one hundred years old, the standard rate of import VAT applies (currently 17.5 percent).

It is possible to import art into the United Kingdom on a temporary basis for certain purposes—for example, to exhibit the art in a museum—provided that certain conditions are met. No import VAT is due while the art is in temporary import, provided that it is exported at the end of the temporary import period (typically two years or less).

It is possible to keep art in a bonded warehouse in exemption of import VAT, subject to certain conditions.

Other exemptions from import VAT may be available, for example when importing inherited art.

Bringing art into the United Kingdom from another EU country is not subject to import VAT.

The export of art from the United Kingdom to non-EU countries is not subject to VAT, and no VAT applies when art is removed from the United Kingdom to another EU country.

Wealth Taxes

There is another tax regime that applies in some European countries, which, although it does not apply directly to works of art, could indeed influence where an art collector or dealer might choose to live. The tax is called a "wealth tax," and it was a fashionable policy for European socialist politicians to adopt in the 1970s, as in France, Spain, Greece, Switzerland, and Sweden. It has never been imposed in the United Kingdom.

Although wealth taxes have now been abandoned by a number of countries—Austria, Denmark, Finland, Germany, Iceland, Luxembourg, and the Netherlands—the implications of the concept of the tax should be considered by any high-net-worth individual contemplating residency in European jurisdictions. *L'impôt de solidarité sur la fortune*, the wealth tax regime in France, for example, levies an annual charge on all those with assets in excess of 760,000 euros. Not only has that law discouraged many wealthy internationals from living there, but it has also made exiles of some French citizens.[10]

Chapter Notes

1. There is no definition of a "set," but Her Majesty's Revenue & Customs, the U.K. revenue authority, has expressed the view that two items alone cannot constitute a set.

2. A body whose purposes include the attainment of political objectives, for example, cannot be deemed charitable.

3. There is no requirement that an English charity exercise its purposes in the United Kingdom; so long as its purposes are charitable, they can be exercised anywhere in the world.

4. Unless they are within the nil-rate band.

5. These are known as excluded-property trusts.

6. Unless the parent is paying a full market rent for keeping it.

7. One is considered to be providing public access if one lends the objects to a public collection, museum, or gallery or displays the objects in a privately owned house that is open to the public.

8. Examples include the death of the owner and disposal of the object by gift.

9. Four questions are considered in deciding if an object can be considered preeminent: Does it have especially close associations with the history and national life of the United Kingdom? Is it of special artistic or art-historical interest? Is it of special importance for the study of some particular form of art or learning? Does it have an especially close association with a particular historic setting?

10. According to a newspaper article titled, "Old Money, New Money Flee France and Its Wealth Tax" (*Washington Post,* July 16, 2006), on average, at least one millionaire leaves France every day to take up residence in more wealth-friendly nations. The article cites only "a government study" as a source but says the ranks of the wealthy expats include such world-recognizable names as Taittinger, Peugeot, Carrefour, and Darty.

11

Art Conservation and Restoration

Barbara A. Ramsay and John K. Jacobs,
ARTEX Fine Art Services

EDITOR'S NOTE: The conservation and restoration of works of art and antiques is critical both as a means to secure the preservation of the cultural heritage of the future and to protect the value of works of art over time for an individual investor. This chapter defines the concepts of art conservation and restoration and looks at the different professional individuals and groups engaged in these activities. It examines how collectors can preserve their art investment and engage with the correct professionals, and discusses preventive conservation and restoration treatment. Finally, it considers the specialized concerns related to safely storing and shipping art.

One of the hallmarks of an enlightened society is accepting responsibility for the conservation and restoration, or preservation, of art. Modern society is fortunate in having access to many magnificent works of art, artifacts, and monuments that have been passed along from generation to generation, making the lives of many within it richer and more meaningful. The continued existence of whatever artistic and cultural heritage has survived intact to this day means that past generations have borne the responsibility of its care. Our current society has the same obligation to continue this chain of custodianship, so that these historic or contemporary works of art are available to enrich the quality of life of the generations to come. Conservation refers not only to saving a work of art as a physical object but also to clarifying and communicating its meaning and historical and aesthetic significance. As an individual art collector or investor, you can contribute to this effort by preserving your own art collection and by supporting the conservation of art in your family, your community, your favorite museum, your local historical society, and beyond.

In addition to the not-insignificant considerations of heritage, there are also, on an individual level, financial considerations, because conservation is an essential part of preserving your collection's investment value. Damage to the condition of an artwork—whether the result of a specific accident, inappropriate restoration, benign neglect, or a more gradual deterioration over time—can significantly reduce its potential value and salability. Although conservation and restoration costs are unique to this asset class of art and must be considered in calculating returns over time, the costs of negligence are often much greater.

Distinguishing Among Conservation, Restoration, and Preservation

Art conservation refers to the activities of the profession dedicated to the care and preservation of heritage or cultural property of all kinds—fine art, furniture, textiles, documents and books, photographs, minerals, archaeological objects, natural-history specimens, monuments or other structures, historic sites, and so on. Within the field of art conservation, however, the terms "conservation," "restoration," and "preservation" have been defined in various ways and often used interchangeably.

Preservation is a more general term that encompasses a wide array of actions taken to help ensure the protection of art from damage, deterioration, and loss, and involves a range of activities to reduce or minimize the deterioration induced by physical, chemical, or biological agents over a period of time. *Heritage preservation* is a term that is in common usage today.

Restoration is a more traditional term that includes the repair or replacement of damaged or missing elements in a work of art, with the goal of returning the object to its original appearance. In addition, restoration of original works of art involves a range of cosmetic or aesthetic treatments, such as cleaning, to remove grime or discolored varnishes or removal of later additions such as overpainting. Restoration can also include compensation of losses in the support or reintegration of the damaged paint layers.

Historically, restorers carefully guarded their treatment methods as trade secrets, but this practice gradually evolved toward a greater openness and sharing of information among professionals. Restoration techniques and materials now encompass both traditional materials and modern materials made available through the development of new technologies and scientific research. When guided by respect for the artist's intention and the original materials used in creating the art, restoration can return a work of art to a state that more closely approximates its original or previous condition. Unfortunately, however, some work done in the name of restoration has resulted in art that might appear to be in good condition but will show under close scrutiny that it has, in fact, suffered further damage, through the elimination or covering of original elements or through the use of methods or materials that cannot be easily modified in the future without harm to the art. It is precisely such incidences of significant alteration of the original work or loss of historical information that have contributed to the emergence of the profession of art conservation.

Conservation is a term that was first employed in an art context in the 1930s. Its continued use reflects an increased respect for the original aspects of an artwork, as opposed to the desire simply to make the art "look good." Conservation is an interdisciplinary field that comprises the activities of both preservation (preventive care) *and* restoration. Its objective is to slow any progressive deterioration of a work of art and to keep it intact for as long as possible, and it is practiced according to professional principles, ethics, and standards. In conservation examination, documentation, treatment, and research, conservators use art historical and technological information, scientific knowledge and methods, intellectual assessment, and reasoning as well as technical competency and craftsmanship. Equally important are a humanistic approach and the recognition of a work of art as an aesthetic entity.

In addition to the treatment of art, conservation includes management of the conditions in the environment of a work of art to preserve or restore the integrity of the object. It aims to prevent or mitigate damage and deterioration, employing such efforts as the following:

❑ Controlling and monitoring ambient temperature, relative humidity, and light levels

❑ Reducing chemical threats from atmospheric pollutants and biological hazards from mold, insects, and other pests

❏ Safe framing or mounting
❏ Implementing appropriate handling, packing, and shipping practices
❏ Providing secure locations for display or storage

Art Conservators and Restorers

Art conservators are professionals with highly specialized training and experience in the conservation of cultural property. Historically, these practitioners were called "restorers," a more traditional term that is still used in many parts of the art market. It was not until sometime in the mid-1950s that the term "conservator" emerged in the United Kingdom, then in Canada and the United States. This title was used to distinguish the new breed of art practitioners who were responsible for preserving art as well as restoring it, and it reinforced the fact that the profession had embraced the role of science in assisting in the conservation of art. Another variant in the title is "conservator-restorer," which is a more recent appellation originating in the 1970s in Europe, adopted as a compromise in terminology to bring together similar professionals from different countries.

Traditionally, most aspiring restorers were either self-taught or served in apprenticeships under experienced restorers for many years. Today, it is more common for professional conservators in North America, the United Kingdom and Ireland, Australia, and parts of Europe to enter the field through university-level training, by earning a master's degree in art conservation, historic preservation, or science and techniques; or a master's degree plus a diploma or certificate in conservation. Prerequisites for admission to these highly specialized graduate programs in North America vary, but they normally include a bachelor's degree in either art or science, with coursework in the alternate discipline, some studio-art studies, and some pre-program conservation experience. Apart from the academic studies they offer, these conservation programs also require students to complete curriculum internships under the supervision of experienced conservators. New graduates of the conservation programs then gain hands-on experience working with established conservators or eventually launch their own independent practices. Ongoing professional development is a requirement for all conservators, regardless of their type of training.

Conservators require a knowledge of art, science, and technology as well as an understanding of processes of deterioration and conservation methods. They must also possess finely tuned technical skills, an inquiring mind, a critical thought process, an aptitude for problem solving, patience, and an altruistic ability to put the object first. In addition, since some conservation processes can involve potential—but usually avoidable—danger to the object, sound judgment and competent risk management are essential qualities in a conservator.

Conservators may be employed by a wide array of institutions—such as museums, art galleries, historical societies, libraries, archives, archaeological or historic sites, government agencies, regional conservation centers, universities, or conservation research institutes. Alternatively, they may work in the private sector, which is where individual art collectors and investors will most often deal with them.

Conservation scientists are also an important part of the conservation field, and work with conservators in the technical study and analysis of the materials used to create works of art. These specialized scientists investigate processes of deterioration and preventive conservation, in addition to the risks of transportation and the development of safer crating and shipping procedures. They may also conduct research into materials and techniques employed by conservators. Conservation scientists may be called upon to become involved in authentication studies or forensic work that involves the study of suspected fakes or forgeries.

Preserving Your Investment—The Basics

As a collector, you have the responsibility of taking good care of the art you own. Once you have acquired a work of art of any kind, you will want to ensure that it does not disintegrate or become damaged and that it maintains its value over time. Proper care and treatment will help to preserve your art and to protect its monetary or market value. If you have bought wisely and you are housing your art in a safe place, you will want to avoid making the mistake of waiting until you observe some form of damage or deterioration before calling in a professional to examine your works of art. Requesting a condition assessment early on and monitoring your collection periodically can help you identify existing problems before they become more serious and potential problems before they occur.

Consulting an appropriate conservation professional when you first acquire your art will allow the conservator to

❑ confirm the materials, techniques, and structure of the work of art;

❑ assess the physical condition of the art and identify signs of deterioration or damage;

❑ provide reassurance that the art is in good condition or not at risk of damage;

❑ advise on preservation and maintenance;

❑ assess the need for any treatment that might stabilize the structure of a work of art or improve its appearance in a manner consistent with the artist's original intent; and

❑ make recommendations for its care in handling, storage, and display.

Whether you collect ancient glass objects or contemporary paintings, whether you are concerned primarily with your art's escalating market value or its purely sentimental value, the timely advice of a conservator can spare you grief in the future.

Choosing a Conservator

In choosing a conservator, you need to locate a professional with the appropriate training, knowledge, and experience to deal with the type of object that you have. Unfortunately, this is not always as simple a matter as it might appear. Since conservators do not have to be licensed, anyone can advertise or call himself a provider of "restoration services," whether or not he has the necessary qualifications or adheres to any professional code of practice. Some of these practitioners have the skill and knowledge to perform excellent work, while others can do irreparable damage to works of art.

So, how exactly do you choose a good conservator? One sound approach is to obtain a list of accredited conservators from a professional conservation association. National and international associations of conservation have been established in many countries, and have developed codes of ethics and guidelines for professional conduct specifically for the conservator. Some have instituted professional accreditation for their member conservators. This voluntary accreditation procedure constitutes the profession's commitment to self-regulation through a peer review process, with the goal of helping to protect the public and private art collector from unqualified or unethical individuals who pose as conservators or restorers. For example, in Canada, there is the Canadian Association of Professional Conservators (CAPC), and in the United Kingdom and Ireland, there are the Professional Accreditation of Conservator-Restorers (PACR) operated by the Institute of Conservation (ICON), the British Horological Institute (BHI), and the Society of Archivists.

Another option is to contact a non-self-regulating professional conservation association for a list of members. There are a number of such associations throughout the world that do not accredit conservators, but do require members to agree to abide by their code of ethics in order to register for or renew their membership. Some of these organizations provide listings of members who have demonstrated a commitment to a code of ethics as approved by that body. For example, the American Institute for Conservation of Historic and Artistic Works (AIC) has established membership categories of "Fellow" and "Professional Associate," which require a certain level of conservation experience and demonstrated ethical behavior and peer endorsement that distinguish them from "Associate" members. AIC also provides access to a directory of its members who have either Fellow or Professional Associate status.

Another approach is to contact a local or major museum that can provide a list of qualified conservators whose services they are familiar with and can recommend with confidence. Once you have a list of names of potentially suitable conservators, interviews can give you the opportunity to obtain references and information about their background and practices.

You will want to choose a professional who is open about his conservation training and experience, his affiliations (such as membership in professional organizations), and his ethical obligations.

The code of ethics for conservators in the United States, which has been adopted by the AIC, prescribes a number of standards for the professional conservator, including the following:

❑ To act honestly and respectfully with regard to the work of art, its owner, fellow conservators, and society

❑ To maintain high standards of practice in all aspects of conservation work

❑ To recognize the limits of one's own knowledge, experience, and competency

❑ To evaluate and use materials and methods in examination and treatment according to the present state of knowledge and use them only if they are reversible or readily removable and will not (now or later) harm the work of art or interfere with its future examination or study

❑ To take responsibility for preventive conservation and treatment of the work of art

❑ To document examination and treatment in conservation reports

❑ To continue to develop one's professional skills

❑ To contribute to the profession through sharing experience with colleagues, teaching, mentoring, publishing, and promoting a broader understanding of conservation to others

A prospective conservator should be pleased to provide information on

❑ his previous work experience;

❑ his technical reports and photographic documentation; and

❑ his facility's location, fire-protection and security systems, insurance, and art-transportation practices.

What to Expect in Terms of Conservation

Once you've selected a conservator, he can carry out a condition assessment of just one work of art or of your entire collection.

THE EXAMINATION

Work begins with a detailed examination of a work of art to identify its material and structure, including documentation of the physical condition of the piece, both in writing and in photographs. If restoration, or treatment, of the art is necessary, the conservator should examine and test the work of art, so that he understands the materials and techniques, structure, damage, and other significant factors. When they are available, he should consult previous condition records or conservation reports. Routine examination may include use of a stereomicroscope and ultraviolet light. Your conservator may recommend sampling and scientific analysis in order to answer specific questions about original materials or later additions.

After analyzing the work of art, the conservator will consider what surface cleaning agents, solvents, adhesives, or consolidants might be used, and these will be pretested in order to determine the sensitivity of the materials of the work of art and the removability of nonoriginal components. He will supplement his written treatment records with drawings and photographs before, during, and after treatment.

THE CONDITION REPORT AND TREATMENT PROPOSAL

When he has completed his examination, the conservator will then provide you with the following items:

- ❑ A written condition report
- ❑ A conservation treatment proposal
- ❑ An explanation of the procedures and a rationale for their use
- ❑ An expected completion date
- ❑ A description of the anticipated impact of treatment on the structure or appearance of the work
- ❑ An explanation of any particular risks that might be associated with the proposed treatment
- ❑ A cost quote for his conservation services (which may be either an estimate or a fixed rate, something that needs to be confirmed with the conservator before approving the treatment proposal). Like appraiser's fees, conservator's fees should not be based on the value of the work being treated.

Before beginning work, the conservator will usually ask you to sign a written legal agreement authorizing conservation work according to the treatment proposal. If, during treatment of your artwork, he finds that modifications to the original proposal are necessary, he should inform you and ask you to approve any changes and related costs.

CONSERVATION TREATMENT

Signs of a certain amount of aging are to be expected in works of art and, indeed, are often valued as evidence of age and history. In general, most professional conservators now adopt an approach that is referred to as "minimal intervention," which means the execution of treatment that is no more invasive or comprehensive than is absolutely necessary and appropriate for the object.

Any work of art that has been damaged in any way has incurred some loss of integrity. The type and extent of that damage, however, and the manner in which it is restored will determine whether the monetary value will be reduced significantly, somewhat, or not at all.

On the one hand, minor damage that is repaired by an unskilled or unethical practitioner can lead to a considerable reduction in value of that work of art. On the other hand, major structural or aesthetic damage, when treated by a conservator who applies sound technical skills and an ethical approach, can result in much less of a reduction in the value of a work of art. A skilled conservator can also remove nonoriginal additions, such as extensive overpainting that might be covering original details, without damaging the underlying original design. Conservation carried out with this level of skill can thereby increase the value of an otherwise less-valuable work.

Conservation treatment may be required in some situations where

❏ an unacceptable form of physical, chemical, or biological deterioration has occurred;

❏ some accidental damage or act of vandalism has taken place;

❏ there is evidence of "inherent vice" (the effect of instability in the artist's own materials or techniques);

❏ some previous restoration has been rendered unacceptable by virtue of its having been poorly done or carried out using materials and methods that, though appropriate for the time in which they were done, have not aged well;

❏ additions have been made, by someone other than the artist, that misrepresent the work of art, detract from its appearance, or might damage the structure; and

❏ inappropriate repairs, such as unsuitable lining attempts, unacceptable fills, inserts, or other added elements.

A wide array of conservation methods can include stabilization of structural insecurities, removal of nonoriginal materials, and replacement of damaged components or compensation of loss.

Conservation treatment can be undertaken to address structural instability in the work of art:

❏ Paint layers that are lifting can be set down and consolidated by introducing adhesives that have been tested for conservation use.

❑ Tears in paper or canvas and fractures in wood can be re-adhered or reinforced to prevent further tearing or splitting.

❑ Pronounced planar deformation in canvas and paper supports can be reduced with low-pressure treatments using controlled humidity and sometimes temperature.

❑ An old lining fabric or backing with embrittled adhesive can be removed if it poses a risk to the original support or design layers.

❑ A painting with a severely damaged or embrittled canvas that can no longer provide adequate support for the paint layers can be lined (that is, have a new fabric attached to the reverse of the original canvas).

Conservation treatment can also involve the removal of nonoriginal materials or later additions to improve the aesthetic qualities and integrity of the work of art:

❑ Superficial grime, accretions, or mold growth can be removed.

❑ Inappropriate coatings or varnishes that have discolored or become cloudy with age can often be carefully removed or reduced, using solvents or other chemical systems that will not damage the underlying paint.

❑ Overpaint or retouching (not applied by the artist) that is excessive, mismatched, or discolored can be sensitively removed, using solvent solutions and gels, compresses and poultices, or tools such as scalpels, in such a way that the original paint is not damaged in the process.

The keys to maintaining the value of a work of art during conservation treatment are to ensure the appropriateness and quality of the restoration and to demonstrate respect for the original work and the intention of the artist. When a work of art has suffered damage and loss that have an aesthetic impact, the conservator must first decide whether to restore the lost material or design elements. The goal of compensation is not necessarily to make the work look like new but to improve its appearance by bringing it closer to a previously known or unaltered state. There are a number of ethical considerations surrounding this issue, and they may be determined as much by cultural beliefs as by professional practices. The extent of loss and knowledge of the preexisting or original condition of the work must dictate the approach taken to reintegration.

In some contexts, it might not be appropriate to reconstruct large losses of design in paintings or other objects, because such reconstruction would be regarded as falsification. In other contexts, reconstruction might be acceptable if clear evidence of an earlier state exists and if the nonoriginal additions remain distinguishable from the original parts. In most situations, for example, it is considered acceptable to inpaint small loss areas as long as original paint is not covered and the materials used are stable and can be readily removed in the future. Inpainting executed by a conservator may not be apparent from a normal viewing distance, but it should remain detectable on close scrutiny and when viewed under ultraviolet light.

The approach to compensation and the methods used to carry it out must be decided for each unique work and its context or use. The conservator has a wide array of suitable materials and techniques available to use in the treatment of a work of art's structural and aesthetic components, and she selects a treatment based on a respect for the original materials and meaning of the work.

THE TREATMENT REPORT

Upon completion of the conservation work, the conservator will provide you with a written copy of a treatment report (usually with photographs) and also retain a copy for herself. In addition, she will make recommendations for the future care of the work of art, including acceptable environmental conditions or special handling requirements, or she will identify the need to monitor its condition over time. Written reports and photographic images that record the pretreatment and posttreatment condition of a work of art, and any materials and techniques used in restoring it, should be kept as part of the permanent archive for each work, to support your claims as to the real condition of your art.

In certain circumstances, the conservator you hire might find a conservation treatment you have requested for the work of art to be unethical or otherwise inappropriate. In that case, she will refuse to perform the treatment, but if that occurs, she should be able to provide you with a reasonable explanation and justification for such an action.

THE CONSERVATOR'S FEES

It is important that, as an art investor, you weigh the costs of conserving against the costs of not conserving. Conservation fees may be minor or major, depending on the nature of the work of art and the type and extent of treatment required. In order to secure conservation services from an established professional conservator, you can expect to pay professional rates. Whether charged by the hour or by the project, fees can also vary considerably from one conservator to another depending on many factors, from level of expertise to location and overhead costs. A conservator will base charges on

❏ the complexity and inherent risks of the treatment,
❏ the actual hours required,
❏ direct costs, such as for materials used, and
❏ shipping or storage charges, if applicable.

As a collector, when you are faced with the decision of whether to have conservation work carried out, consider the value of the work of art itself (both its monetary value and sentimental value). Reflect on the potential loss of value or meaning that a damaged or deteriorating work of art will suffer, and keep in mind that, in some cases, inaction in the face of severe or ongoing damage may result in total loss of the work. Further, contemplate such a loss not only in the context of your own desires but also in the context of any future owner or any art bequeathals that you might be considering in your estate.

Authentication and Appraisals

It is important to note that most conservators should not be asked to authenticate works of art. In general, this is best left to museum curators, auction houses, or art historians who specialize in particular artists or periods of art history. That said, there are instances where conservators can team up with conservation scientists, art historians, and other specialists, to undertake a systematic study that will result in evidence that either supports or refutes a particular attribution. Except for these cases, however, authentication of a work of art by a conservator may constitute a conflict of interest.

A conservator should also not be asked to provide an appraised value of a work of art unless the individual has been certified as an appraiser. In fact, such activity, for most conservators, is construed as a conflict of interest. The collector should contact an art appraisal association or society to request the names of local certified appraisers in the appropriate area of expertise. (See Chapter 2 for a discussion of the art appraisal process.)

Preventive Conservation and Ongoing Maintenance

All materials used to create works of art are subject to some form of natural decay. Since most art is vulnerable to environmental conditions, preventive conservation is probably the most effective way to help ensure the preservation of your collection over time. Although the responsibility for such conservation rests ultimately with the collector, conservators can offer useful advice about how best to protect your works of art and slow down their rate of deterioration. The factors to beware of, which can both cause immediate damage or accelerate long-term deterioration, include the following:

- ❏ Extremes or rapid fluctuations in temperature
- ❏ Extremes or rapid fluctuations in relative humidity
- ❏ Excessive light
- ❏ Biological agents
- ❏ Atmospheric pollutants

Whether a work of art is stored in an institution, a company office, or a family home, a variety of circumstances can damage it over time. Paper, canvas, textiles, wood, and other materials, when properly made and cared for, can last for hundreds of years—but when improperly stored, they are vulnerable to all sorts of damage and deterioration. Basic information about specific threats follows.

RELATIVE HUMIDITY

Relative humidity (RH) and temperature in the environment have a direct relationship with each other. As the air temperature is raised, the RH generally decreases, and as the temperature drops, the RH increases. Fluctuating levels of RH in the environment can cause the materials making up works of art to expand and contract as they absorb and release moisture. Some materials and structures are more sensitive and responsive to these changes than others. The following are some examples of different mediums affected by inappropriate humidity:

❑ *Wooden sculptures or paintings on wood panel supports* are particularly vulnerable to changing RH. Exposure to very low humidity levels (less than 40 percent) can lead to desiccation and shrinking, warping, or splitting of the wood and flaking of the paint and ground layers.

❑ *Painting canvases* exposed to excessive moisture or very high RH can suddenly and forcefully shrink, causing severe paint loss. Sized canvas kept in low RH can become embrittled, making these supports more vulnerable to fracturing or cracking when handled.

❑ *Paper* kept in low RH can also become embrittled, making it susceptible to fracture, but works of art on paper in a high-RH environment are in danger of cockling.

❑ *Many organic materials,* when exposed to high-RH conditions (greater than 65–75 percent) can develop mold growth and related staining or weakening of structure.

❑ *Metals* are more likely to corrode in a high-RH environment.

The actual RH values that pose a risk to works of art vary from material to material and from object to object. For this reason, it is often recommended that collections of art objects be stored in conditions as close as possible to 50 percent RH, plus or minus 5 percent, with a minimum of rapid fluctuations. The environment of individual objects or groupings of similar objects, however, may be tailored to the specific sensitivities of those materials.

Heating, ventilation, and air conditioning (HVAC) or climate-control systems, by humidifying or dehumidifying the ambient air, can be used to achieve desired RH levels. Systems calibration and regular monitoring of RH are important. Good air circulation is also necessary to ensure the even distribution of the conditioned air. In addition, in order to reduce inappropriate or unacceptably fluctuating levels of RH, art should not be displayed near air vents or radiators.

AMBIENT TEMPERATURE

Apart from its effect on the RH of the environment, temperature can have its own impact on the condition of works of art. Depending on their components, some art objects exposed to low temperatures can become more brittle and therefore more prone to cracking or fracturing during handling. Higher temperatures can lead to an increase in the rate of chemical reactions involved in deterioration in general. A couple of examples of materials with particular sensitivity to temperature are provided below.

❏ *Acrylic paintings* have design layers that will fracture or delaminate more easily when subjected to pressure or shock in ambient temperatures significantly below room temperature. When these paints are subjected to higher temperatures, however, they can suffer increased tackiness and can therefore imbibe dirt and adhere to their wrapping materials.

❏ *Photographs or other image-based materials* can suffer accelerated degradation when exposed to higher temperatures. Cold storage is usually recommended for these collections.

Again, the actual temperatures that can induce damage to works of art will be different for various types of materials. In order to protect a range of object types, it is often recommended that an ambient temperature of 68 degrees Fahrenheit, plus or minus 2 degrees, be maintained.

As is true with humidity control, well-designed HVAC systems can provide appropriate temperature levels, if they are well positioned within the spaces to be conditioned, there is efficient air circulation, and thermostats are accurate and monitored regularly.

Art should never be stored or displayed close to localized heat sources, such as radiators, light fixtures, or direct sunlight. Display-case or vitrine lights should not generate a lot of heat, or else they should have sufficient ventilation to keep the case interior from overheating.

LIGHT EXPOSURE

Light, without which you would be unable to view and enjoy your works of art, can unfortunately also have a destructive effect on the materials making up those works. Ultraviolet (UV) and infrared (IR) radiation are invisible, but they are the usual culprits when it comes to the deterioration of works of art that are made of organic materials, and both are present in regular home and office light fittings. Near-UV light, which is visible to the human eye, can also cause damage to organic materials.

❑ IR radiation heats up the surface of art objects and increases the rate of deterioration of their materials.

❑ UV radiation, emitted to varying degrees by different light sources, can fade, discolor, or otherwise degrade organic materials such as paint, ink, textiles, and paper objects.

The quality and intensity of UV and IR radiation, as well as visible light—and the length of time to which the art is exposed—are critical factors in determining how much damage will be done. It is therefore important to select or modify light sources in ways that will reduce the amount of harmful or excessive light to which your art will be exposed. The following methods can be useful:

❑ *Blinds or UV-absorbing window films,* which offer a shield from direct sunlight.

❑ *Special UV-filtering sleeves* can fit over fluorescent tubes.

❑ *UV-absorbing Plexiglas* can be used in framing light-sensitive works on paper, photographs, or textiles.

Light levels can be measured in order to monitor the amount of UV radiation or the intensity of light in display areas. "Lux" levels (which measure the light intensity) can give an indication of how much light an object is being exposed to. Light-sensitive materials such as the following should be exposed to reduced lux levels:

❑ *Most works on paper,* particularly those created using modern media or lower-quality paper, should be exposed to light levels in the range of 50 to 75 lux.

❑ *Oil paintings* with stable pigments can be exhibited at 150 to 350 lux.

If it is not possible or desirable to display your collection at lower light levels, reducing the length of time that your art is exposed to light will help to preserve it, as the damaging effects of light are cumulative.

BIOLOGICAL AGENTS

If you are maintaining a larger collection of art, you should have a formal pest-management plan in place, to avoid biological risks.

❏ *Mold* (discussed above in the section on relative humidity) can present itself as staining, odor, or etching of painted surfaces or supports. Also keep in mind that if your art is directly exposed to water from a leak or flood, it is important to air it out as quickly as possible and immediately seek the advice of a conservator.

❏ *Insects* can attack collections of books, paper, textiles, wooden objects, and framed paintings. To reduce the chances of insect infestation, it is important to examine your collections carefully, at the time of acquisition and periodically afterward, for any sign of insect eggs, larvae, or adults, or evidence of attacks on wood, such as frass (powder) emanating from holes or tunnels.

❏ *Rodents* can devour and seriously damage wood, paper, or textile-based collections. Animal droppings or nests usually indicate rodent infestation.

ATMOSPHERIC POLLUTION

Unfiltered air contains dust and pollutants that can tarnish silver or make the surfaces of works of art more acidic, causing discoloration, embrittlement, and eventual disintegration of paper fibers over time. Care should be taken not to display works of art in areas near food-preparation areas, open fireplaces, candles, or tobacco smoke, in order to prevent the deposition of harmful chemicals and disfiguring coatings. The materials making up some display cases—wood, paints, varnishes, or adhesives—also emit volatile components that can degrade various kinds of art in contained spaces. Filtering the air passing through your HVAC system and providing good ventilation and air circulation will eliminate many of the chemical and particulate pollutants in your art's environment.

PHYSICAL FORCES

Works of art are continually being exposed to physical forces, such as accidental pressure or impact, that can cause minor to major damage in the form of abrasion, dents, scratches, tears, cracking, or flaking of design layers. Handling adds the risks of vibration and shock that can lead to fracture or breakage, delamination of paint layers, or detachment of other components. The choice of a display area should be made with some consideration of possible risks of accidental damage caused by direct contact with people, pets, or equipment.

Some of the greatest risks for the safety of art occur during shipping or other handling, and a section on safe art shipping and storage follows.

VANDALISM, THEFT, OR NATURAL DISASTERS

Acts of vandalism represent the deliberate damaging of works of art and may occur with inadequate security or inappropriate display locations. Likewise, theft is a risk if works are not installed with security hardware, alarms, or other forms of protection. Natural disasters, such as fire, flood, or earthquake, can seriously damage or completely destroy a collection.

In the event that your art is damaged by an act of vandalism or by a fire, flood, or other disaster, it is important to seek the advice of a conservator immediately. Since a rapid assessment of the type and amount of damage, along with appropriate action, can often do much to prevent further damage or loss, it is wise to have a contingency plan in place to enable you to react quickly.

Shipping and Storing Works of Art

An essential component in the preservation program for your works of art is the manner in which they are housed while they are not on display. There are significant risks to your collection if great care is not taken in planning and implementing the correct shipping and storage of your art.

SHIPPING FINE ART

The field of specialized art transport is one that has developed in the United States only over the past thirty years. Prior to that time, general freight companies or companies specializing in the transport of antiques were the only choices available to museums, galleries, and art collectors. In the late 1970s, as museums began to mount larger and more ambitious exhibitions and the commercial-gallery world expanded, a need arose for highly specialized shipping and installation companies. In response, a number of companies sprang up, many of them founded by artists who enjoyed the process of handling artwork for museums and galleries and who were looking for ways to support themselves.

The majority of these specialized art-shipping companies were established in major cities such as New York, Boston, Los Angeles, San Francisco, and Washington, D.C. These companies now provide such services as local and long-distance transportation, crating and packing, storage, installation, and, in some cases, international import and export. Depending on the focus of the particular company, these services are tailored to the private individual or gallery or to the most stringent requirements of the museum community.

As these companies grew and began to perfect their techniques for handling art, professional standards steadily improved, and new information about equipment and materials also began to emerge. Museum conservators contributed the knowledge they had gleaned from their experiences, both within their institutions and with the private art-services companies they employed. These conservators have since published numerous research papers on the best practices for the packing and shipping of art. As a result there is now a growing consensus among museums about what standards should be followed when packing and shipping works of art.

GROUND TRANSPORT

As museum scientists examined the best practices for the transport of works of art and museum objects, trucks were carefully evaluated. The conclusion was that the use of trucks with air-ride suspension provided the best protection from shock and vibration. While it does not eliminate the need for proper packing and crating, air-ride suspension has been proven to be one of the single most important protections available in ground transport.

Climate control has also become a museum requirement for all shipments because it has been shown that rapid changes in temperature and humidity can have devastating effects on certain types of art. It is important, however, to understand what type of control is possible in trucks. Controlling temperature by adding heating or cooling is the primary function of refrigeration, or "reefer," units on trucks. The control of humidity however is not as straightforward. One byproduct of air conditioning is the removal of moisture from the air, which lowers relative humidity. This is very valuable in the hot summer months, but these units do not add humidity in the winter months when the air is dry. At those times, the proper packing of humidity-sensitive objects is very important. Crates must be insulated, well sealed, and protected as much as possible from rapid changes in temperature. When an object is very sensitive to changes in relative humidity (e.g., wood panel paintings) techniques can be used to moderate humidity changes within the crate.

Tractor-trailer trucks, which are used for shipping larger works of art, frequently come equipped with other technology such as global positioning systems or onboard computers and with driver amenities necessary for long-distance transport. The size of these trucks limits where they can go, both legally and physically, as a full-sized modern tractor-trailer combination may be more than 85 feet (26 meters) in length, and up to 13 feet 6 inches (or over 4 meters) tall. When arranging transport in a vehicle of this size, it is important to plan not only the beginning of the trip and the space requirements for loading but also the delivery. Although museums are used to accommodating vehicles of this size, many art galleries and most private residences cannot, and so special arrangements must be made.

When shipping over short distances, or when the objects being transported are not highly fragile, it is quite possible, even preferable, not to use a tractor trailer but to consider a wider variety of trucks and packing techniques. Understanding the dangers that specific objects might be exposed to during a particular shipment is the first step in determining what kind of shipping should be used. Experienced shippers should be able to provide their clients with a variety of options to consider.

CRATING AND PACKING

Packing works of art depends on the needs of the art, the type of shipping planned, and the available budget. Crates designed for museum usage are frequently insulated to protect against temperature changes, painted to prevent water damage, and covered by lids secured with screws or bolts rather than nails, to allow for repeated opening and closing. The interiors of these crates are fitted with customized foam bumpers to protect against shock and vibration. In some cases, a double-crate system will be used to provide extra protection against shock and vibration and to isolate the object. This type of crate provides maximum protection for the work of art and is particularly beneficial during traveling exhibitions.

When packing and crating less-valuable works of art, less-expensive options for crating may be requested, such as simpler exterior construction, uninsulated interiors, and less-expensive disposable packaging.

Galleries, auction houses, and private individuals often use this kind of packaging, and when such crates are well conceived and constructed, they are perfectly adequate for one-way shipping, even for relatively high-value works of art—as long as professional art shippers are involved.

STORAGE

Professional art-storage facilities need to control temperature and humidity according to the specifications discussed earlier. Unfortunately, many facilities that advertise "climate control" are referring only to temperature control, and so it is important to be sure that the climate in an art warehouse is maintained at close to 50 percent relative humidity (plus or minus 5 percent) and 70 degrees Fahrenheit (plus or minus 5 degrees). The conditions in storage should be monitored on a regular basis, and records should be available for inspection if required.

FACILITY SECURITY

Electronic security systems that consist of door contacts, motion and vibration sensors, and antitamper devices connected to an alarm company's central station are the minimum security requirements for an art-storage facility. Additional equipment, such as water detection, heat and smoke detection, and digital closed-circuit television (CCTV) recording are also highly valuable. The facility must also have a sprinkler system connected to the central-station alarm. Over the past ten years, many museums have decided that a standard "wet-pipe" sprinkler system is the most reliable and effective means of controlling fire. Other systems are also available, but they are very expensive to install and maintain, and so most commercial art warehouses use wet-pipe sprinkler systems, which must be properly maintained and monitored but provide excellent fire protection.

There are few absolutes in providing protection for works of art in storage or transit. Factors to consider are the art's value, the budget, and the risks, and, within these parameters, there are many different acceptable solutions. What is appropriate for a commercial gallery or auction house may not be right for a museum or for an individual collector or investor. Museums and other art professionals can usually recommend trustworthy fine-art service companies, and such companies are expert in developing appropriate and creative solutions to most shipping and storage problems.

Summary of Considerations for Art Conservation

There are a number of ways to ensure that your art collection is well-preserved and maintains its integrity and market value for years to come.

❏ Find a qualified professional conservator who can advise you on the condition and preservation of your art and carry out conservation treatment as required.

❏ Use preventive-care methods in framing or mounting your works of art, to reduce the risk of needless damage.

❏ Plan suitable display and storage of your art to minimize risks to your collection.

❏ Monitor relative humidity, temperature, and light, to indicate whether harmful conditions exist and make adjustments as necessary.

❏ Watch out for evidence of pests, so they can be tracked, identified, and eliminated before they do serious damage to your collections.

❏ Implement security measures to prevent vandalism or theft.

❏ Have an emergency or disaster plan in place, to prevent or mitigate serious damage or loss.

❏ Hire professional art handlers to wrap and transport your works of art to ensure that appropriate care is taken in situations when your art is most vulnerable.

Whether you have one valued art object or a significant art collection, it is wise to seek out and work closely with an art conservator and a reputable art shipping company who can provide the counsel and services you require to help ensure that your art does not lose value or integrity. Working together, you can make certain that your art is safely housed, displayed, and transported. A program of appropriate monitoring of condition and the development of conservation treatment strategies can be established to meet the specific needs of your art and your particular context. A conservator can assist you not only with your existing collection but can advise you with respect to proposed art acquisitions to identify conditions that may be cause for concern now or in the future. Learning more about the technique, condition, and conservation of your art can also add a fascinating new dimension to your collecting and help you to protect your art for your own enjoyment as well as that of future generations.

12

The Illegal Art Trade

Thomas C. Danziger and Charles T. Danziger[1]

EDITOR'S NOTE: The legitimate trade in art has thrived during the last ten years, reportedly exceeding $60 billion in annual global sales in 2008.[2] Running in tandem with this enormous market is a substantial illegal trade in works of art and antiquities. Because of the clandestine nature of this underground market, no one knows its precise commercial value, but some estimate that the illicit art market may be running in excess of $6 billion per year.

This complex black market has many layers and includes the trade in stolen goods, the illegal import and export of art, and the market for fakes and forgeries. There is also a small but important "gray" market, composed of art of uncertain provenance, art with disputes over title and ownership, and art traded legally in one nation but contravening another nation's patrimony restrictions or other trade policies.

Two of the unique risks associated with investing in art concern authenticity and provenance. A risk associated with investing in art is that a work could turn out to be fake, forged, stolen, or illicitly imported or exported. Unless the authenticity of a work can be established, its valuation—and marketability—is likely to be substantially constrained.

This final chapter looks at some of the key issues related to authenticity, ownership history, and art theft that are pertinent to art collectors and investors, drawing on the experience and observations of Charles and Thomas Danziger, two prominent New York art attorneys (and brothers). It deals with the issues related to ownership of previously stolen art, including examples of some controversial cases of works looted by Nazis during World War II. It looks at the importance of ensuring authenticity and provenance when investing in art and discusses the implications and remedies for investors in cases of dubious authenticity or uncertain provenance. Finally, the serious problem of art theft from museums in the United States is also addressed.

Recovering Stolen Art: Whose Is It?

One of the most interesting areas of art law concerns works looted by the Nazis. Even though the Second World War ended well over sixty years ago, the issues relating to looted works remain alive and well in today's art market—and occupy the time of various art attorneys. Many disputes concerning such works involve two innocent parties: the heirs of the original rightful owner and the innocent purchaser of the work (or his heirs) who had no knowledge of its shady past.

So, what should you do if a painting that was stolen from your family by the Nazis turns up two generations later hanging above your neighbor's mantelpiece? As a starting point, before taking action, you should gather as much information as possible about the work at the time it was last seen. This may include uncovering formal documentation of ownership (such as bills of sale and shipping receipts), and often involves digging through correspondence and old photographs to place the work in your family at the time the work was lost. Since a number of art dealers who operated in occupied Europe during the war were known to be acting as agents for prominent Nazis, a bill of sale from one of them may be a tip-off that a work was not sold in an arm's-length transaction but was, instead, sold under duress.

If you or your family has been the victim of Nazi looting, collect available documentation and contact an attorney. But beware: cases involving Nazi looted art are notoriously slow (and expensive) to resolve, so do not expect a quick recovery, even with a mountain of supporting evidence to buttress your claim.

When evaluating a possible claim based on looted art, most attorneys begin with the general rule in the United States that a purchaser cannot acquire good title to a stolen work and may be exposed to a claim by the original owner almost indefinitely. This general principle applies no matter how innocent the buyer and no matter how often the piece was purchased, sold, or donated in the years after its initial theft. Although there are a few narrow exceptions to this rule (which are discussed below), generally, once a work is stolen it remains stolen until it is returned to its rightful owners. By contrast, in civil-law countries such as France, Germany, and Switzerland,[3] a good-faith purchaser may indeed acquire good title from a thief, even against the rightful owner. In some countries, this right can arise within a very short period of time.

The application of this general rule to real-life claims can sometimes produce seemingly inequitable results, and often raises interesting questions not just of choice of law but also of basic fairness. For example, what should happen in the following cases?

❏ An art gallery that unwittingly acquired Nazi-looted art, restored it at its own expense, and sold it years later;

❏ A dealer who openly exhibited a painting and included it in publications such as the artist's *catalogue raisonné* (a comprehensive catalogue of the artist's works) without the slightest objection from a prior (but still rightful) owner;

❏ The case of a buyer of looted art who can prove that technically the work was not stolen, but legally confiscated and sold under the laws of Nazi Germany; or

❏ Art that was simply abandoned by owners who were fleeing the country.

Do any of these cases change the basic rule that once works have been stolen, they remain stolen until returned to their rightful owners (or the owners' heirs)? The answer—at least in New York—is no, according to the landmark 1966 New York Supreme Court decision *Menzel v. List*.

Menzel v. List: In the Case of Nazi Looting, a Decision for the Original Owner

Erna Menzel, the plaintiff in that case, tried to recover a Marc Chagall painting that she and her husband had left in their apartment in Brussels in 1940, when they fled the invading Nazis. The Menzels searched for the painting after the war, finally locating it in 1962 in an art book that named the owner as Albert List. For his part, List had bought the work in 1955 for $4,000 from the highly respected Perls Galleries in

New York. List refused to turn the work over to Mrs. Menzel, arguing that her claim was barred by the statute of limitations. Menzel sued List, demanding that he return the work or reimburse her for its value at the time suit was brought, $22,500. The court ultimately ordered List to return the painting and held that the taking of private property not necessary for the waging of war is unlawful.

Not surprisingly, most cases case involving looted works of art turn on the issue of the applicable statute of limitations. In New York, for example, the statute of limitations for the recovery of personal property is only three years. The key question then becomes: When does the statute of limitations start to run? The answer depends on the state. Many states apply the "discovery rule", which says that the clock starts from the date the original owner discovered, or should have discovered, the work's location and the identity of the person who possessed it, taking into account such variables as its visibility in exhibitions, catalogues, and other places where the original owner might be likely to spot it. Certain states, however—most notably New York (which is generally protective of the rights of the original owner who wishes to recover a work)—apply the "demand-and-refusal rule". Under that rule, the clock starts from the date the original owner demands return of the work and the current possessor refuses to return it—which is usually long after the date when the work was originally stolen.

O'Keeffe v. Snyder: The Discovery Rule and the Statute of Limitations

A good example of the discovery rule is the 1980 New Jersey case of *O'Keeffe v. Snyder*, in which the artist Georgia O'Keeffe sought to have three stolen paintings returned to her. The paintings were taken from a New York gallery in 1946, but O'Keeffe did not report the theft until 1972, when she contacted the Art Dealers Association of America. In 1976, she learned that the paintings had been sold to defendant Barry Snyder, and demanded their return. Snyder refused, arguing that the case should be dismissed because O'Keeffe's claim was time barred— that is, that the applicable statute of limitations had expired. The court ruled for O'Keeffe, holding that the statute of limitations did not begin to run until the injured party discovered, or reasonably should have discovered, the location of the stolen property. Significantly, the court noted that "under the discovery rule, if an artist diligently seeks the recovery of a lost or stolen painting, but cannot find it or discover the identity of the possessor, the statute of limitations will not begin to run."

Guggenheim v. Lubell: New York's Demand-and-Refusal Rule

An oft-cited example of New York's demand-and-refusal rule is found in the 1991 New York Court of Appeals decision *Guggenheim v. Lubell*. In that case, New York's Guggenheim Museum demanded that a good-faith purchaser return a stolen gouache by Marc Chagall. The museum had realized in 1970 that the work was missing but did not notify the authorities for fear of driving it further underground. In 1967, a reputable New York gallery sold the work to Jules and Rachel Lubell. When the Lubells later brought the work to Sotheby's for an auction estimate, a former Guggenheim employee recognized it and notified the museum. The Guggenheim demanded the gouache's return, but the Lubells refused, and the museum sued. Since the museum had brought its claim within three years of its "demand and refusal," its claim was not time barred. However, the court remanded the case to the trial court to establish whether the suit should nevertheless be dismissed on the grounds of laches[4]—that is, whether the Guggenheim had unreasonably delayed in asserting its rights to the detriment of the current owner, the Lubells. In common legal parlance, the question of laches invariably turns on whether the original owner had "slumbered on his rights." As it happens, under U.S. law, a purchaser has the best hope of gaining title to a stolen work if the applicable statute of limitations has run out on the original owner's claim or if the purchaser can mount a successful laches defense.

Wertheimer v. Cirker's Hayes Storage Warehouse: A Successful Laches Defense

One example of a laches defense is found in the famous 2002 case of *Wertheimer v. Cirker's Hayes Storage Warehouse*, in which the plaintiff, Alain Wertheimer, failed to recover a Camille Pissarro painting from a reputable dealer. The picture had been owned by Wertheimer's grandfather, who had entrusted it to someone who had allegedly misappropriated it during the Nazi occupation of France. The court granted summary judgment to the gallery on its laches defense after finding that the Wertheimer family had done nothing since the 1950s to recover the painting. The court found that the family's lack of due diligence in searching for it had seriously disadvantaged the gallery because everyone with direct knowledge of the matter had died long ago. Accordingly, it was virtually impossible for the gallery to show that any of its predecessors in interest had acquired good title. The gallery prevailed in court, even though it had done little due diligence before acquiring the work. Indeed, another dealer who had been offered the painting checked with the Art Loss Register (the largest private international database for lost and stolen art) and was told that while the painting was not in its registry, it had been reported as missing in a 1947 publication.

In short, in New York the statute of limitations will not begin to run until after demand and refusal are made, but an original owner should still make reasonable efforts to locate a lost work to avoid facing a successful laches defense.

Interestingly, California has enacted a law specifically applying to art stolen during the Holocaust. Under that law, the original owners or their heirs may bring an action to reclaim the work from certain entities and may avoid any statute of limitations complications if the action is brought on or before December 31, 2010.

When art passes through states that apply different legal theories, the determination of which rule of law is tricky—and even trickier when the art is located abroad. A recent case in point involves five Gustav Klimt paintings, most famously *Portrait of Adele Bloch-Bauer I*, which had been stolen by the Nazis in World War II from Ferdinand and Adele Bloch-Bauer. For the next sixty years, the portrait was kept in Vienna's Belvedere Palace. Eventually, the Bloch-Bauers' niece, Maria Altmann, uncovered documentation relating to her family's ownership of the paintings and sought to recover them from Austria on the grounds that when her uncle Ferdinand died in 1945, he had left his entire estate, including the art, to her relatives and to her. Austria's recently passed restitution law required that an advisory board determine whether works such as the Klimt paintings should be returned to their original owners, and the advisory board denied Ms. Altmann's request for their return. Because Ms. Altmann was unable to file suit successfully in Austria, she and her fellow heirs instead tried to sue Austria in a U.S. court, and, after much jurisdictional wrangling, the U.S. Supreme Court decided that they could proceed. Eventually, an arbitration panel unanimously held in favor of Ms. Altmann and her family, and the dispute was settled.

The upshot was that, at the age of ninety, Ms. Altmann finally got the paintings back. She sold the *Portrait of Adele Bloch Bauer I* to cosmetics magnate Ronald Lauder for a reported $135 million. The portrait has found a new home at a small museum on upper Fifth Avenue in New York City, the Neue Galerie.

Purchasing Art: Ensuring Authenticity and Avoiding Forgeries

When acquiring a work from a dealer, artist, or auction house, a buyer must, as a starting point, determine if the work is genuine. The process of authenticating art can be daunting, especially for the non-expert, and the best place to start is with the *catalogue raisonné*. After that, rely on connoisseurship and research, and end, if necessary, with scientific analysis.

Connoisseurship involves stylistic analysis coupled with an expert's intuition born of long experience. In Malcolm Gladwell's book *Blink*, Thomas Hoving, former director of New York's Metropolitan Museum of Art, describes his immediate reaction to the Getty kouros, a supposedly ancient Greek statue of a youth in the Getty collection that had been vetted by scientists but whose authenticity remained unresolved after years of debate: "[It]looked like it had been dipped in the very best *café latte* from Starbucks." In short, an expert's gut reaction can be more compelling than a truckload of testimonials.

The Challenge of Obtaining Expert Authentication

Actually finding an unbiased expert to authenticate art can be surprisingly challenging. In addition to seeking the advice of recognized experts who may work at auction houses or art galleries (and who may have an economic interest in the outcome of an authentication), one might try contacting a respected museum curator, who, at least theoretically, is likely to be impartial. The drawback is that curators who authenticate art can be overly cautious—suffering from so-called fake fever—because they realize how easily works can be faked. Furthermore, museums may fear legal liability for false authentications and, as a result, often prohibit curators from participating in outside evaluations.

With Contemporary art, might be able to ask the artist directly to authenticate it, but even this approach is not without risk: A famous painter reportedly told a collector that, although the collector's piece was indeed authentic, the painter would not issue a written authentication because it was "just a student work." Other artists may be less than candid about when their works were created. To take just one example, Giorgio de Chirico was known for painting, and then predating, copies of works from earlier periods when his art was in higher demand.

To authenticate art in France, one might consult with the holder of the artist's *droit moral* (moral right), which includes the right to attribute a piece as being by a particular artist. It is important to remember, however, that the holder of the right (usually the heir) may not have any particular expertise in the artist's oeuvre, and even a French court need not accept the holder's opinion as definitive. Sending art for evaluation can also be risky, because some authenticating committees take, quite literally, a "destroy the work first, ask questions later" approach if authorship is even in question.

As part of the authentication process, authenticating committees in the United States and elsewhere usually ask to see not only the work itself but also background information relating to its ownership history, such as publications that cite the piece. Unfortunately, certain committees may have economic incentives to authenticate a work or, perhaps more importantly, decline to authenticate it—for example, the desire to limit the supply of "originals." The decision by a leading authenticating committee not to recognize a work as by the artist can effectively render it unmarketable, and in most cases no major auction house will knowingly offer such a piece for sale.

Another valuable resource for authentication is the independent art expert. However, Peter Sutton, Director of the Bruce Museum in Greenwich, Connecticut, cautions collectors to be wary of anyone who charges for an opinion, since experts who "get into the cottage industry of authenticating are tempted to give the object more credence." Reputable dealers also authenticate art and will usually stand behind what they sell. For an added degree of comfort, collectors can buy from dealers at "vetted" art fairs, since recognized experts typically spend several days before the opening of such fairs examining objects, questioning attributions, and often requiring dealers to relabel or remove questionable works.

When a dealer issues an invoice or bill of sale stating that a work is authentic, is this merely an opinion, or a warranty of fact? The laws in four U.S. states—New York, Michigan, Iowa, and Florida—expressly protect the consumer by eliminating this murky distinction. The New York statute, for example, provides that, when an arts merchant (such as an art dealer) sells fine art to a non-arts merchant and furnishes a certificate of authenticity or similar instrument, it:

❑ "(a) shall be presumed to be part of the basis of the bargain; and
❑ (b) shall create an express warranty for the material facts stated as of the date of such sale or exchange."

Once a fact is deemed to be part of the "basis of the bargain," then the buyer may be entitled to damages if the work is not authentic. The warranty applies even if the merchant tries to waffle in the authenticity language (e.g., by saying, "We *believe* the work is authentic" and not "The work *is* authentic").

In short, when buying art from a dealer, at least in New York, a smart purchaser will always request that the seller provide both

❑ a specific warranty of authenticity in the bill of sale, and
❑ a certificate of authenticity.

Purchasing at auction presents its own authenticity challenges since, depending on the location of the sale, buyers may have limited time or opportunity to research a work. Dr. Hugo Weihe, Christie's International Director of Asian art, advises would-be bidders to handle a work of art, sleep on it (preferably not literally), and then look at it again. "It should be eternally fresh," he says. "If, on the second day, you don't feel the freshness, there may be a problem—or it may be just a poor work of art. Masterpieces speak to you again and again." And what masterpieces have to say may be more compelling than the typical auction catalogue entry.

When researching authenticity, bear in mind that documents as well as art can be faked. In a well-publicized 2006 controversy involving Costco's Web site and dealers working with the company,

Maya Widmaier-Picasso, the artist's daughter and holder of Picasso's *droit moral*, claimed that the certificates of authenticity accompanying certain "Picasso" drawings were fakes. Clearly, buyers should be wary of purchasing a piece simply because of its supporting documentation. In fact, in certain areas of the art world, the more documentation that comes with an unknown work, the greater the likelihood that it is fake.

Another essential factor in determining authenticity is the work's provenance, or ownership history. A cautionary tale from one collector involved an impressive-looking *catalogue raisonné* of a famous artist's oeuvre. Though the catalogue purported to contain a comprehensive list of the prior owners of the artist's paintings, few of the supposed past owners could actually be located or verified, and many works listed were outright fakes. The moral of this story: Whenever possible, do your own due diligence, or at the very least, ask who researched what and when.

Since different scholars may create different *catalogues raisonnés,* and no particular qualifications are necessary to write one, authors may arrive at conflicting conclusions concerning authenticity. Nevertheless, if a major auction house consistently relies on a particular *catalogue raisonné,* it is likely to be deemed authoritative in the trade. Conversely, a work that is omitted from what is generally viewed as an artist's definitive *catalogue raisonné* may be difficult to sell and should be approached with caution by a would-be buyer.

When connoisseurship and research suggest that a work is "right," but an iron-clad authentication is not possible, the next step may be technical analysis, such as radiocarbon and thermoluminescent (TL) dating. Such techniques have been heralded by some as the art world's wave of the future, but they are often more useful for disproving or disputing authorship than for actually authenticating. Science can determine that an object is old, but not necessarily that it is by the hand of a particular artist. For instance, most of the questionable Rembrandt attributions involve works done during the artist's time—and some that were even done in Rembrandt's own studio—but just not by him.

It may be wise to revisit certain works in one's collection periodically to determine whether an earlier authentication still stands. Opinions, especially regarding older works, may change over time as more information becomes available, and so today's "hand of the master" may turn out to be tomorrow's "done by a cousin"—or the reverse. An up-to-date authentication is especially important before trying to sell art, and can save the seller a considerable amount of legal difficulty both with the buyer and with those further down the chain of ownership.

When all else fails, courts of law may resolve authentication issues. However, courts are often the worst places to rule on authenticity, since judges and lawyers tend to think in terms of clear rules and final judgments—quite inappropriate standards in an area where opinions may change based on new, and presumably better, information.

The Authenticity Is Suspect: What Now?

Even a work that is accompanied by a solid certificate of authenticity may later turn out to be suspect. In such a case, the owner may be entitled to a legal remedy if he files a claim in time. But what does "in time" mean?

One collector (let's call him Peter) inherited a nineteenth-century painting of a noble steed from his grandfather, who had purchased it, complete with a certificate of authenticity, from a prominent Madison Avenue gallery. Some forty years later, the leading scholar on the artist decided that the painting was actually fake and excluded it from his upcoming *catalogue raisonné*. Peter was livid and sought payment from the gallery in the amount equal to what the work would have fetched had it been authentic. He was pleased to hear about the 1966 New York State law (discussed above) that stipulates that whenever an art merchant delivers a certificate of authenticity to a buyer who is not an art merchant, the certificate creates an express warranty and is deemed part of the "basis of the bargain." But he was less than charmed to learn that the statute of limitations for claims of breach of warranty under the New York Uniform Commercial Code is four years after the "cause of action has accrued," which generally means from delivery of the goods.

Wilson v. Hammer Holdings: The Statute of Limitations on an Authenticity Challenge

An example of this statutory four-year rule is found in the 1988 U.S. Court of Appeals decision *Wilson v. Hammer Holdings*. In 1961, the plaintiffs, Dorothy and John Wilson, paid more than $11,000 to the Hammer

Galleries in New York for an original painting by Edouard Vuillard. The gallery assured the Wilsons in writing that the work's authenticity was "guaranteed." Problems arose in 1984, when Mrs. Wilson attempted to sell the Vuillard and an expert declared it a fake. Mrs. Wilson and her late husband's executors sued the gallery, arguing that "a warranty of authenticity of a painting necessarily relates to the future condition of the artwork," and their cause of action therefore should begin not at the time they purchased the painting, but at the time they discovered the work was a fake. In other words, they argued that the statute was "tolled" (suspended) until the time they discovered the breach. The federal court of appeals hearing their case rejected this tolling argument, and instead held that the four-year clock, under the Uniform Commercial Code in Massachusetts, starts running at the date of delivery of the work, not at the time of discovery of the breach. The court reasoned that the Wilsons' ability to discover that the work was fake was no less possible at the time of purchase than at the time of the attempted sale of the work. As a result, their claim for breach of warranty was time barred.

Returning to Peter's case, he had hoped that his grandfather's various discussions with the dealer during the years since the purchase might extend the statute of limitations, but the following case suggested otherwise.

Firestone v. Union League of Philadelphia: Adversary's Refusal to Agree on Validity of a Claim Does Not Extend Statute

In *Firestone v. Union League of Philadelphia*, which was brought in the Eastern District of Pennsylvania, the plaintiffs in 1981 had purchased a painting purportedly by Albert Bierstadt from the Union League of Philadelphia for $500,000. In 1986, an important art historian declared in *Antiques* magazine that the work was actually by John Ross Key. The plaintiffs sued the Union League to rescind the purchase contract and to seek damages for lost profits, claiming that, as a work by Key, the painting was worth only $50,000. They argued that the statute of limitations should have been tolled because the sellers continued to insist that the painting was by Bierstadt, even after others had raised serious doubts as to the attribution. The court in that case held that "the time limit for filing suit is not extended by reason of the adversary's refusal to agree that the claim is valid."

Again returning to Peter's situation, the prior case law was not all bad for him however. A 1990 federal decision offered a glimmer of hope for purchasers who suddenly find they are the owners of fake works—at least for purchasers in Hawaii.

Balog v. Center Art Gallery–Hawaii: Tolling the Statute of Limitations

In *Balog v. Center Art Gallery–Hawaii*, the plaintiffs were private collectors who, beginning in 1978, paid Hawaii's Center Art Gallery approximately $36,200 for works that the gallery claimed were either originals or limited editions by Salvador Dalí. After the purchase, the gallery sent the collectors a "Confidential Appraisal–Certificate of Authenticity" for each work, which showed its purported increase in market value. Some seven years after their last purchase of art, the collectors saw a news report questioning the authenticity of art sold by the Center Art Gallery, and in 1989 they sued for breach of warranty. Surprisingly, the *Balog* court did not find that the statute of limitations had expired and did not dismiss the collectors' suit. Instead, the court agreed with them that the four-year statute of limitations should be tolled because the gallery's warranty extended to "future performance of goods." The court declined to follow *Wilson* and *Firestone*, observing that those cases applied the Uniform Commercial Code too literally.

Unfortunately for Peter, *Balog* is an outlier that has generally not been followed by subsequent courts, and Peter's claim had no connection to Hawaii. But all was not lost for Peter, since—depending on the circumstances surrounding the original purchase of the painting—he might have been able avoid the relatively short statute of limitations for breach of warranty by alleging fraud. Indeed, an allegation of fraud is a classic way to circumvent the statute of limitations for breach of contract. In New York, cases involving fraud may be brought within six years from the sale date, or (importantly) two years from the date that the fraud was, or could have been, discovered.

The problem with Peter's filing a fraud claim is that it would have required a showing that the dealer had knowingly made false representations about the painting, or had made representations with a reckless disregard for the truth. Since forty years had passed since the dealer had provided the certificate of authenticity for the work, such a showing would have been extremely difficult. Indeed, even though claims of fraud are almost invariably made in cases involving reattribution of art, the necessity to show that the seller knowingly made false representations at the time of sale is daunting. Accordingly, most such claims that we have seen have failed.

Foxley v. Sotheby's: A Claim of Fraud

In the 1995 Southern District of New York case *Foxley v. Sotheby's*, the plaintiff, William Foxley, was unsuccessful in his fraud claim. Foxley had purchased a Mary Cassatt painting in 1987 from Sotheby's for $632,500. Sotheby's auction catalogue stated that the painting would be sold complete with a letter from a leading Cassatt authority "discussing" the work, and the catalogue guaranteed the painting's authenticity for five years from the sale date. Foxley claimed that he received the letter only in 1993, at which point he realized that the expert's comments were based on her reviewing only a color transparency of the painting and not the original. That same year, almost six years after purchasing the work and just as Foxley was about to resell it at an upcoming Sotheby's auction, Sotheby's notified Foxley that the Cassatt Committee had questioned the work's authenticity. Foxley withdrew the painting from the sale, and when Sotheby's refused to refund the original purchase price, Foxley sued for fraud, among other causes of action. The court granted summary judgment to Sotheby's on the fraud claim because Foxley had not presented facts sufficient to allege fraud.

When all else fails in authenticity cases, an appeal to the original art dealer's good name can sometimes do the trick. In Peter's case, this meant not making a full-blown legal argument (which we believe he would have lost), but rather approaching the now-elderly dealer and suggesting that his fine reputation had been built on treating customers fairly, irrespective of any statute of limitations. Fortunately, the dealer was highly ethical and ended up making a reasonable settlement offer. As Peter's case illustrates, buying from a reputable dealer has obvious advantages.

Provenance Problems: How to Protect Your Investment

Although good provenance for a work of art does not guarantee that a buyer will be free from legal problems down the line, significant gaps in provenance can, and often should, raise red flags for a savvy purchaser, including the fear that a work may have been stolen or forged.

A solid purchase agreement that covers provenance issues can avoid much misunderstanding and expensive litigation later on. Accordingly, when buying art with questionable provenance, one might wish to include a provision in the agreement or bill of sale stating that the purchaser is expressly relying on the provenance as part of the purchase. Under New York's Uniform Commercial Code, which governs the sale of goods, including art, a seller's assertion of provenance can create an express warranty if it forms the "basis of the bargain." Including this type of representation in the purchase agreement will be helpful if the buyer or a subsequent owner of the work is unlucky enough to end up in court with the seller.

Weber v. Peck: When a Dealer's Statement Creates an Express Warranty

In the 1999 federal case *Weber v. Peck*, a dealer's statement about provenance was found to have created an express warranty in favor of the buyer. The dealer, who claimed that an oil painting was by Jacob van Ruisdael, incorrectly stated the ownership history in the bill of sale. The purchaser, Francis Weber, later attempted to auction off the painting at Sotheby's, but the auction house advised him that it could not verify the provenance and deleted the reference to previously listed owners and publications. Despite the deletion, Weber proceeded with the sale, which went badly: A bid of $300,000 was accepted, but payment was never made. Weber sued the dealer based on the false provenance. The court found that the written provenance constituted an express warranty, which the dealer had breached. The court ruled that Weber was entitled to damages, and the amount of these damages was to be based on the extent to which the breach caused the painting's loss in value. The court did not, however, allow Weber to rescind the sale.

Even if the seller's assurances about ownership history are not included in a written contract, the buyer may still be entitled to legal redress. For example, in the United States a seller's advertisements may constitute warranties of provenance if the buyer can show that he relied on them in making the purchase. If the seller knowingly makes misleading assertions, he may also face criminal liability for his actions, including fraudulent misrepresentation, larceny by false pretenses, or other crimes. Even if the seller's misstatements were made honestly, without the intent to mislead, he may still be civilly liable for breach of warranty.

Because of the potential legal liability that arises from false statements of provenance, smart sellers commonly try to insert a disclaimer regarding provenance in the purchase agreement, so buyers should beware. While a New York court would probably disregard a vaguely worded disclaimer that is inconsistent with the bill of sale, buyers should nonetheless delete disclaimers from the sales contract wherever possible. Savy sellers also try to exclude all "implied" warranties and instead insert language in contracts making them responsible only for those warranties that are explicitly stated in either the signed contracts or bills of sale.

As a related matter, when purchasing art from a dealer, a buyer should insist that the sales contract include a representation that the dealer is transferring good title. Ideally, the contract should also include an indemnification provision that survives delivery of the work, since this may allow the buyer to recover not just his purchase price but also his attorney's fees and expenses (often a tidy sum) if the work turns out to be stolen or otherwise not as represented by the seller.

If a purchaser's due diligence does not uncover any potential problems and he ultimately buys the work, then any research carried out before the purchase should come in handy if an ownership dispute later arises. This is because courts, in balancing the equities, are generally more likely to side with purchasers who have gone to the trouble of investigating the title of a piece *before* buying it.

For museums purchasing art, the International Code of Professional Ethics of the International Council of Museums (ICOM) specifically states that "no object or specimen should be acquired by purchase, gift, loan, bequest, or exchange unless the acquiring museum is satisfied that a valid title is held." In other words, the museum, before acquiring a work, has a responsibility to make a good-faith effort to ensure that the piece had been legally obtained. Similarly, the American Association of Museums Code of Ethics states that the "stewardship of collections entails the highest public trust and carries with it the presumption of rightful ownership."

Both the J. Paul Getty Museum in Los Angeles and the Metropolitan Museum of Art in New York have encountered very public problems in this area. Marion True, a curator at the Getty, was criminally prosecuted in Athens for conspiring to acquire looted art (the charges were ultimately dismissed) and faced similar charges in Italy. The Metropolitan Museum, for its part, recently agreed to return twenty-one looted artifacts to Italy. So even the most reputable institutions can run into problems of provenance if they are not extremely careful.

Autocephalous Greek-Orthodox Church of Cyprus v. Goldberg & Feldman Fine Arts: The Need for Purchaser's Due Diligence

The need for purchasers to conduct proper due diligence was stressed in the 1990 U.S. Court of Appeals case *Autocephalous Greek-Orthodox Church of Cyprus v. Goldberg & Feldman Fine Arts*. In that case, Cyprus successfully brought an action to recover stolen sixth-century mosaics that the American dealer Peg Goldberg had purchased from a Turkish archaeologist for more than $1.2 million. After learning of the theft, Cyprus reported it to the United Nations and UNESCO, among others. The Getty Museum's Marion True heard about Goldberg's mosaics and contacted Cypriot officials. The court observed that, especially when a potential purchase raises red flags, "dealers can (and probably should) take steps such as a formal IFAR (International Foundation for Art Research) search; a documented authenticity check by disinterested experts; a full background search of the seller and his claim of title; insurance protection and a contingency sales contract; and the like." The court also noted that "those who wish to purchase artwork on the international market, undoubtedly a ticklish business, are not without means to protect themselves."

Erisoty v. Rizik: When It's Not a Case of "Finders, Keepers"

The value of proper due diligence was also emphasized in the 1995 Eastern District of Pennsylvania case *Erisoty v. Rizik*, which involved a Corrado Giaquinto painting that had been stolen from a family in Washington, D.C. in 1960 and was discovered torn into five pieces in a garbage bag in 1988 by a furniture-removal company. In 1989, the painting (in pieces) was consigned to an auction house, where it was purchased by a professional art restorer. The original owner had reported the loss to the FBI and the police in 1960, and had contacted IFAR in 1992. The FBI and IFAR located the painting and removed it from the purchaser's home, and the purchaser then sued the original owner in federal court for the work's return. The court awarded the painting to the original owner's family. It criticized the purchaser for failing to investigate "the painting's prior ownership or the identity of the consignor, or making any inquiry of art or law enforcement agencies, and with the knowledge that the painting was in five pieces—suspicious circumstances to say the least." The court also suggested that the current possessor of stolen art is subject to a higher standard of due diligence than the original owner.

When one is investigating whether a work might be stolen, computerized databases are a good place to start. Although no single, all-encompassing registry of stolen art exists today, an increasing number of excellent databases are used in the international art world to determine whether works are missing, stolen, or subject to other claims. The best known of these databases is the Art Loss Register (referred to earlier), with offices in New York, London, and elsewhere. It was established in 1991 as a partnership among auction houses, the insurance industry, art trade associations, and IFAR. The Art Loss Register's database includes records from private sources and government agencies such as the FBI and Interpol.

One can also investigate provenance through scholars, museums, auction houses, dealers, and insurance agents. This approach, however, may be less successful for older works, since their titles may have changed and their exhibition catalogues may be difficult to track down.

Art Theft and Museums

In the United States, museums that are the victims of theft benefit from legal protections that individuals and other types of institutions do not share. For instance, if a work is sufficiently valuable (either monetarily or culturally), its theft from a museum may violate the 1994 federal law known as the Museum Statute, which makes stealing an object of cultural heritage from a U.S. museum a federal crime punishable by up to ten years in prison. The statute defines "an object of cultural heritage" as one that is either

❑ worth at least $10,000, or
❑ worth more than $5,000 and is over one hundred years old.

The statute has the advantage of not requiring interstate or international transport—which is customarily a condition for the prosecution of many other types of federal crimes. It also expressly makes the buyer of stolen art liable, since it criminalizes the "receiving, concealing, exhibiting, or disposing" of a stolen work.

United States v. Pritchard: The Museum Statute Applied to a Historic Home

The Museum Statute was used in the 2003 federal case *United States v. Pritchard*. Here, the curator Russ Pritchard Jr. was convicted of stealing a Civil War officer's uniform valued at $45,000 from the Hunt-Phelan Home Foundation, a historic house in Memphis. Pritchard argued that the statute did not apply to him because the house was not a museum in the sense that it did not actually own the objects inside. The court rejected his argument and found him guilty.

Because the Museum Statute requires specific technical definitions to be met, prosecution for art theft is more common under the National Stolen Property Act (NSPA), which criminalizes the interstate transportation of stolen goods worth more than $5,000. Significantly, the NSPA is not limited to thefts from cultural institutions, and it has a short five-year statute of limitations (calculated from the date of theft), in contrast to the Museum Statute's more liberal twenty-year statute of limitations period. Both the Museum Statute and the NSPA bring the theft of art from a museum under the purview of the FBI, which maintains the National Stolen Art File, a database of stolen art and cultural property similar to the Art Loss Register.

When a museum suspects that the thief is one of its own employees, special problems may arise. For example, museum unions often impose various conditions on the questioning of an employee or the administration of a lie-detector test. Assuming for the moment that a museum has solid grounds for believing that an employee has stolen a work of art, the museum must consider other legal issues—such as the protections offered under the U.S. Constitution—before it may try to find and recover the work. The Fourth Amendment to the Constitution, for example, prevents unreasonable searches and seizures and would prohibit a museum (or anyone else) from searching the employee's property without adequate proof and protections—in this case, a court-ordered search warrant.

State v. Kennedy: Illegal Search and Seizure

In the 1989 case *State v. Kennedy*, involving the theft of Japanese and Korean pottery and ivory carvings from Connecticut's Slater Museum, the court stressed this point, and held that, even with a search warrant, police officers had violated the defendant's reasonable expectation of privacy when they broke into his family's locked garage.

An intriguing related question arises in the context of theft and forgeries: What happens when a hapless thief inadvertently steals a work that turns out to be a worthless fake? The answer is that the thief is out of luck and remains liable for the theft. This point was illustrated in the 1978 ruling *United States v. Tobin*.

United States v. Tobin: Stealing a Fake Is Still a Crime

In the *Tobin* case, the defendants were convicted of attempting to sell stolen sculptures by Frederic Remington and Emile Picault to an undercover FBI agent for $15,000, even though the Remington was actually fake. The U.S. Court of Appeals for the Fifth Circuit ruled that, since the defendants had intended to commit a crime, their mistake concerning the work's authenticity did not exonerate them (although it did mitigate their punishment). The court noted that the value of the stolen Remington should be calculated as the price that a willing seller would pay a willing buyer at the time when it was taken.

United States v. Crawford: Lack of Clear Title Doesn't Preclude a Charge of Theft

Another interesting sidelight in this area: You do not need to prove that you actually owned a work in order for it be considered stolen from you.

In the 2001 Ninth Circuit case *United States v. Crawford*, a defendant working at UCLA falsely claimed that a painting in her California office had been removed for restoration when, in fact, she had simply sold it in New York. She argued that she was not guilty because technically the university lacked title to the painting. (It was owned by a UCLA affiliate that had since been dissolved.) Unfortunately for her, the court disagreed.

In sum, to avoid thorny legal issues related to art, remember to investigate authenticity and provenance, and know your rights. If, despite your best efforts, you find yourself the victim of forgery, art theft, or worse, do not despair. With a bit of perseverance—and the assistance of a capable lawyer—even serious legal problems in these areas can be artfully resolved.

The Illegal Art Trade: List of Legal Cases Cited

Menzel v. List: In the Case of Nazi Looting, a Decision for the Original Owner

O'Keeffe v. Snyder: The Discovery Rule and the Statute of Limitations

Guggenheim v. Lubell: New York's Demand-and-Refusal Rule

Wertheimer v. Cirker's Hayes Storage Warehouse: A Successful Laches Defense

Wilson v. Hammer Holdings: The Statute of Limitations on an Authenticity Challenge

Firestone v. Union League of Philadelphia: Adversary's Refusal to Agree on Validity of a Claim Does Not Extend Statute

Balog v. Center Art Gallery–Hawaii: Tolling the Statute of Limitations

Foxley v. Sotheby's: A Claim of Fraud

Weber v. Peck: When a Dealer's Statement Creates an Express Warranty

Autocephalous Greek-Orthodox Church of Cyprus v. Goldberg & Feldman Fine Arts: The Need for Purchaser's Due Diligence

Erisoty v. Rizik: When It's Not a Case of "Finders, Keepers"

United States v. Pritchard: The Museum Statute Applied to a Historic Home

State v. Kennedy: Illegal Search and Seizure

United States v. Tobin: Stealing a Fake Is Still a Crime

United States v. Crawford: Lack of Clear Title

Doesn't Preclude a Charge of Theft

Chapter Notes

1. The authors gratefully acknowledge the assistance of Danielle Gaier in the preparation of this chapter. Nothing in this chapter is intended to provide specific legal advice.

2. The number may decline in 2009–2010 with the weakening global economy.

3. A civil-law country is one where the primary source of law is legislation founded on ancient Roman principles rather than on legal precedent established by prior cases, which controls in common-law countries.

4. The word "laches" is from the Latin for "estoppel," meaning delay. Legally, it is an equitable defense.

Index

ABOUT BLOOMBERG

Bloomberg L.P., founded in 1981, is a global information services, news, and media company. Headquartered in New York, the company has sales and news operations worldwide.

Serving customers on six continents, Bloomberg, through its wholly-owned subsidiary Bloomberg Finance L.P., holds a unique position within the financial services industry by providing an unparalleled range of features in a single package known as the Bloomberg Professional® service. By addressing the demand for investment performance and efficiency through an exceptional combination of information, analytic, electronic trading, and straight-through-processing tools, Bloomberg has built a worldwide customer base of corporations, issuers, financial intermediaries, and institutional investors.

Bloomberg News, founded in 1990, provides stories and columns on business, general news, politics, and sports to leading newspapers and magazines throughout the world. Bloomberg Television, a 24-hour business and financial news network, is produced and distributed globally in seven languages. Bloomberg Radio is an international radio network anchored by flagship station Bloomberg 1130 (WBBR-AM) in New York.

In addition to the Bloomberg Press line of books, Bloomberg publishes *Bloomberg Markets* magazine. To learn more about Bloomberg, call a sales representative at:

London:	+44-20-7330-7500
New York:	+1-212-318-2000
Tokyo:	+81-3-3201-8900